Frommer's®

German
PhraseFinder &
Dictionary

1st Edition

WILEY

Wiley Publishing, Inc.

Published by:

Wiley Publishing, Inc.

111 River St.
Hoboken, NJ 07030-5774

ISBN-13: 978-0-470-17839-3

Editor: Jim Cohen
Series Editor: Maureen Clarke
Photo Editor: Richard H. Fox
Illustrations by Maciek Albrecht

Translation, Copyediting, Proofreading, Production, and Layout by:
Lingo Systems, 15115 SW Sequoia Pkwy, Ste 200, Portland, OR 97224

For information on our other products and services or to obtain technical support,
please contact our Customer Care Department within the U.S. at 800/762-2974, outside the U.S. at 317/572-3993 or fax 317/572-4002.
Wiley also publishes its books in a variety of electronic formats. Some content that
appears in print may not be available in electronic formats.

Manufactured in the United States of America

5   4   3   2   1

Contents

Introduction   vii

1 Survival German (& Grammar Basics)   1

Basic Greetings **1**, The Key Questions **3**, Numbers &
Counting **7**, Measurements **10**, Time **11**,
The Alphabet **16**, Pronunciations **16**, Personal
Pronouns **20**, Regular Verb Conjugations **20**,
To Be or not To Be (SEIN) **23**, Irregular Verbs **24**, Reflexive
Verbs **29**

2 Getting There & Getting Around   30

At the Airport **30**, Renting a Vehicle **42**, By Taxi **50**,
By Train **51**, By Bus **52**, By Boat or Ship **54**,
By Subway **55**, Considerations for Travelers with
Special Needs **57**

3 Lodging   58

Room Preferences **58**, In-Room Amenities **64**,
Happy Camping **70**

4 Dining   72

Finding a Restaurant **72**, Ordering **76**, Drinks **80**,
Settling Up **82**, Menu Reader **83**, Buying Groceries **89**

5 Socializing   99

Greetings **99**, Curse Words **101**, Getting Personal **102**,
Topics of Conversation **113**, Getting to Know
Someone **116**

6   **Money & Communications**   **120**

Money 120, Phone Service 122, Internet Access 126,
Getting Mail 128

7   **Culture**   **132**

Cinema 132, Performances 133, Museums,
Galleries & Sights 135

8   **Shopping**   **137**

General Shopping Terms 137, Clothes Shopping 138,
Artisan Market Shopping 141, Bookstore / Newsstand
Shopping 144, Shopping for Electronics 144,
At the Barber / Hairdresser 146

9   **Sports & Fitness**   **149**

Getting Fit 149, Catching a Game 152, Hiking 154,
Boating or Fishing 157, Diving 158, Surfing 159,
Golfing 160

10 **Nightlife**   **163**

Club Hopping 163, Across a Crowded Room 167,
Getting Intimate 170, In the Casino 173

11 **Health & Safety**   **175**

At the Pharmacy 175, At the Doctor's Office 177,
At the Police Station 182

English–German Dictionary   **185**

German–English Dictionary   **224**

An Invitation to the Reader

In researching this book, we discovered many wonderful sayings and terms useful to travelers in German-speaking countries. We're sure you'll find others. Please tell us about them so we can share them with your fellow travelers in upcoming editions. If you were disappointed about any aspect of this book, we'd like to know that, too. Please write to:

Frommer's German PhraseFinder & Dictionary, 1st Edition
Wiley Publishing, Inc.
111 River St. • Hoboken, NJ 07030-5774

An Additional Note

The packager, editors and publisher cannot be held responsible for the experience of readers while traveling. Your safety is important to us, however, so we encourage you to stay alert and aware of your surroundings. Keep a close eye on cameras, purses, and wallets, all favorite targets of thieves and pickpockets.

Frommers.com

Now that you have the language for a great trip, visit our website at **www.frommers.com** for travel information on more than 3,600 destinations. With features updated regularly, we give you instant access to the most current trip-planning information available. At Frommers.com you'll also find the best prices on airfares, accommodations, and car rentals—and you can even book travel online through our travel booking partners. Frommers.com also features:

- Online updates to our most popular guidebooks
- Vacation sweepstakes and contest giveaways
- Newsletter highlighting the hottest travel trends
- Online travel message boards with featured travel discussions

ABOUT THE EDITOR

Jim Cohen is a professional translator and editor living in New York City. He spent a year in Heidelberg, Germany, before attending the University of Massachusetts at Amherst, where he received an M.A. in German. When he is not translating and editing, he enjoys running and spending time with his fiancée, Blythe.

INTRODUCTION: HOW TO USE THIS BOOK

More than 80 million people in Germany, Switzerland, Austria, and Luxembourg are native speakers of German. Tens of millions more speak it as a second language. German is the language of music, art, philosophy, science, and literature. Like English, German is a Germanic language, and they share many cognates, or words that look alike with similar meanings.

Our intention is not to teach you German; a class or audio program is better for that. Our aim is to provide a portable travel tool that's easy to use. The problem with most phrasebooks is that you practically have to memorize the contents before you know where to look for the term you need on the spot. This phrasebook is designed for fingertip referencing, so you can whip it out and find the words you need fast.

Part of this book organizes terms by chapters, like the sections in a Frommer's guide—getting a room, getting a good meal, etc. Within those divisions, we tried to organize phrases intuitively, according to how frequently most readers would be likely to use them. The most unique feature, however, is the two-way PhraseFinder dictionary in the back, which lists words as well as phrases organized by key word. Say a taxi driver hands you €5 instead of €10. Look up "change" in the dictionary and discover how to say: "Sorry, but this isn't the correct change."

To make best use of the content, we recommend that you spend some time flipping through it before you depart for your trip. Familiarize yourself with the order of the chapters. Read through the pronunciations section in chapter one and practice pronouncing random phrases throughout the book. Try looking up a few phrases in the phrasebook section as well as in the dictionary. This way, you'll be able to locate phrases faster and speak them more clearly when you need them.

What will make this book most practical? What will make it easiest to use? These are the questions we asked ourselves repeatedly as we assembled these travel terms. Our immediate goal was to create a phrasebook as indispensable as your passport. Our far-ranging goal, of course, is to enrich your experience of travel. And with that, we wish you *Viel Spass!* (Have a great trip!)

CHAPTER ONE

If you tire of toting around this phrasebook, tear out this chapter. You should be able to navigate your destination with only the terms found in the next 29 pages.

BASIC GREETINGS

For a full list of greetings, see p99.

Hello.	**Hallo.**
	Hah-LOH.
How are you?	**Wie geht es Ihnen?**
	Vee GHEHHT as eehnen?
I'm fine, thanks.	**Mir geht es gut, danke.**
	Mere ghehht as GOOT, dunk-eh.
And you?	**Und Ihnen?**
	Oonnd EEHNEN?
My name is ____.	**Ich heiße ____.**
	Ee[ch] HYE-sseh ____.
And yours?	**Wie heißen Sie?**
	Vee hye-ssenn ZEE?
It's a pleasure to meet you.	**Freut mich, Sie kennen zu lernen.**
	Froyd mi[ch], zee CANON tsoo lehr-nen.
Please.	**Bitte.**
	BIT-eh.
Thank you.	**Danke.**
	DUNK-eh.
Yes.	**Ja.**
	Yahh.
No.	**Nein.**
	Nine.
Okay.	**OK.**
	Okay.

No problem.	**Kein Problem.**
	Kyne proh-BLEHM.
I'm sorry, I don't understand.	**Entschuldigung, ich verstehe Sie nicht.**
	Ennt-SHOOLL-dee-ghoong, ee[ch] fair-SHTEH-heh zee ni[ch]t.
Would you speak slower please?	**Könnten Sie bitte etwas langsamer sprechen?**
	K[oe]nn-ten zee bit-eh at-vahs LUNG-sah-mehr shpre-[ch]en?
Would you speak louder please?	**Könnten Sie bitte etwas lauter sprechen?**
	K[oe]nn-ten zee bit-eh at-vahs LOU-tehr shpre-[ch]en?
Do you speak English?	**Sprechen Sie Englisch?**
	Shpre-[ch]en zee ENG-lish?
Do you speak any other languages?	**Sprechen Sie irgendeine andere Sprache?**
	Shpre-[ch]en zee irr-ghend eye-ne UN-deh-reh shpra-[ch]eh?
I speak ____ better than German.	**Ich spreche besser ____ als Deutsch.**
	Ee[ch] shpre-[ch]eh bess-er ____ ahlls doytsh.
Would you spell that?	**Könnten Sie das bitte buchstabieren?**
	K[oe]nn-ten zee dahs bit-eh bu[ch]-shtah-BEE-ren?
Would you please repeat that?	**Könnten Sie das bitte wiederholen?**
	K[oe]nn-ten zee dahs bit-eh veeder-HOH-len?
Would you point that out in this dictionary?	**Könnten Sie mir das bitte in diesem Wörterbuch zeigen?**
	K[oe]nn-ten zee mere dahs bit-eh in dee-sem V[OE]R-tehr-boo[ch] tsai-ghen?

SURVIVAL GERMAN

THE KEY QUESTIONS

With the right hand gestures, you can get a lot of mileage from the following list of single-word questions and answers.

Who?	**Wer?**
	Vehr?
What?	**Was?**
	Vahs?
When?	**Wann?**
	Vahnn?
Where?	**Wo?**
	Voh?
To where?	**Wohin?**
	Voh-HINN?
Why?	**Warum?**
	Vah-ROOM?
How?	**Wie?**
	Vee?
Which?	**Welcher (m) / Welche (f) / Welches (n)?**
	VELL-[ch]err / VELL-[ch]eh / VELL-[ch]ess?
How many? / How much?	**Wie viele?**
	Vee FEE-leh?

THE ANSWERS: WHO

For full coverage of pronouns, see p20.

I	**Ich**
	Ee[ch]
you	**Sie (formal, sing. + pl.) / du (informal, sing.) / ihr (informal, pl.)**
	zee / doo / eehr
him	**er**
	air
her	**sie**
	zee
us	**wir**
	veer

them	**sie (pl.)**
	zee

THE ANSWERS: WHEN

For full coverage of time, see p11.

now	**jetzt**
	yetst
later	**später**
	SHP[AE]-tehr
in a minute	**gleich**
	glye[ch]
today	**heute**
	HOY-teh
tomorrow	**morgen**
	MORR-ghenn
yesterday	**gestern**
	GHESS-tehrn
in a week	**in einer Woche**
	in eye-nehr VOH-[ch]eh
next week	**nächste Woche**
	n[ae][ch]s-teh VOH-[ch]eh
last week	**letzte Woche**
	lets-teh VOH-[ch]eh
next month	**nächsten Monat**
	n[ae][ch]s-ten MOH-naht
At _____	**Um** _____
	Oomm _____
ten o'clock this morning.	**zehn Uhr heute Morgen.**
	TSEHN oohr hoy-teh MORR-ghenn.
two o'clock this afternoon.	**zwei Uhr heute Nachmittag.**
	TSVAIH oohr hoy-teh NAH[CH]-mitt-tahhg.
seven o'clock this evening.	**sieben Uhr heute Abend.**
	ZEE-ben oohr hoy-teh AHH-bend.

For full coverage of numbers, see p7.

THE ANSWERS: WHERE

here	**hier**
	hear
there	**dort**
	dohrrt
near	**in der Nähe von**
	in dehr N[AE]H-heh fonn
closer	**näher**
	N[AE]H-herr
closest	**am nächsten**
	umm N[AE][CH]s-ten
far	**weit weg**
	VYTE vegg
farther	**weiter weg**
	VYE-tehr vegg
farthest	**am weitesten weg**
	umm VYE-tess-ten vegg
across from	**gegenüber von**
	ghe-ghenn-[UE]H-behr fonn
next to	**neben**
	NEH-ben
behind	**hinter**
	HINN-tehr
straight ahead	**geradeaus**
	ghe-rah-deh-OUS
left	**links**
	links
right	**rechts**
	re[ch]ts
up	**aufwärts**
	OUF-v[ae]rts
down	**abwärts**
	UPP-v[ae]rts

lower	**niedriger (height) / geringer (price)**
	NEE-drigger / ghe-RING-er
higher	**höher**
	H[OE]-hehr
forward	**vorwärts**
	FOHR-v[ae]rts
back	**zurück**
	tsoo-R[UE]KK
around	**herum**
	heh-ROOMM
across the street	**auf der anderen Straßenseite**
	ouf dehr UN-deh-renn SHTRAH-ssen-sye-teh
down the street	**am Ende der Straße**
	umm enn-deh dehr SHTRAH-sseh
on the corner	**an der Ecke**
	unn dehr EKKEH
kitty-corner	**schräg gegenüber**
	shr[ae]gg gheh-ghenn-[UE]H-behr
____ blocks from here	**____ Straßen von hier**
	SHTRAH-ssen fonn hear

For a full list of numbers, see the next page.

THE ANSWERS: WHICH

this one	**dieser (m) / diese (f) / dieses (n)**
	DEE-sehr / DEE-seh / DEE-sess
that (that one, close by)	**dieser (m) / diese (f) / dieses (n)**
	DEE-sehr / DEE-seh / DEE-sess
(that one, in the distance)	**jener (m) / jene (f) / jenes (n)**
	YEH-nehr / YEH-neh / YEH-ness
these	**diese**
	DEE-seh
those (those there, close by)	**diese (pl.)**
	DEE-seh

NUMBERS & COUNTING

one	**Eins**	seventeen	**Siebzehn**
	Aihnts		*ZEEB-tsehn*
two	**Zwei**	eighteen	**Achtzehn**
	Tsvaih		*A[CH]-tsehn*
three	**Drei**	nineteen	**Neunzehn**
	Drrye		*NOYN-tsehn*
four	**Vier**	twenty	**Zwanzig**
	Feer		*TSVANN-tsigg*
five	**Fünf**	twenty-one	**Einundzwanzig**
	F[ue]nff		*AIHNN-oonnd-*
six	**Sechs**		*tsvann-tsigg*
	Zeks	thirty	**Dreißig**
seven	**Sieben**		*DRRYE-sigg*
	ZEE-ben	forty	**Vierzig**
eight	**Acht**		*FEER-tsigg*
	A[ch]t	fifty	**Fünfzig**
nine	**Neun**		*F[UE]NFF-tsigg*
	Noyn	sixty	**Sechzig**
ten	**Zehn**		*ZE[CH]-tsigg*
	Tsehn	seventy	**Siebzig**
eleven	**Elf**		*ZEEB-tsigg*
	Ellf	eighty	**Achtzig**
twelve	**Zwölf**		*A[CH]-tsigg*
	Tsv[oe]llf	ninety	**Neunzig**
thirteen	**Dreizehn**		*NOYN-tsigg*
	DRRYE-tshen	one hundred	**Einhundert**
fourteen	**Vierzehn**		*AIHN-hoonn-*
	FEER-tsehn		*dehrt*
fifteen	**Fünfzehn**	two hundred	**Zweihundert**
	F[UE]NFF-tsehn		*TSVAIH-hoonn-*
sixteen	**Sechzehn**		*dehrt*
	ZE[CH]-tsehn	one thousand	**Eintausend**
			aihn-TOWSEND

FRACTIONS & DECIMALS

one eighth	**ein Achtel**
	aihn A[CH]-tell
one quarter	**ein Viertel**
	aihn FEER-tell
one third	**ein Drittel**
	aihn DRITT-tell
one half	**die Hälfte**
	dee H[AE]LLF-teh
two thirds	**zwei Drittel**
	tsvaih DRITT-tell
three quarters	**drei Viertel**
	drrye FEER-tell
double	**doppelt**
	DOP-pellt
triple	**dreifach**
	DRRYE-fah[ch]
one tenth	**ein Zehntel**
	aihn TSEHN-tell
one hundredth	**ein Hundertstel**
	aihn HOON-derts-tell
one thousandth	**ein Tausendstel**
	aihn TOW-sends-tell

MATH

addition	**Addition**
	AH-dee-tsee-ohn
2 + 1	**zwei plus eins**
	tsvaih plooss aihnts
subtraction	**Subtraktion**
	ZOOBB-trahkk-tsee-ohn
2 - 1	**zwei minus eins**
	tsvaih mee-nooss aihnts
multiplication	**Multiplikation**
	MUHLL-tee-plee-kah-tsee-ohn

2 x 3	**zwei mal drei**
	tsvaih mahl drye
division	**Division**
	DEE-vee-see-ohn
6 ÷ 3	**sechs geteilt durch drei**
	zekks gheh-TYLET doorr[ch] drye

ORDINAL NUMBERS

first	**erster (m) / erste (f) / erstes (n)**
	AIHRS-tehr / AIHRS-teh / AIHRS-tess
second	**zweiter (m) / zweite (f) / zweites (n)**
	TSVAIH-tehr / TSVAIH-teh / TSVAIH-tess
third	**dritter (m) / dritte (f) / drittes (n)**
	DRITT-ehr / DRITT-eh / DRITT-tess
fourth	**vierter (m) / vierte (f) / viertes (n)**
	FEER-tehr / FEER-teh / FEER-tess
fifth	**fünfter (m) / fünfte (f) / fünftes (n)**
	F[UE]NFF-tehr / F[UE]NFF-teh / F[UE]NFF-tess
sixth	**sechster (m) / sechste (f) / sechstes (n)**
	ZEKS-tehr / ZEKS-teh / ZEKS-tess
seventh	**siebter (m) / siebte (f) / siebtes (n)**
	ZEEB-tehr / ZEEB-teh / ZEEB-tess
eighth	**achter (m) / achte (f) / achtes (n)**
	A[CH]-tehr / A[CH]-teh / A[CH]-tess
ninth	**neunter (m) / neunte (f) / neuntes (n)**
	NOYN-tehr / NOYN-teh / NOYN-tess
tenth	**zehnter (m) / zehnte (f) / zehntes (n)**
	TSEHN-tehr / TSEHN-teh / TSEHN-tess
last	**letzter (m) / letzte (f) / letztes (n)**
	LETS-tehr / LETS-teh / LETS-tess

MEASUREMENTS

millimeter	**Millimeter**
	MIL-lee-meh-tehr
centimeter	**Zentimeter**
	TSENN-tee-meh-tehr
meter	**Meter**
	MEH-tehr
kilometer	**Kilometer**
	KEE-loh-meh-tehr
squared	**quadriert**
	kvah-DREEHRT
short	**kurz**
	koorrts
long	**lang**
	lahng

VOLUME

milliliters	**Milliliter**
	MIL-lee-lee-tehr
liter	**Liter**
	LEE-tehr
kilo	**Kilo**
	KEE-loh
cup	**Tasse**
	TAHSS-eh

QUANTITY

some	**etwas**
	AT-vahs
none	**nichts**
	ni[ch]ts
all	**alles**
	AHLL-ehs
many / much	**viele / viel**
	FEEL-eh / feel

a little bit (can be used for quantity or for time)	**etwas**
	AT-vahs
dozen	**Dutzend**
	DUTT-send

SIZE

small	**klein**
	klyne
the smallest	**der / die / das Kleinste**
	dehr / dee / dahs KLYNES-teh
medium	**mittel**
	MITT-ell
big	**groß**
	grohs
fat	**dick**
	dick
wide	**breit**
	brryte
narrow	**schmal**
	shmahl

TIME

Time in German is referred to, literally, by the clock. "What time is it?" translates literally as "How much clock is it?"
For full coverage of number terms, see p7.

HOURS OF THE DAY

What time is it?	**Wie spät ist es?**
	Vee SHP[AE]HT isst as?
At what time?	**Um wie viel Uhr?**
	Oomm VEE-feel oohr?
For how long?	**Wie lange?**
	Vee LUNG-eh?
It's one o'clock.	**Es ist ein Uhr.**
	As isst AIHN oohr.

It's two o'clock.	**Es ist zwei Uhr.**
	As isst TSVAIH oohr.
It's two thirty.	**Es ist halb drei.**
	As isst hahllb DRRYE.
It's two fifteen.	**Es ist Viertel nach zwei.**
	As isst feer-tell nah[ch] TSVAIH.
It's a quarter to three.	**Es ist Viertel vor drei.**
	As isst feer-tell fohr DRRYE.
It's noon.	**Es ist Mittag.**
	As isst MITT-tahgg.
It's midnight.	**Es ist Mitternacht.**
	As isst MITT-ehr-na[ch]t.
It's early.	**Es ist früh.**
	As isst FR[UE]HH.
It's late.	**Es ist spät.**
	As isst SHP[AE]HT.
in the morning	**morgens**
	MORR-ghenns
in the afternoon	**nachmittags**
	NA[CH]-mitt-tahggs
at night	**nachts**
	na[ch]ts
dawn	**Morgendämmerung**
	MORR-ghenn-d[ae]mm-eh-roong

DAYS OF THE WEEK

Sunday	**Sonntag**
	ZONN-tahgg
Monday	**Montag**
	MOHN-tahgg
Tuesday	**Dienstag**
	DEENS-tahgg
Wednesday	**Mittwoch**
	MITT-voh[ch]
Thursday	**Donnerstag**
	DONN-airs-tahgg

Friday	**Freitag**
	FRYE-tahgg
Saturday	**Samstag**
	ZAMMS-tahgg
today	**heute**
	HOY-teh
tomorrow	**morgen**
	MORR-ghenn
yesterday	**gestern**
	GHESS-tehrn
the day before yesterday	**vorgestern**
	FOHR-ghess-tehrn
one week	**eine Woche**
	eye-neh VOH-[ch]eh
next week	**nächste Woche**
	n[ae][ch]s-teh VOH-[ch]eh
last week	**letzte Woche**
	lets-teh VOH-[ch]eh

MONTHS OF THE YEAR

January	**Januar**
	YAHNN-oo-ahr
February	**Februar**
	FEHH-broo-ahr
March	**März**
	M[ae]rts
April	**April**
	ah-PRILL
May	**Mai**
	Maih
June	**Juni**
	YOU-nee
July	**Juli**
	YOU-lee
August	**August**
	ou-GHOOSST

September	**September**
	zepp-TEMM-behr
October	**Oktober**
	okk-TOH-behr
November	**November**
	no-FEMM-behr
December	**Dezember**
	deh-TSEMM-behr
next month	**nächsten Monat**
	n[ae][ch]s-ten MOH-naht
last month	**letzten Monat**
	lets-ten MOH-naht

SEASONS OF THE YEAR

spring	**Frühling**
	FR[UE]H-linng
summer	**Sommer**
	ZOMM-ehr
autumn	**Herbst**
	Herrbst
winter	**Winter**
	VINN-tehr

Falsche Freunde

If you try winging it with Denglish, beware of false cognates, known as *"falsche Freunde"* (false friends)— German words that sound like English ones, but with different meanings. Here are some examples of false cognates.

bald	soon
kahl	bald
Menü	today's special
Speisekarte	menu
Gift	poison
Geschenk	gift
Billion	trillion
Milliarde	billion
Puff	bordello
Hauch / Zug	puff
konsequent	consistent(ly)
folglich	consequently
Dom	cathedral
Kuppel	dome
aktuell	current
eigentlich, wirklich	actual
also	thus, therefore
auch	also
Art	kind, type
Kunst	art
Bad	bath, spa
schlecht	bad
blenden	dazzle, blind
mischen	blend
brav	well behaved
tapfer	brave

GERMAN GRAMMAR BASICS

Like English, German is a Germanic language. Both languages have the same basic alphabet of 26 letters. German has three additional letters with the addition of the umlaut (the two dots over the a, o and u). German is a very phonetic language, meaning words are generally (though not always) pronounced the way they look.

THE ALPHABET

German is a straightforward language with a simple alphabet. It has 29 letters: all of the same letters found in the English alphabet, plus three additional vowels formed by adding an umlaut (two dots) over a, o and u. The umlaut changes the pronunciation of these vowels in a small but important way.

Letter	Name	Pronunciation
a	a	*ah (as in "fAther")*
ä	aeh	*aeh (as in "hEAven")*
b	beh	*b (as in "brave")*
c	tseh	*k (as in "caviar");*
("ch" at beginning of word: hard "k" sound (as in "character"), "ch" in the middle or at the end of a word: softer sound (as in Scottish pronunciation of "Loch"))		
d	deh	*d (as in "day")*
e	ehh	*eh (as in "help")*
f	eff	*f (as in "friend")*
g	gheh	*gh (as in "ghost")*
h	hah	*h (as in "hand")*
stresses all vowels; for combinations with "c" see letter "c"		
i	eeh	*ee (as in "bee")*
j	yott	*y (as in "yellow")*
k	kah	*c (as in "can")*
l	ell	*l (as in "lake")*
m	emm	*m (as in "mother")*

Letter	Name	Pronunciation
n	enn	n (as in "name")
o	ohh	o (as in "often")
ö	oeh	u (as in "burger")
p	peh	p (as in "page");

the combination "ph" is pronounced as "f" (as in "philosophy")

q	coo	q (as in "quest")
r	err	r (as in "ERRor";

however, the German "r" has to be spoken as a rolling "r"

s	ess	s (as in "stay");

the combination "st" at the beginning of a word is pronounced as "sh" (as in "shuttle"), while in the middle or at the end of a word it is pronounced as "st" (as in "stick"); the combination "sch" is pronounced as "sh" (as in "shelf")

t	teh	t (as in "tea");

the combination "tio" is pronounced as "tsee-yoh" (as in the German word "Aktion" - akk-tsee-YOHN)

u	ooh	ooh
ü	ueh	ueh (a slight variant of the "ooh" sound)
v	fauh	f (as in "front")
w	vehh	v (as in "value")
x	ikks	x (as in "extra")
y	YP-see-lohn	ueh (see letter "ü")
z	tsett	ts (as in "iTS")

PRONUNCIATION GUIDE
Vowels

a	ah as the a in father: Vater *(FAH-tehr)*
ä	eh like the ea in heaven: hätte *(hat-teh)*
au	ow as in cow: Haus *(hows)*
ai	aye as in "All in favor, say aye": Mai *(my)*
e	long as the a in tame: zehn *(tsayn)*
eu	oy as in toy: euch *(oy[ch])*

i	ee as in feed
o	oh as in boat
ö	ew as in blue
u	oo as in coo
ü	like the oo in cool

Consonants

b	as in bean: Boot *(boht)*
ch	like the "ch" in loch (as in Loch Ness)
d	as the d in day
f	as in fox: Feuer *(FOY-er)*
g	as in guy: Geist *(guyst)*
h	as in hay: hallo *(HALL-oh)*
j	pronounced like the "y" as in yes: Ja *(yahh)*
k	as in English: Kilometer *(KEE-lo-may-ter)*
l	as in English: links
m	as in English: Mai *(my)*
n	as in English: nein *(nine)*
p	as in English: Pass *(pahs)*
q	qu is pronounced as kv: Quittung *(KVih-toong)*
r	as in English but more rolled: rot *(rote)*
s	at the beginning of words (followed by a vowel) pronounced as z; in the middle and at or near the end of words as in English: selbst *(ZELpst)*
st, sch	like the "sh" in shoe: Stein *(shtine)*; Schule *(SHOO-la)*
ß	like English "s": Straße *(SHTRAH-sseh)*
t	as in English: Tee *(tay)*
v	like the "f" in fox, but more explosive: verwirrt *(fehr-VIRRT)*
w	like the "v" in vase: weiss *(vice)*
x	like English x: extra *(EX-tra)*
z	like "ts" or the "zz" in pizza: Zoo *(tsoh)*

WORD PRONUNCIATION

Syllables in words are also accented in a standard pattern. Generally, in words with two syllables the first syllable is stressed. For longer words, an accent mark is shown to indicate the stress.

Ending in -ieren

studieren	*shtoo-DEE-ren*

Loan word

Computer	*com-PEW-ter*

Compound adjective with hin, her, da or wo

damit	*da-MIT*

GENDER, ADJECTIVES, MODIFIERS

Each noun takes a masculine, feminine or neutral gender and is most often accompanied by a masculine, feminine or neutral definite article, like the English "the" (*der, die* or *das*), or by an indefinite article, like the English "a" or "an" (*ein* or *eine*). Definite articles ("the"), indefinite articles ("a," "an"), and related adjectives change their endings depending on whether they are the subject, direct or indirect object, or possessive. For example, "*Ich bin ein Mann*" (I am a man) becomes "*Ich sehe einen Mann*" (I see a man) because "Mann" is the subject of the first sentence and the direct object of the second. (What is being seen? The man.)

The Definite Article ("the")

	Masculine	Feminine	Neutral
Singular	*der* Hund (the dog)	*die* Katze (the cat)	*das* Tier (the animal)
Plural	*die* Hunde (the dogs)	*die* Katzen (the cats)	*die* Tiere (the animals)

The Indefinite Article ("a" or "an")

	Masculine	Feminine	Neutral
Singular	*ein* Hund (a dog)	*eine* Katze (a cat)	*ein* Tier (an animal)

PERSONAL PRONOUNS

	LIEBEN: "to love"	
I love.	*Ich* liebe.	LEE-beh
You (singular familiar) love.	*Du* liebst.	leebst
He / She / It loves. You (singular formal) love.	*Er / Sie / Es* liebt. Sie lieben.	leebt / LEE-ben
We love.	*Wir* lieben.	LEE-ben
You (plural familiar) love.	*Ihr* liebt.	leebt
They / You (plural formal) love.	*Sie / Sie* lieben.	LEE-ben

Hey, you!

German has two words for "you"— *du*, spoken among friends and familiars, and *Sie*, used among strangers or as a sign of respect toward authority figures. When speaking with a stranger, expect to use *Sie*, unless you are invited to do otherwise. The second-person familiar plural form (*ihr*) is used among friends and family. The second-person formal plural is the same as the second-person formal singular: *Sie*. Both the singular and plural forms of the second-person formal are always written with an upper-case S: "*Sie*."

REGULAR VERB CONJUGATIONS

Most German verbs end in "-en" (*lieben, gehen, kommen*, etc.). To conjugate the present tense of regular verbs, drop the -en and add the following endings:

Present Tense

Regular verbs	GEHEN "to go"	
I go.	Ich gehe.	GHEH-heh
You (singular familiar) go.	Du gehst.	ghehst
He / She / It goes.	Er / Sie (singular feminine) / Es geht.	gheht
You (singular formal) go.	Sie (singular formal) gehen.	GHEH-hen
We go.	Wir gehen.	GHEH-hen
You (plural familiar) go.	Sie gehen.	GHEH-hen
They / You (plural formal) go.	Sie / Sie gehen.	GHEH-hen

Simple Past Tense

These are the simple past tense conjugations for regular verbs.

Regular verbs	LIEBEN "To Live"	
I lived.	Ich lebte.	LEHB-te
You (singular familiar) lived.	Du lebtest.	LAYb-test
He / She / It lived.	Er / Sie / Es lebte.	LAYb-tah
You lived. (singular formal)	Sie lebten.	LAYb-tahn
We lived.	Wir lebten.	LAYb-ten
You (plural familiar) lived.	Ihr lebtet.	LAYb-tet
They / You (plural formal) lived.	Sie / Sie lebten.	LAYb-ten

The Future

For novice German speakers, the easiest way to express the future is to conjugate the verb WERDEN (to go) + any infinitive ("I am going to speak", "you are going to speak", etc.).

I am going to speak.	Ich *werde* reden.	VER-de
You (singular familiar) are going to speak.	Du *wirst* reden.	Virrst
He / She / It is going to speak.	Er / Sie / Es *wird* reden.	Virrd
You (singular formal) are going to speak.	Sie *werden* reden.	Verr-den
We are going to speak.	Wir *werden* reden.	Verr-den
You (plural familiar) are going to speak.	Ihr *werdet* reden.	Verr-det
They / You (plural formal) are going to speak.	Sie / Sie *werden* reden.	Vehrr-den

TO BE OR NOT TO BE (SEIN)

The German verb for "to be," SEIN, is irregular. It is conjugated as follows:

Present Tense

SEIN "To Be"		
I am.	**Ich** *bin.*	bin
You (singular, familiar) **are.**	**Du** *bist.*	bist
He / She / It is.	**Er / Sie / Es** *ist.*	ist
You (singular formal) **are.**	**Sie sind.**	zint
We are.	**Wir** *sind.*	zint
You (plural familiar) **are.**	**Ihr** *seid.*	zeit
They / You (plural formal) **are.**	**Sie sind.**	zint

Simple Past Tense

SEIN "To Be"		
I was.	**Ich** *war.*	vahr
You were.	**Du** *warst.*	vahrst
He / She / It was.	**Er / Sie / Es** *war*	vahr
You (formal) **were.**	**Sie** *waren.*	VAHR-en
We were.	**Wir** *waren.*	VAHR-en
You were.	**Ihr** *wart.*	vahrt
They / You (plural formal) **were.**	**Sie** *waren.*	VAHR-en

IRREGULAR VERBS

German has numerous irregular verbs that stray from the standard -EN conjugations. Rather than bog you down with too much grammar, we're providing the present tense conjugations for the most commonly used irregular verbs.

HABEN "To Have"

I have.	Ich *habe.*	HAH-beh
You (singular familiar) **have.**	Du *hast.*	hahsst
He / She / It has.	Er / Sie / Es *hat.*	haht
You (singular formal) **have.**	Sie *haben.*	HAH-ben
We have.	Wir *haben.*	HAH-ben
You (plural familiar) **have.**	Ihr *habt.*	hahbt
They / You (plural formal) **have.**	Sie / Sie *haben.*	HAH-ben

---

Haben

Haben means "to have," but it's also used to describe conditions such as hunger and thirst. For example:
Ich habe Hunger. I'm hungry.
(Literally: I have hunger.)
Ich habe Durst. I'm thirsty.
(Literally: I have thirst.)

SPRECHEN "To Speak, To Talk"

I speak.	Ich spreche.	SHPRE[CH]-eh
You (singular familiar) speak.	Du sprichst.	shpri[ch]st
He / She / It speaks.	Er / Sie / Es spricht.	shpri[ch]t
You (singular formal) speak.	Sie sprechen.	SHPRE[CH]-en
We speak.	Wir sprechen.	SHPRE[CH]-en
You (plural familiar) speak.	Ihr sprecht.	shpre[ch]t
They / You (plural formal) speak.	Sie / Sie sprechen.	SHPRE[CH]-en

WOLLEN "To Want"

I want.	Ich will.	vill
You (singular familiar) want.	Du willst.	villsst
He / She / It wants.	Er / Sie / Es will.	vill
You (singular formal) want.	Sie wollen.	VOHLL-en
We want.	Wir wollen.	VOHLL-en
You (plural familiar) want.	Ihr wollt.	vohllt
They / You plural formal) want.	Sie / Sie wollen.	VOHLL-en

KOENNEN "To Be Able"

I can.	Ich kann.	KHANN
You (singular familiar) **can.**	Du kann*st.*	khannst
He / She / It can.	Er / Sie / Es kann.	khann
You (singular formal) **can.**	Sie könn*en.*	KH[OE]NN-en
We can.	Wir könn*en.*	KH[OE]NN-en
You (plural familiar) **can.**	Ihr könn*t.*	kh[oe]nnt
They / You (plural formal) **can.**	Sie / Sie könn*en.*	KH[OE]NN-en

KENNEN vs. WISSEN: There are two ways to say "To Know" in German: *kennen* and *wissen*. *Kennen* is to know someone or something, while *wissen* is to know a fact. For example, "*Ich kenne Peter.*" (I know Peter.) BUT "*Ich weiß, wo das Restaurant ist.*" (I know where the restaurant is.)

KENNEN "To Know" (someone)

I know.	Ich kenn*e.*	KHENN-eh
You (singular familiar) **know.**	Du kenn*st.*	khennst
He / She / It knows.	Er / Sie / Es kenn*t.*	khennt
You (singular formal) **know.**	Sie kenn*en.*	KHENN-en
We know.	Wir kenn*en.*	KHENN-en
You (plural familiar) **know.**	Ihr kenn*t.*	khennt
They / You (plural formal) **know.**	Sie / Sie kenn*en.*	KHENN-en

WISSEN "To Know" (something)

I know.	Ich weiß.	vice
You (singular familiar) know.	Du weißt.	vyesst
He / She / It knows.	Er / Sie / Es weiß.	vice
You (singular formal) know.	Sie wissen.	VISS-en
We know.	Wir wissen.	VISS-en
You (plural familiar) know.	Ihr wisst.	visst
They / You (plural formal) know.	Sie / Sie wissen.	VISS-en

Stem-changing Verbs

Some irregular verbs change their stem in addition to their ending. For example:

ESSEN (To Eat)
Ich esse (I eat)
Du isst (You eat)
Er / Sie / Es isst (He / She / It eats)
Wir essen (We eat)
Ihr esst (You eat) (informal)
Sie / Sie essen (You eat / They eat) (formal / pl.)

Notice that the stem only changes in the first three conjugations (I, you, and he/she/it). All of the plural forms are conjugated like regular verbs by adding the correct ending to the stem.

Gefallen

To say you like something, use the verb *gefallen*. *Gefallen* is different from other verbs because the person doing the liking is the subject of the sentence, not the object. For example, to say you like music, you would say:

Mir gefällt Musik. I like music.
(Literally: Music is pleasing to me.)

When what is liked is plural, the verb is plural:

Mir gefallen die Blumen. I like the flowers.
(Literally: The flowers are pleasing to me.)

The person doing the liking is represented by an indirect object pronoun placed in front of the verb, as illustrated below. Remember, gefallen can only be conjugated in two ways: *gefällt* (for singular things that are liked) and *gefallen* (for plural things that are liked). The pronoun changes to reflect who is doing the liking.

GEFALLEN "To Like"

I like Germany.	*Mir* gefällt Deutschland.	geh-FELT
You (informal singular) **like Germany.**	*Dir* gefällt Deutschland.	geh-FELT
He / She/ It likes Germany.	*Ihm / Ihr / Ihm* gefällt Deutschland.	geh-FELT
You (formal singular) **like Germany.**	*Ihnen* gefällt Deutschland.	geh-FELT
We like Germany.	*Uns* gefällt Deutschland.	geh-FELT
You (informal plural) **like Germany.**	*Euch* gefällt Deutschland.	geh-FELT
They / You (formal plural) **like Germany.**	*Ihnen* gefällt Deutschland.	geh-FELT

REFLEXIVE VERBS

German has many reflexive verbs (when the subject and object both refer to the same person or thing). The following common verbs are used reflexively: *sich anziehen* (to get dressed, literally to dress oneself), *sich rasieren* (to shave, literally to shave oneself), *sich duschen* (to shower, literally to shower oneself), and *sich treffen* (to meet, literally to meet one another).

SICH ANZIEHEN "To Dress"

I get dressed.	Ich ziehe mich an.	tsee-he mee[ch]UN
You (singular familiar) **get dressed.**	Du ziehst dich an.	tseeh-st di[ch] UN
He / She / It gets dressed.	Er / Sie / Es zieht sich an.	tseet si[ch] UN
You (singular formal) **get dressed.**	Sie ziehen sich an.	tsee-hen si[ch] UN
We get dressed.	Wir ziehen -uns an.	*tsee-hen oonns UN*
You (plural familiar) **get dressed.**	Ihr zieht euch an.	*tseet oy[ch] UN*
They / You (plural formal) **get dressed.**	Sie / Sie ziehen sich an.	tsee-hen si[ch] UN

CHAPTER TWO

GETTING THERE & GETTING AROUND

This section deals with every form of transportation. Whether you've just reached your destination by plane or you're renting a car to tour the countryside, you'll find the phrases you need in the next 30 pages.

AT THE AIRPORT

I am looking for ____	**Ich suche ____**
	Ee[ch] su[ch]e ____
a porter.	**einen Träger für mein Gepäck.**
	eye-nen tr[ae]ger f[ue]r mine ghe-P[AE]CK.
the check-in counter.	**den Abfertigungsschalter.**
	dehn AB-fertigungs-shahlter.
the ticket counter.	**den Kartenschalter.**
	dehn KAHRR-ten-shahlter.
arrivals.	**den Ankunftsbereich.**
	dehn AN-kunfts-beh-rei[ch].
departures.	**den Abreisebereich.**
	dehn AB-rise-eh-beh-rei[ch].
gate number ____.	**Gate ____.**
	Gate ____.

For full coverage of numbers, see p7.

the waiting area.	**den Wartebereich.**
	dehn WARTEH-beh-rei[ch].
the men's restroom.	**die Herrentoilette.**
	dee hair-renn-toi-LET-teh.
the women's restroom.	**die Damentoilette.**
	dee dah-menn-toi-LET-teh.
the police station.	**die Polizeidienststelle.**
	dee poli-TSAI-deenst-shtelle.
a security guard.	**einen Sicherheitsbeamten.**
	eye-nen SI[CH]ER-heights-beh-ahmten.

the smoking area.	**den Raucherbereich.**
	dehn RAU[CH]-er-beh-rei[ch].
the information booth.	**den Informationsstand.**
	dehn informahtsihons-stahnd.
a public telephone.	**ein öffentliches Telefon.**
	aihn [oe]ffentli[ch]es tehleh-PHON.
an ATM.	**einen Geldautomaten.**
	eye-nen GELD-auto-MAH-ten.
baggage claim.	**die Gepäckausgabe.**
	dee ghe-P[AE]CK-ousgah-beh.
a luggage cart.	**einen Gepäckwagen.**
	eye-nen ghe-P[AE]CK-wah-ghen.
a currency exchange.	**eine Geldwechselstube.**
	eye-neh GELD-whecksel-shtoobeh.
a café.	**ein Café.**
	aihn kaff-EHH.
a restaurant.	**ein Restaurant.**
	aihn restau-RONG.
a bar.	**eine Bar.**
	eye-neh bar.
a bookstore or newsstand.	**eine Buchhandlung oder einen Zeitungsstand.**
	eye-neh BOO[CH]-hahnd-lung ohdehr eye-nen TSITE-oongs-shtahnd.
a duty-free shop.	**einen Duty-Free-Shop.**
	eye-nen duty-FREE shop.
Is there Internet access here?	**Gibt es hier einen Internetzugang?**
	Gheebt as heer eye-nen INTERNET-tsoo-gahng?
I'd like to page someone.	**Ich möchte jemanden ausrufen lassen.**
	Ee[ch] m[oe][ch]teh yeh-mahn-denn OUS-roofen lahssen.
Do you accept credit cards?	**Akzeptieren Sie Kreditkarten?**
	Acktsep-TEEREN zee cre-DEET-kahrr-ten?

CHECKING IN

I would like a one-way ticket to ____.	**Ich hätte gern ein einfaches Ticket nach ____.** *Ee[ch] HAT-teh ghern aihn AIHN-fa[ch]es ticket nah[ch] ____.*
I would like a round trip ticket to ____.	**Ich hätte gern ein Ticket nach ____ inklusive Rückreise.** *Ee[ch] HAT-te ghern aihn AIHN-fa[ch]-as ticket nah[ch] ____ inclu-ZEE-veh R[UE]CK-rise-eh.*
How much are the tickets?	**Wie viel kosten die Tickets?** *Vee-feel costen dee tickets?*
Do you have anything less expensive?	**Haben Sie auch etwas Günstigeres im Angebot?** *Ha-ben zee au[ch] at-WAHS G[UE]NS-tee-geh-res im ahn-ghe-BOHT?*
How long is the flight?	**Wie lange dauert der Flug?** *Vee lahng-eh dauert dehr floog?*
What time does flight ____ leave?	**Welche Abflugzeit hat Flug Nummer ____?** *VELL-[ch]eh UP-floog-tsite hut floog noommer ____?*
What time does flight ____ arrive?	**Welche Ankunftszeit hat Flug Nummer ____?** *VELL-[ch]eh UN-koonfts-tsite hut floog noommer ____?*
Do I have a connecting flight?	**Gibt es einen Anschlussflug?** *Gheebt as eye-nen AN-shluss-floog?*
Do I need to change planes?	**Muss ich umsteigen?** *Muhss ee[ch] UM-shteye-ghenn?*
My flight leaves at __:__.	**Mein Flug geht um __:__ Uhr.** *Mine floog gheht oomm __:__ oor.*

For full coverage of numbers, see p7.
For full coverage of time, see p11.

Common Airport Signs

Ankunft	Arrivals
Abreise	Departures
Terminal	Terminal
Gate	Gate
Tickets	Ticketing
Zoll	Customs
Gepäckausgabe	Baggage Claim
Drücken	Push
Ziehen	Pull
Rauchen verboten	No Smoking
Eingang	Entrance
Ausgang	Exit
Herren	Men's
Damen	Women's
Pendelbusse	Shuttle Buses
Taxis	Taxis

What time will the flight arrive?

Welche Ankunftszeit hat der Flug?
VELL-[ch]eh UN-koonfts-tsite hut dehr floog?

Is the flight on time?

Ist der Flug pünktlich?
Ist dehr floog P[UE]NKT-li[ch]?

Is the flight delayed?

Hat der Flug Verspätung?
Hut dehr floog fair-SP[AE]-toong?

From which terminal is flight ____ leaving?

Welches Abflugterminal hat Flug ____?
VELL-[ch]ess UP-floog-terminal hut floog ____?

From which gate is flight ____ leaving?

Welches Abfluggate hat Flug ____?
VELL-[ch]ess UP-floog-gate hut floog ____?

How much time do I need for check-in?

Wie lange dauert das Einchecken?
Vee lahng-eh douert dahs EYN-checken?

Is there an express check-in line?	**Gibt es einen schnelleren Check-In?** *Gheebt as eye-nen SHNELL-eren check-in?*
Is there electronic check-in?	**Gibt es einen elektronischen Check-In?** *Gheebt as eye-nen ehlec-TROH-nishen check-in?*

Seat Preferences

I would like ____ ticket(s) in ____	**Ich hätte gern ____ Ticket(s) in ____** *Ee[ch] HUT-te ghern ____ Ticket(s) in ____*
first class.	**der ersten Klasse.** *dehr AIR-sten klasseh.*
business class.	**Business-Klasse.** *business klasseh.*
economy class.	**Economy-Klasse.** *economy klasseh.*
I would like ____	**Geben Sie mir bitte einen ____** *Ghehben zee mere bit-eh eye-nen*
Please don't give me ____	**Geben Sie mir bitte keinen ____** *Ghehben zee mere bit-eh k-eye-nen ____*
a window seat.	**Fensterplatz.** *FAN-stir-plahts.*
an aisle seat.	**Gangplatz.** *GAHNG-plahts.*
an emergency exit row seat.	**Platz an einem Notausgang.** *plahts un eye-nem NOHT-ous-gahng.*
a bulkhead seat.	**Fensterplatz.** *FAN-stir-plahts.*
a seat by the restroom.	**Platz in der Nähe der Toiletten.** *plahts in dehr N[AE]-he dehr toi-LET-ten.*
a seat near the front.	**Platz im vorderen Teil.** *plahts im FOR-deren tile.*

a seat near the middle.	**Platz im mittleren Teil.**
	plahts im MITT-leren tile.
a seat near the back.	**Platz im hinteren Teil.**
	plahts im HIN-teren tile.
Is there a meal on the flight?	**Gibt es Verpflegung während des Flugs?**
	Gheebt as fair-PFLEH-goong v[ae]h-rend des floogs?
I'd like to order ____	**Ich hätte gern ____**
	Ee[ch] hut-te ghern ____
a vegetarian meal.	**ein vegetarisches Essen.**
	aihn veh-gheh-TA-rishes essen.
a kosher meal.	**ein koscheres Essen.**
	aihn KO-sheres essen.
a diabetic meal.	**ein Essen für Diabetiker.**
	aihn essen f[ue]r dee-ah-BEH-ticker.
I am traveling to ____.	**Ich bin auf dem Weg nach ____.**
	Ee[ch] bin ouf dehm vehg na[ch] ____.
I am coming from ____.	**Ich komme gerade aus ____.**
	Ee[ch] com-me ghe-RA-de ous ____.
I arrived from ____.	**Ich bin aus ____ angekommen.**
	Ee[ch] bin ous ____ UN-gheh-com-menn.

For full coverage of country terms, see English / German dictionary.

I'd like to change / cancel / confirm my reservation.	**Ich möchte meine Reservierung ändern / stornieren / bestätigen.**
	Ee[ch] m[oe][ch]te mine-eh rehsehr-VEE-rung [ae]n-dern / shtor-NEE-ren / beh-ST[AE]H-ti-ghen.
I have ____ bags to check.	**Ich habe ____ Taschen aufzugeben.**
	Ee[ch] hah-beh ____ tashen OUF-tsoo-GEH-ben.

For full coverage of numbers, see p7.

Passengers with Special Needs

Is that wheelchair accessible?	**Ist dieser Rollstuhl frei?**
	Isst DEE-sehr ROLL-shtool frei?
May I have a wheelchair / walker please?	**Könnte ich bitte einen Rollstuhl / eine Gehhilfe bekommen?**
	K[oe]nnte ee[ch] bit-eh eye-nen ROLL-shtool / eye-neh GHEH-hilfeh beh-COM-men?
I need some assistance boarding.	**Ich benötige Hilfe beim Einsteigen.**
	Ee[ch] beh-N[OE]-tiggeh HILL-feh buym AIHN-shty-ghen.
I need to bring my service dog.	**Ich bin auf die Begleitung meines Blindenhundes angewiesen.**
	Ee[ch] bin ouf dee beh-GLEYE-toong minus BLIN-den-hoon-des un-gheh-VEE-sen.
Do you have services for the hearing impaired?	**Haben Sie Angebote für Hörgeschädigte?**
	Hah-ben zee un-gheh-BOH-teh f[ue]r H[OE]R-gheh-SH[AE]H-digg-teh?
Do you have services for the visually impaired?	**Haben Sie Angebote für Sehbehinderte?**
	Hah-ben zee un-gheh-BOH-teh f[ue]r SEH-behhinderteh?

Trouble at Check-In

How long is the delay?	**Wie viel beträgt die Verspätung?**
	Vee feel beh-TR[AE]GT dee fair-SHP[AE]H-tung?
My flight was late.	**Mein Flug hatte Verspätung.**
	Mine floog hut-eh fair-SHP[AE]H-tung.
I missed my flight.	**Ich habe meinen Flug verpasst.**
	Ee[ch] hah-beh my-nen floog fair-PASSED.
When is the next flight?	**Wann geht der nächste Flug?**
	Vann gheht dehr n[ae][ch]s-teh floog?

May I have a meal voucher? **Bekomme ich einen Essensgutschein?**
Beh-COM-meh ee[ch] eye-nen ESSENCE-goot-shine?

May I have a room voucher? **Bekomme ich einen Zimmergutschein?**
Beh-COM-meh ee[ch] eye-nen TSIMMER-goot-shine?

AT CUSTOMS / SECURITY CHECKPOINTS

I'm traveling with a group. **Ich bin Mitglied einer Reisegruppe.**
Ee[ch] bin mit-GLEED eye-ner RISE-EH-gruppeh.

I'm on my own. **Ich reise allein.**
Ee[ch] rise-eh ah-LINE.

I'm traveling on business. **Ich befinde mich auf Geschäftsreise.**
Ee[ch] beh-FINN-deh mi[ch] ouf gheh-SHAFTS-rise-eh.

I'm on vacation. **Ich mache Urlaub.**
Ee[ch] ma[ch]eh OOR-laub.

I have nothing to declare. **Ich habe nichts zu verzollen.**
Ee[ch] hah-beh ni[ch]ts tsoo fair-TSOLLEN.

I would like to declare ____. **Ich habe ____ zu verzollen.**
Ee[ch] hah-beh ____ tsoo fair-TSOLLEN.

I have some liquor. **Ich habe etwas Alkohol dabei.**
Ee[ch] hah-beh AT-vahs alkohol dah-BY.

I have some cigars. **Ich habe ein paar Zigarren dabei.**
Ee[ch] hah-beh aihn pahr tsi-GARREN dah-BY.

They are gifts. **Das sind Geschenke.**
Dahs sind gheh-SHENK-eh.

They are for personal use. **Sie sind für den Privatgebrauch.**
Zee sind f[ue]r dehn pree-VAAT-gheh-brau[ch].

GETTING THERE

That is my medicine.	**Das ist meine Medizin.**
	Dahs isst my-neh mehdi-TSIHN.
I have my prescription.	**Ich habe ein Rezept.**
	Ee[ch] hah-beh aihn reh-TSEPT.
My children are traveling on the same passport.	**Meine Kinder reisen mit demselben Ausweis.**
	My-neh KIN-der rise-en mit dehm selben OUS-vise.
I'd like a male / female officer to conduct the search.	**Ich hätte gern, dass die Durchsuchung von einem Mann / einer Frau durchgeführt wird.**
	Ee[ch] hat-teh ghern, dahss dee dur[ch]-SUH-[ch]ung fonn eye-nem mahnn / eye-ner frau dur[ch]-gheh-F[UE]HRT wird.

Trouble at Security

Help me. I've lost ____	**Könnten Sie mir bitte helfen? Ich habe ____**
	K[oe]nnten zee mere bit-eh HELL-fen? Ee[ch] hah-beh ____
my passport.	**meinen Ausweis verloren.**
	my-nen OUS-vise fer-LOH-ren.
my boarding pass.	**meine Bordkarte verloren.**
	my-ne BORT-kahrr-teh fer-LOH-ren.
my identification.	**meine Papiere verloren.**
	my-ne pa-PEE-reh fer-LOH-ren.
my wallet.	**meine Geldbörse verloren.**
	my-ne GELD-b[oe]rseh fer-LOH-ren.
my purse.	**meine Handtasche verloren.**
	my-ne HAHND-tasheh fer-LOH-ren.
Someone stole my purse / wallet!	**Jemand hat meine Handtasche / meine Geldbörse gestohlen!**
	YEH-mahnd hut my-ne HANHD-tasheh / my-ne GELD-b[oe]rseh gheh-SHTOH-len!

Listen Up: Security Lingo

Bitte ziehen Sie Ihre Schuhe aus.	Please remove your shoes.
Ziehen Sie Ihre Jacke aus.	Remove your jacket / sweater.
Legen Sie Ihren Schmuck ab.	Remove your jewelry.
Legen Sie Ihre Taschen auf das Band.	Place your bags on the conveyor belt.
Treten Sie zur Seite.	Step to the side.
Wir müssen Sie abtasten.	We have to do a hand search.

IN-FLIGHT

It's unlikely you'll need much German on the plane, but these phrases will help if a bilingual flight attendant is unavailable or if you need to talk to a German-speaking neighbor.

I think that's my seat.	**Ich glaube, das ist mein Platz.** *Ee[ch] GLAU-beh, das isst MINE plahts.*
May I have ___	**Ich hätte gern ___** *Ee[ch] hat-eh ghern ___*
water?	**ein stilles Wasser.** *aihn shtilles vahsser.*
sparkling water?	**ein Wasser mit Kohlensäure.** *aihn vahsser mit COHLEN-soi-reh.*
orange juice?	**einen Orangensaft.** *eye-nen oh-RUNSHEHN-saft.*
soda?	**eine Limonade.** *eye-ne limo-NAH-deh.*
diet soda?	**eine Diätlimonade.** *eye-ne dee-ATE-limo-NAH-deh.*
a beer?	**ein Bier.** *aihn beer.*
wine?	**ein Glas Wein.** *aihn glahs vine.*

For a complete list of drinks, see p80.

GETTING THERE

a pillow?	**ein Kissen.** *aihn KISS-en.*
a blanket?	**eine Decke.** *eye-ne DECK-eh.*
a hand wipe?	**ein Tuch für die Hände.** *aihn tuh[ch] f[ue]r dee H[AE]N-deh.*
headphones?	**Kopfhörer.** *KOPF-h[oe]rer.*
a magazine or newspaper?	**eine Zeitschrift oder eine Zeitung.** *eye-ne TSAIT-shrift ohdehr eye-ne TSAI-toong.*
When will the meal be served?	**Wann wird das Essen serviert?** *Vann vird dahs ESSEN sehr-VEERT?*
How long until we land?	**Wie lange noch bis zur Landung?** *Vee lahng-he no[ch] bis tsoor LANN-doong?*
May I move to another seat?	**Dürfte ich mich bitte woanders hinsetzen?** *D[ue]rfte ee[ch] mi[ch] bit-eh wo-AHNN-ders HIN-settsen?*
How do I turn the light on / off?	**Wie kann ich das Licht einschalten / ausschalten?** *Vee kann ee[ch] dahs li[ch]t AIHN-shahllten / OUS-shahllten?*

Trouble In-Flight

These headphones are broken.	**Dieser Kopfhörer funktioniert nicht.** *DEE-sehr KOPF-h[oe]rer funktsio-NEERT ni[ch]t.*
I spilled.	**Ich habe etwas verschüttet.** *Ee[ch] hah-beh AT-vas fair-SH[UE]T-tet.*
My child spilled.	**Mein Kind hat etwas verschüttet.** *Mine kinnd hut AT-vahs fair-SH[UE]T-tet.*

My child is sick.

Meinem Kind ist schlecht.
Mine-m kinnd isst shle[ch]t.

I need an airsickness bag.

Ich brauche eine Spucktüte.
Ee[ch] BRAU-[ch]eh eye-ne SHPUCK-t[ue]teh.

I smell something strange.

Hier riecht etwas seltsam.
Hear REE[CH]T at-vahs SELLT-sahm.

That passenger is behaving suspiciously.

Dieser Passagier verhält sich verdächtig.
Dee-sehr passa-SHEER fair-H[AE]LT si[ch] fair-D[AE][CH]-tig.

BAGGAGE CLAIM

Where is baggage claim for flight ____?

Wo finde ich die Gepäckausgabe für Flug ____?
Voh fin-de ee[ch] dee ghe-P[AE]CK-ousgahbeh f[ue]r floog ____?

Would you please help with my bags?

Könnten Sie mir bitte mit meinem Gepäck behilflich sein?
K[oe]nn-ten zee mere bit-eh mit mine-em ghe-P[AE]CK beh-HILLF-li[ch] sine?

I am missing ____ bags.

Mir fehlen ____ Taschen.
Mere FEH-lenn ____ tashen.

For full coverage of numbers, see p7.

My bag is ____

Meine Tasche ____
My-neh tasheh ____

lost.

ist verschwunden.
isst fair-SHWOON-den.

damaged.

wurde beschädigt.
voor-deh beh-SH[AE]H-diggt.

stolen.

wurde gestohlen.
voor-deh gheh-SHTOH-len.

a suitcase.

ist ein Koffer.
isst aihn COUGH-er.

a briefcase.

ist ein Aktenkoffer.
isst aihn ACKTEN-cough-er.

GETTING THERE

a carry-on.	**ist eine Tragetasche.**
	isst eye-ne TRAH-gheh-tasheh.
a suit bag.	**ist ein Kleidersack.**
	isst aihn kl-EYE-dehr-sahck.
a trunk.	**ist ein Schrankkoffer.**
	isst aihn SHRANK-cough-er.
golf clubs.	**sind Golfschläger.**
	sinnd GOLF-shl[ae]h-gher.

For full coverage of color terms, see English / German Dictionary.

hard.	**ist hart.**
	isst harrt.
made out of ____	**ist aus ____**
	isst ous ____
canvas.	**Stoff.**
	shtoff.
vinyl.	**Vinyl.**
	vee-N[UE]HL.
leather.	**Leder.**
	LEH-der.
hard plastic.	**Hartplastik.**
	HARRT-plahstick.
aluminum.	**Aluminium.**
	ahlu-MIH-nium.

RENTING A VEHICLE

Is there a car rental agency in the airport?	**Gibt es am Flughafen eine Autovermietung?**
	Gheebt as ahm FLOOG-hahfen eye-ne OUTOH-fair-meetung?
I have a reservation.	**Ich habe eine Reservierung.**
	Ee[ch] hah-beh eye-ne reh-sehr-VEE-rung.

Vehicle Preferences

I would like to rent ____	**Ich möchte gern ____ mieten.**
	Ee[ch] m[oe][ch]-te ghern ____ meeten.

an economy car.	**ein sparsames Auto** *aihn SHPAHR-summes outoh*
a midsize car.	**einen Mittelklassewagen** *eye-nen MITTEL-clahsseh-wahghen*
a sedan.	**eine Limousine** *eye-ne limo-SEENEH*
a convertible.	**ein Cabrio** *aihn CAAH-bree-oh*
a van.	**einen Van** *eye-nen van*
a sports car.	**einen Sportwagen** *eye-nen SHPORT-wahghen*
a 4-wheel-drive vehicle.	**ein Auto mit Vierradantrieb** *aihn outoh mit FEAR-rahd-antreeb*
a motorcycle.	**ein Motorrad** *aihn moh-TO-rahd*
a scooter.	**einen Roller** *eye-nen roller*
Do you have one with ____	**Ist ein Fahrzeug mit ____ verfügbar?** *Isst aihn FAAR-tsoig mit ____ fair-F[UE]G-bahr?*
air conditioning?	**Klimaanlage** *CLEE-mah-un-lahgheh*
a sunroof?	**Sonnendach** *SONNEN-da[ch]*
a CD player?	**CD-Player** *TSEH-DEH player*
satellite radio?	**Satellitenradio** *sattel-ITTEN-rah-dee-oh*
satellite tracking?	**Navigationssystem** *nah-vee-ghah-TSEEONS-sys-tehm*
an onboard map?	**Straßenatlas** *SHTRAHSSEN-aht-lahss*

a DVD player?	**DVD-Player** *DHE-FOUH-DEH player*
child seats?	**Kindersitzen** *KIN-dehr-sitsen*
Do you have a ____	**Haben Sie ein ____** *Hah-ben zee aihn ____*
smaller car?	**kleineres Auto?** *CLYE-neres outoh?*
bigger car?	**größeres Auto?** *gr[oe]ceres outoh?*
cheaper car?	**günstigeres Auto?** *GH[UE]N-stee-gheres outoh?*
Do you have a non-smoking car?	**Haben Sie ein Nichtraucherauto?** *Hah-ben zee aihn NI[CH]T-rau-[ch]er-outoh?*
I need an automatic transmission.	**Ich hätte gern ein Automatikgetriebe.** *Ee[ch] hut-teh ghern aihn outoh-MAH-tik-ghe-treebeh.*
A standard transmission is okay.	**Schaltgetriebe ist in Ordnung.** *Shallt-ghe-treebeh isst in ORD-noong.*
May I have an upgrade?	**Könnte ich bitte eine höhere Kategorie bekommen?** *K[oe]nn-te ee[ch] bit-eh eye-ne h[oe]her-eh kahte-gho-REE beh-COM-men?*

Money Matters

What's the daily / weekly / monthly rate?	**Wie hoch sind die Kosten pro Tag / Woche / Monat?** *Vee hoh[ch] sind dee COS-ten proh tahg / wo[ch]eh / MOH-naht?*
What is the mileage rate?	**Wie hoch sind die Kosten pro Kilometer?** *Vee hoh[ch] sind dee COS-ten proh KILO-mehter?*

How much is insurance?	**Wie viel kostet die Versicherung?**
	Vee feel costet dee fair-SI[CH]E-roong?
Are there other fees?	**Fallen weitere Kosten an?**
	Fahllen VYE-tereh COS-ten un?
Is there a weekend rate?	**Gibt es einen Wochenendtarif?**
	Gheebt as eye-nen WO-[ch]en-end-ta-REEF?

Technical Questions

What kind of fuel does it take?	**Welche Kraftstoffart muss ich verwenden?**
	Vell-[ch]e KRAFFT-shtoff-art muss ee[ch] fair-VENN-denn?
Do you have the manual in English?	**Haben Sie ein englisches Handbuch?**
	Hah-ben zee aihn ENG-lishes hahnd-boo[ch]?
Do you have a booklet in English with the local traffic laws?	**Haben Sie eine englische Broschüre mit den örtlichen Verkehrsregeln?**
	Hah-ben zee eye-ne ENG-lisheh bro-SH[UE]-reh mit dehn [oe]rt-li-[ch]en fair-CARES-reh-gheln?

Technical Issues

Fill it up, please.	**Volltanken, bitte.**
	FOLL-tunken, bit-eh.
It is already dented.	**Das Fahrzeug ist bereits beschädigt.**
	Dahs FAAR-tsoig isst beh-raits beh-SH[AE]H-diggt.
It is scratched.	**Das Fahrzeug hat einen Kratzer.**
	Dahs FAHR-tsoig hut eye-nen KRATT-ser.

The ____ doesn't work.	**Der / Die / Das ____ funktioniert nicht.**
	Dehr / Dee / Dahs ____ funk-tsio-NEERT ni[ch]t.

See diagram on p47 for car parts.

The tires look low.	**Die Reifen scheinen wenig Druck zu haben.**
	Dee RYE-fan shy-nen wehnig droock tsoo hah-ben.
It has a flat tire.	**Das Fahrzeug hat einen Platten.**
	Dahs FAAR-tsoig hut eye-nen plahtten.
Whom do I call for service?	**Wo kann ich anrufen, wenn ich Hilfe benötige?**
	Voh kann ee[ch] UN-roofen, venn ee[ch] HILL-fe beh-N[OE]-tiggeh?
It won't start.	**Der Motor springt nicht an.**
	Dehr MO-tor shpringt ni[ch]t un.
It's out of gas.	**Der Tank ist leer.**
	Dehr tahnk isst lehr.
The Check Engine light is on.	**Das Lämpchen für ein Problem mit dem Motor leuchtet.**
	Dahs L[AE]MP-[ch]en f[ue]r aihn proh-BLEHM mit dehm MO-tor loy[ch]ted.
The oil light is on.	**Das Öllämpchen leuchtet.**
	Dahs [OE]HL-l[ae]mp-[ch]en loy[ch]ted.
The brake light is on.	**Die Bremsleuchte leuchtet.**
	Dee BREMS-loy[ch]teh loy[ch]ted.
It runs rough.	**Das Fahrzeug läuft unruhig.**
	Dahs FAAR-tsoig loyft OON-ruhig.
The car is over-heating.	**Das Fahrzeug überhitzt.**
	Dahs FAAR-tsoig [ue]ber-HITST.

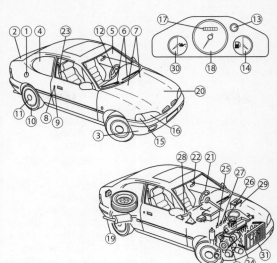

1. Tank
2. Kofferraum
3. Stoßstange
4. Fenster
5. Windschutzscheibe
6. Scheibenwischer
7. Scheibenwaschanlage
8. Tür
9. Schloss
10. Reifen
11. Radkappe
12. Lenkrad
13. Warnleuchte
14. Tankanzeige
15. Blinker
16. Scheinwerfer
17. Kilometerzähler

18. Tacho
19. Auspuff
20. Motorhaube
21. Lenkrad
22. Rückspiegel
23. Sicherheitsgurt
24. Motor
25. Gaspedal
26. Kupplung
27. Bremse
28. Handbremse
29. Batterie
30. Ölstandsanzeige
31. Kühler
32. Keilriemen

Asking for Directions

Excuse me, please.	**Verzeihung bitte.**
	Fair-TSYE-hoong bit-eh.
How do I get to _____?	**Wie komme ich zum _____?**
	Vee COMM-eh ee[ch] tsoomm _____?
Go straight.	**Gehen Sie geradeaus.**
	Ghe-hen zee ghe-RA-deh ous.
Turn left.	**Gehen Sie nach links.**
	Ghe-hen zee na[ch] links.
Continue right.	**Gehen Sie nach rechts.**
	Ghe-hen zee na[ch] re[ch]ts.
It's on the right.	**Das Ziel befindet sich auf der rechten Seite.**
	Dahs tseel beh-FIN-det si[ch] ouf dehr RE[CH]-ten SYE-teh.
Can you show me on the map?	**Könnten Sie mir das bitte auf der Karte zeigen?**
	K[oe]nn-ten zee mere dahs bit-eh ouf dehr KAHRR-teh tsye-ghen?
How far is it from here?	**Wie weit ist das von hier entfernt?**
	Vee vye-t isst dahs fonn heer ent-FAIRNT?
Is this the right road for _____?	**Ist das die Straße nach _____?**
	Isst dahs dee shtrahseh na[ch] _____?
I've lost my way.	**Ich habe mich verirrt.**
	Ee[ch] hah-beh mi[ch] fair-IRRT.
Would you repeat that?	**Könnten Sie das bitte wiederholen?**
	K[oe]nn-ten zee dahs bit-eh veeder-HOH-len?
Thanks for your help.	**Vielen Dank für Ihre Hilfe.**
	FEEL-en dunk f[ue]r ee-reh HILL-feh.

For full coverage of direction-related terms, see p5.

Road Signs

Geschwindigkeitsbegrenzung	Speed Limit
Stopp	Stop
Vorfahrt gewähren	Yield
Gefahr	Danger
Sackgasse	No Exit
Einbahnstraße	One Way
Einfahrt verboten	Do Not Enter
Straße gesperrt	Road Closed
Maut	Toll
Nur Bargeld	Cash Only
Parken verboten	No Parking
Parkgebühr	Parking Fee
Parkhaus	Parking Garage

Sorry, Officer

What is the speed limit?

Welche Geschwindigkeitsbegrenzung gilt hier?
Vell-[ch]eh ghe-SHWINN-digg-keits-beh-gren-tsoong guilt heer?

I wasn't going that fast.

So schnell bin ich nicht gefahren.
Soh shnell bin i[ch] ni[ch]t ghe-FAH-renn.

How much is the fine?

Wie hoch ist die Strafe?
Vee hoh[ch] isst dee SHTRA-fe?

Where do I pay the fine?

Wo muss ich die Strafe bezahlen?
Voh muhss i[ch] dee shtra-fe beh-ZAH-len?

Do I have to go to court?

Komme ich vor Gericht?
Com-me ee[ch] fohr ghe-RI[CH]T?

I had an accident.

Ich hatte einen Unfall.
Ee[ch] hut-eh eye-nen OON-fahll.

The other driver hit me.

Der andere Fahrer hat den Unfall verursacht.
Dehr un-dehreh FAH-rer hut dehn OON-fahll fair-OOR-sa[ch]t.

I'm at fault.	**Es war mein Fehler.** *Ess vahr MINE fehler.*

BY TAXI

Where is the taxi stand?	**Wo ist der Taxistand?** *Voh isst dehr TAHXEE-stahnd?*
Is there a limo / bus / van for my hotel?	**Fährt eine Limousine / ein Bus / ein Van zu meinem Hotel?** *F[ae]hrt eye-ne limo-SEENHE / aihn booss / aihn van tsoo my-nem ho-TELL?*
I need to get to _____.	**Bringen Sie mich bitte zum _____.** *Bring-hen zee mi[ch] bit-eh tsoom _____.*
How much will that cost?	**Wie viel wird das kosten?** *Vee feel vird dahs costen?*
How long will it take?	**Wie lange dauert die Fahrt?** *Vee lahng-eh douert dee fahrt?*
Can you take me / us to the train / bus station?	**Können Sie mich / uns bitte zum Bahnhof / Busbahnhof bringen?** *K[oe]n-nen zee mi[ch] / oons bit-eh tsoom BAHN-hohf / BOOSS-bahn-hohf bring-hen?*
I am in a hurry.	**Ich bin in Eile.** *Ee[ch] bin in AY-leh.*

Listen Up: Taxi Lingo

Steigen Sie ein!	Get in!
Lassen Sie Ihr Gepäck stehen. Ich kümmere mich darum.	Leave your luggage. I got it.
Das kostet sieben Euro pro Tasche.	It's seven Euros for each bag.
Wie viele Fahrgäste?	How many passengers?
Sind Sie in Eile?	Are you in a hurry?

Slow down.	**Fahren Sie bitte langsamer.** *Fah-ren zee bit-eh LAHNG-summer.*
Am I close enough to walk?	**Kann ich von hier aus zu Fuß gehen?** *Cahnn ee[ch] fonn heer ous tsoo FOOS ghe-hen?*
Let me out here.	**Lassen Sie mich hier bitte aussteigen.** *Lahssen zee mi[ch] heer bit-eh OUS-shtye-ghen.*
That's not the correct change.	**Das Wechselgeld stimmt leider nicht.** *Dahs VECK-sell-geld shtimmt lye-der ni[ch]t.*

BY TRAIN

How do I get to the train station?	**Wie komme ich zum Bahnhof?** *Vee COM-meh ee[ch] tsoom BAHN-hohf?*
Would you take me to the train station?	**Könnten Sie mich bitte zum Bahnhof bringen?** *K[oe]nn-ten zee mi[ch] bit-eh tsoom BAHN-hohf bring-hen?*
How long is the trip to ____?	**Wie lange dauert die Fahrt nach ____?** *Vee lahng-eh douert dee fahrt na[ch] ____?*
When is the next train?	**Wann geht der nächste Zug?** *Vahnn gheht dehr n[ae][ch]s-teh tsoog?*
Do you have a schedule / timetable?	**Haben Sie einen Fahrplan?** *Hah-ben zee eye-nen FAAR-plahn?*
Do I have to change trains?	**Muss ich umsteigen?** *Muhss ee[ch] OOMM-shtye-ghen?*
a one-way ticket	**ein einfaches Ticket** *aihn AIHN-fa-[ch]es ticket*

a round-trip ticket	**ein Hin- und Rückreiseticket** *aihn hin oonnd R[UE]CK-rise-eh-ticket*
Which platform does it leave from?	**Von welchem Gleis fährt der Zug ab?** *Fonn vell-[ch]emm glise f[ae]hrt dehr tsoog ab?*
Is there a bar car?	**Gibt es einen Barwagen?** *Gheebt as eye-nen BAR-vah-ghen?*
Is there a dining car?	**Gibt es einen Speisewagen?** *Gheebt as eye-nen SHPY-seh-vah-ghen?*
Which car is my seat in?	**In welchem Wagen befindet sich mein Platz?** *In VELL-[ch]em VAH-ghen beh-FIN-det si[ch] mine PLAHTS?*
Is this seat taken?	**Ist dieser Platz besetzt?** *Isst DEE-sehr plahts beh-SETST?*
Where is the next stop?	**Wo ist der nächste Halt?** *Voh isst dehr n[ae][ch]s-teh HALLT?*
How many stops to ____?	**Wie viele Haltestellen noch bis ____?** *Vee fee-leh HALLT-teh-shtell-en noh[ch] biss ____?*
What's the train number and destination?	**Welche Zugnummer und welchen Zielort hat dieser Zug?** *Vell-[ch]eh TSOOG-noommer oonnd vell-[ch]enn TSEEL-ort hut deeser tsoog?*

BY BUS

How do I get to the bus station?	**Wie komme ich zum Busbahnhof?** *Vee COM-meh ee[ch] tsoom BOOSS-bahn-hohf?*

Would you take me to the bus station?	**Könnten Sie mich bitte zum Busbahnhof bringen?**
	K[oe]nn-ten zee mi[ch] bit-eh tsoom BOOSS-bahn-hohf bring-hen?
May I have a bus schedule?	**Könnte ich bitte einen Busfahrplan bekommen?**
	K[oe]nn-teh ee[ch] bit-eh eye-nen BOOSS-faar-plahn beh-COM-men?
Which bus goes to ____?	**Welcher Bus fährt nach ____?**
	Vell-[ch]er booss f[ae]hrt na[ch] ____?
Where does it leave from?	**Von wo fährt er ab?**
	Fonn VOH f[ae]hrt ehr ab?
How long does the bus take?	**Wie lange dauert die Fahrt?**
	Vee LAHNG-eh douert dee fahrt?
How much is it?	**Wie viel kostet das?**
	Vee feel COSS-tet dahs?
Is there an express bus?	**Gibt es einen Expressbus?**
	Gheebt as eye-nen ex-PRESS-booss?
Does it make local stops?	**Hält der Bus unterwegs?**
	H[ae]llt dehr booss oonter-VEHGS?
Does it run at night?	**Fährt der Bus nachts?**
	F[ae]hrt dehr booss NA[CH]TS?
When does the next bus leave?	**Wann geht der nächste Bus?**
	Vann gheht dehr n[ae][ch]s-teh BOOSS?
a one-way ticket	**ein einfaches Ticket**
	aihn AIHN-fa-[ch]es ticket
a round-trip ticket	**ein Hin- und Rückreiseticket**
	aihn hin oonnd R[UE]CK-rise-eh-ticket
How long will the bus be stopped?	**Wie lange steht der Bus?**
	Vee lahng-eh SHTEHT dehr booss?
Is there an air conditioned bus?	**Gibt es einen klimatisierten Bus?**
	Gheebt as eye-nen kleema-tee-SEER-ten booss?

Is this seat taken?	**Ist dieser Platz besetzt?**
	Isst DEE-sehr plahts beh-SETST?
Where is the next stop?	**Wo ist der nächste Halt?**
	Voh isst dehr n[ae][ch]s-teh HALLT?
Please tell me when we reach ___.	**Könnten Sie mir bitte sagen, wann wir ___ erreichen?**
	K[oe]nn-ten zee mere bit-eh SAH-ghen, vann veer ___ err-RYE-[ch]en?
Let me off here.	**Lassen Sie mich hier bitte aussteigen.**
	Lahssen zee mi[ch] heer bit-eh OUS-shtye-ghen.

BY BOAT OR SHIP

Would you take me to the port?	**Könnten Sie mich bitte zum Hafen bringen?**
	K[oe]nn-ten zee mi[ch] bit-eh tsoom HAH-fenn bring-hen?
When does the ship sail?	**Wann legt das Schiff ab?**
	Vann lehgt dahs shiff ab?
How long is the trip?	**Wie lange dauert die Reise?**
	Vee lahng-eh douert dee rise-eh?
Where are the life preservers?	**Wo befinden sich die Schwimmwesten?**
	Voh beh-fin-den si[ch] dee SHVIMM-vess-ten?
I would like a private cabin.	**Ich hätte gern eine Einzelkabine.**
	Ee[ch] h[ae]tteh ghern eye-ne AIHN-tsell-kah-beeneh.
Is the trip rough?	**Ist mit hohem Seegang zu rechnen?**
	Isst mit HOH-hemm SEH-gahng tsoo re[ch]nen?
I feel seasick.	**Ich bin seekrank.**
	Ee[ch] bin SEH-krahnk.

I need some seasick pills.	**Ich benötige Tabletten gegen Seekrankheit.** *Ee[ch] beh-N[OE]-tiggeh tah-BLETT-en ghe-ghen SEH-krahnk-height.*
Where is the bathroom?	**Wo finde ich die Toiletten?** *Voh fin-deh ee[ch] dee toi-LET-ten?*
Does the ship have a casino?	**Gibt es auf dem Schiff ein Casino?** *Gheebt as ouf dehm shiff aihn kah-ZEE-noh?*
Will the ship stop at ports along the way?	**Legt das Schiff unterwegs an?** *Lehggt dahs shiff oonter-vehggs AN?*

BY SUBWAY

Where's the subway station?	**Wo finde ich die U-Bahn-Haltestelle?** *Voh fin-deh ee[ch] dee OOH-bahn-hallt-eh-shtell-eh?*
Where can I buy a ticket?	**Wo kann ich ein Ticket kaufen?** *Voh cann ee[ch] aihn ticket COW-fehn?*
Could I have a map of the subway?	**Könnte ich bitte einen Plan des U-Bahn-Netzes bekommen?** *K[oe]nn-teh ee[ch] bit-eh eye-nen plahn dess OOH-bahn-netsess beh-COM-men?*
Which line should I take for ____?	**Welche Linie fährt nach ____?** *Vell-[ch]eh LEE-nee-eh f[ae]hrt nah[ch]?*
Is this the right line for ____?	**Ist das die Linie nach ____?** *Isst dahs dee LEE-nee-eh na[ch] ____?*
Which stop is it for ____?	**An welcher Haltestelle muss ich für ____ aussteigen?** *Un vell-[ch]er HALL-teh-shtell-eh muhss ee[ch] f[ue]r ____ OUS-shtye-ghen?*

SUBWAY TICKETS

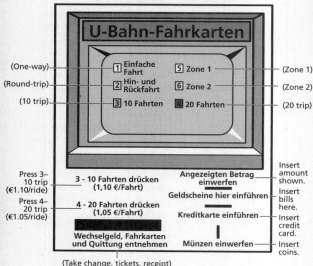

U-Bahn-Fahrkarten

(One-way) — 1 Einfache Fahrt

(Round-trip) — 2 Hin- und Rückfahrt

(10 trip) — 3 10 Fahrten

5 Zone 1 — (Zone 1)

6 Zone 2 — (Zone 2)

4 20 Fahrten — (20 trip)

Press 3– 10 trip (€1.10/ride) — 3 - 10 Fahrten drücken (1,10 €/Fahrt)

Press 4– 20 trip (€1.05/ride) — 4 - 20 Fahrten drücken (1,05 €/Fahrt)

Wechselgeld, Fahrkarten und Quittung entnehmen

(Take change, tickets, receipt)

Angezeigten Betrag einwerfen — Insert amount shown.

Geldscheine hier einführen — Insert bills here.

Kreditkarte einführen — Insert credit card.

Münzen einwerfen — Insert coins.

How many stops is it to ____?	**Wie viele Haltestellen noch bis ____?** *Vee feeleh HALL-teh-shtell-en noh[ch] biss ____?*
Is the next stop ____?	**Ist ____ die nächste Haltestelle?** *Isst ____ dee n[ae][ch]s-teh HALL-teh-shtell-eh?*
Where are we?	**Wo befinden wir uns gerade?** *Voh beh-FIN-denn veer oons ghe-RAH-deh?*
Where do I change to ____?	**Wo muss ich nach ____ umsteigen?** *Voh muhss ee[ch] nah[ch] ____ OOMM-shtye-ghen?*

What time is the last train to ____?

Wann geht der letzte Zug nach ____?
Vann gheht dehr LETS-teh tsoog nah[ch] ____?

CONSIDERATIONS FOR TRAVELERS WITH SPECIAL NEEDS

Do you have wheelchair access?

Ist der Zugang behindertengerecht?
Isst dehr TSOO-gahng beh-HIN-dehr-ten-gheh-re[ch]t?

Do you have elevators? Where?

Gibt es Aufzüge? Wo?
Gheebt as OUF-ts[ue]-gheh? Voh?

Do you have ramps? Where?

Haben Sie Rampen? Wo?
Hah-ben zee RAHM-penn? Voh?

Are the restrooms wheelchair accessible?

Sind die Toiletten behindertengerecht?
Sinnt dee toi-LET-ten beh-HIN-dehr-ten-gheh-re[ch]t?

Do you have audio assistance for the hearing impaired?

Haben Sie Audioinformationen für Hörgeschädigte?
Hah-ben zee OU-dee-oh-informahtsiho-nen f[ue]r H[OE]R-gheh-sh[ae]-digg-teh?

I am deaf.

Ich bin taub.
Ee[ch] bin TAUP.

May I bring my service dog?

Kann ich meinen Blindenhund mitnehmen?
Kann ee[ch] my-nen BLIN-den-hoonnd mit-nehmen?

I am blind.

Ich bin blind.
Ee[ch] bin BLINND.

I need to charge my power chair.

Ich muss meinen elektrisch betriebenen Rollstuhl aufladen.
Ee[ch] muhss my-nen eh-LECK-trish beh-TREE-bennen ROLL-shtool ouf-lah-denn.

CHAPTER THREE

LODGING

This chapter will help you find the right accommodations, at the right price, and the amenities you might need during your stay.

ROOM PREFERENCES

Please recommend ____	**Bitte empfehlen Sie mir ____** *Bit-eh em-PFEHH-len zee meer ____*
a clean hostel.	**eine saubere Jugendherberge.** *eye-ne SOU-beh-reh YOU-ghend-hair-bair-gheh.*
a moderately priced hotel.	**ein Hotel der mittleren Preiskategorie.** *aihn ho-TELL dehr MITT-leh-ren PRYES-kah-teh-gho-ree.*
a moderately priced B&B.	**eine Pension der mittleren Preiskategorie.** *eye-ne pen-SION dehr MITT-leh-ren PRYES-kah-teh-gho-ree.*
a good hotel / motel.	**ein gutes Hotel / Motel.** *aihn GOO-tess ho-TELL / mo-TELL.*
Does the hotel have ____	**Verfügt das Hotel über ____** *fair-F[UE]GHT dahs ho-TELL [ue]-behr ____*
a pool?	**einen Pool?** *eye-nen pool?*
a casino?	**ein Kasino?** *aihn kah-ZEE-noh?*
suites?	**Suiten?** *SWEE-ten?*

a balcony?	**einen Balkon?**
	eye-nen bahll-COHN?
a fitness center?	**ein Fitness-Center?**
	aihn FIT-ness-center?
a spa?	**ein Heilbad?**
	aihn HYLE-bahd?
a private beach?	**einen Privatstrand?**
	eye-nen pree-VAHT-shtrahnd?
a tennis court?	**einen Tennisplatz?**
	eye-nen TENN-is-plahts?
I would like a room for ____.	**Ich hätte gern ein Zimmer für ____.**
	Ee[ch] hat-teh ghern aihn TSIMmer f[ue]r ____.

For full coverage of number terms, see p7.

I would like ____	**Ich hätte gern ____**
	Ee[ch] hat-teh ghern ____
a king-sized bed.	**ein breites Doppelbett.**
	aihn brye-tess DOPPEL-bet.
a double bed.	**ein Doppelbett.**
	aihn DOPPEL-bet.

Listen Up: Reservations Lingo

Wir haben nichts mehr frei. *Veer ha-ben ni[ch]ts mehr fraih.*	We have no vacancies.
Wie lange möchten Sie bleiben? *Vee lahng-he m[oe][ch]-ten zee BYLE-ben?*	How long will you be staying?
Raucher oder Nichtraucher? *RAU-[ch]er oh-dehr NI[CH]T-rau-[ch]er?*	Smoking or nonsmoking?

LODGING

twin beds.	**zwei Betten.**
	tswaih bet-ten.
adjoining rooms.	**angrenzende Zimmer.**
	AHN-grenn-tsenn-deh tsimmer.
a smoking room.	**ein Raucherzimmer.**
	aihn RAU-[ch]er-tsimmer.
a non-smoking room.	**ein Nichtraucherzimmer.**
	aihn NI[CH]T rau-[ch]er-tsimmer.
a private bathroom.	**ein eigenes Bad.**
	aihn EYE-ghenn-es bahd.
a shower.	**eine Dusche.**
	eye-ne DOO-sheh.
a bathtub.	**eine Badewanne.**
	eye-ne BAH-deh-vann-eh.
air conditioning.	**eine Klimaanlage.**
	eye-ne CLEE-mah-un-lahgheh.
television.	**einen Fernseher.**
	eye-nen FEHRN-sehh-her.
cable.	**Kabelfernsehen.**
	KAH-bell-fehrn-sehhn.
satellite TV.	**Satellitenfernsehen.**
	sattel-IT-ten-fehrn-sehhn.
a telephone.	**ein Telefon.**
	aihn tehleh-PHON.
Internet access.	**einen Internetzugang.**
	eye-nen IN-ternet-tsoo-gahng.
high-speed Internet access.	**einen schnellen Internetzugang.**
	eye-nen SHNELL-en IN-ternet-tsoo-gahng.
a refrigerator.	**einen Kühlschrank.**
	eye-nen K[UE]HL-shrahnnk.
a beach view.	**Blick auf den Strand.**
	blick ouf dehn SHTRAHND.

a city view.	**Blick auf die Stadt.**
	blick ouf dee SHTAHTT.
a kitchenette.	**eine Kochnische.**
	eye-ne KO[CH]-nee-sheh.
a balcony.	**einen Balkon.**
	eye-nen bahll-COHN.
a suite.	**eine Suite.**
	eye-ne SWEET.
a penthouse.	**ein Penthaus.**
	aihn PENT-house.
I would like a room ____	**Ich hätte gern ein Zimmer ____**
	Ee[ch] hat-teh ghern aihn tsimmer ____

on the ground floor.	**im Erdgeschoß.**
	imm AIRD-gheh-shohhs.
near the elevator.	**in Aufzugnähe.**
	inn OUF-tsoogh-n[ae]h-he.
near the stairs.	**in der Nähe des Treppenhauses.**
	inn dher N[AE]-he dess TREP-penn-how-sess.
near the pool.	**in Poolnähe.**
	inn POOL-n[ae]h-he.
away from the street.	**das nicht in Richtung der Straße liegt.**
	dahs ni[ch]t inn RI[CH]-toonng der SHTRAH-se leeght.
I would like a corner room.	**Ich hätte gern ein Eckzimmer.**
	Ee[ch] hat-eh ghern aihn EKK-tsimmer.
Do you have ____	**Haben Sie ____?**
	Hah-ben zee ____?
a crib?	**ein Kinderbett?**
	aihn KIN-dehr-bet?

a foldout bed?

ein ausklappbares Bett?
aihn OUS-klahpp-bah-rhes bet?

FOR GUESTS WITH SPECIAL NEEDS

I need a room with _____

Ich benötige ein Zimmer mit _____
Ee[ch] beh-N[OE]-tiggeh aihn tsimmer mitt _____

wheelchair access.

Zugang per Rollstuhl.
TSOO-gang pair ROLL-shtool.

services for the visually impaired.

Hilfe für Sehbehinderte.
HILL-feh f[ue]r SEH-behin-derteh.

services for the hearing impaired.

Hilfe für Hörgeschädigte.
HILL-feh f[ue]r H[OE]R-gheh-sh[ae]-digg-teh.

I am traveling with a service dog.

Ich reise mit einem Blindenhund.
Ee[ch] RYE-seh mitt eye-nem BLIN-den-hoonnd.

MONEY MATTERS

I would like to make a reservation.

Ich möchte reservieren.
Ee[ch] m[oe][ch]-te reh-sehr-VEE-renn.

How much per night?

Wie viel pro Übernachtung?
Vee-feel proh [ue]behr-NA[CH]-toong?

Do you have a _____

Bieten Sie _____
BEE-ten zee _____

weekly / monthly rate?

einen Wochentarif / Monatstarif an?
eye-nen VO-[ch]en-tah-reef / MO-nahts-tah-reef un?

a weekend rate?

einen Wochenendtarif an?
eye-nen VO-[ch]enn-end-tah-reef un?

We will be staying for ____ days / weeks.	**Wir möchten ____ Tage / Wochen bleiben.**
	Veer m[eo][ch]-ten ____ TAH-gheh / VO-[ch]enn blye-ben.

For full coverage of number terms, see p7.

When is checkout time?	**Wann wird ausgecheckt?**
	Vann vird OUS-gheh-checkt?

For full coverage of time-related terms, see p11.

Do you accept credit cards / travelers checks?	**Akzeptieren Sie Kreditkarten / Reiseschecks?**
	Acktsep-TEEREN zee cre-DEET-kahrr-ten / RYE-seh-shecks?
May I see a room?	**Kann ich mir ein Zimmer ansehen?**
	Kahnn ee[ch] mere aihn tsimmer UN-sehh-hen?

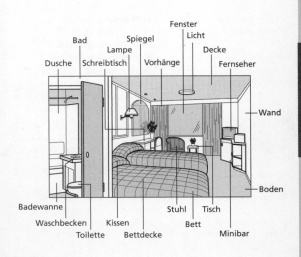

Fenster
Licht
Bad
Spiegel
Decke
Lampe
Dusche Schreibtisch Vorhänge Fernseher

Wand

Boden

Badewanne
Waschbecken Kissen Stuhl Tisch
Toilette Bettdecke Bett Minibar

LODGING

How much are taxes?	**Wie viel Steuer muss ich bezahlen?**
	Vee feel shtoyer muss ee[ch] beh-TSAH-len?
Is there a service charge?	**Gibt es eine Servicegebühr?**
	Gheebt as eye-ne SER-vis-ghe-b[ue]hr?
I'd like to speak with the manager.	**Ich möchte den Manager sprechen.**
	Ee[ch] m[oe][ch]-te dehn MA-nager shpre-[ch]en.

IN-ROOM AMENITIES

I'd like ____	**Ich möchte ____**
	Ee[ch] m[oe][ch]-te ____
to place an international call.	**ein Auslandsgespräch führen.**
	aihn OUS-lahnds-gheh-shpr[ae][ch] f[ue]h-ren.
to place a long-distance call.	**ein Ferngespräch führen.**
	aihn FEHRN-gheh-shpr[ae][ch] f[ue]h-ren.
directory assistance in English.	**eine englischsprachige Telefonauskunft.**
	eye-ne ENG-lish-shprah[ch]igghe tehleh-PHON-ous-koonft.

Instructions for Dialing the Hotel Phone

Wählen Sie für einen Anruf auf einem anderen Zimmer die entsprechende Zimmernummer.	To call another room, dial the room number.
Wählen Sie für ein Ortsgespräch die 9 vor.	To make a local call, first dial 9.
Wählen Sie für einen Anruf bei der Vermittlung die 0.	To call the operator, dial 0.

room service.	**den Zimmerservice.** *dehn TSIMMER-service.*
maid service.	**den Raumpflegedienst.** *dehn RAUHM-pfleh-ghe-deenst.*
the front desk operator.	**die Vermittlung an der Rezeption.** *dee fehr-MITT-loong un dehr reh-tsepp-tsee-OHN.*
Do you have room service?	**Haben Sie Zimmerservice?** *Hah-ben zee TSIMMER-service?*
When is the kitchen open?	**Ab wann ist die Küche geöffnet?** *Up vann isst dee k[ue][ch]e ghe-[OE]FF-net?*
When is breakfast served?	**Wann wird das Frühstück serviert?** *Vann vird dahs FR[UE]H-sht[ue]ck sehr-VEERT?*

For full coverage of time-related terms, see p11.

Do you offer massages?	**Bieten Sie Massagen an?** *Bee-ten zee ma-SSAH-shen un?*
Do you have a lounge?	**Haben Sie ein Foyer?** *Hah-ben zee aihn foy-YEH?*
Do you have a business center?	**Haben Sie ein Geschäftcenter?** *Hah-ben zee aihn gheh-SHAFTS-tsennt-senn-tehr?*
Do you serve breakfast?	**Gibt es bei Ihnen Frühstück?** *Gheebt as by eehnen FR[UE]H-sht[ue]ck?*
Do you have Wi-Fi?	**Haben Sie Wi-Fi?** *Hah-ben zee vee-fee?*
May I have a newspaper in the morning?	**Kann ich morgens bitte eine Zeitung bekommen?** *Khann ee[ch] MOR-ghens bit-eh eye-ne TSAI-toong beh-com-men?*

Do you offer a tailor service?	**Haben Sie eine Schneiderei?**
	Hah-ben zee eye-ne shnai-de-RYE?
Do you offer laundry service?	**Haben Sie eine Wäscherei?**
	Hah-ben zee eye-neh v[ae]-sheh-RYE?
Do you offer dry cleaning?	**Haben Sie eine chemische Reinigung?**
	Hah-ben zee eye-ne KHE-mi-sheh RYE-nee-goong?
May we have ____	**Könnten wir bitte ____**
	K[oe]nn-ten veer bit-eh ____
clean sheets today?	**frische Bettwäsche bekommen?**
	frisheh BET-v[ae]sheh beh-com-men?
more towels?	**mehr Handtücher bekommen?**
	mehr HAHND-t[ue]-[ch]er beh-com-men?
more toilet paper?	**mehr Toilettenpapier bekommen?**
	mehr toi-LET-ten-pah-peer beh-com-men?
extra pillows?	**zusätzliche Kissen bekommen?**
	TSOO-sats-lee-[ch]e kissen beh-com-men?
Do you have an ice machine?	**Haben Sie eine Eismaschine?**
	Hah-ben zee eye-ne ICE-mah-shee-ne?
Did I receive any ____	**Haben Sie ____**
	Hah-ben zee ____
messages?	**Nachrichten für mich?**
	NA[CH]-ree[ch]ten f[ue]r mee[ch]?
mail?	**Post für mich?**
	POSST f[ue]r mee[ch]?

faxes?	**ein Fax für mich?** *aihn FAHCKS f[ue]r mee[ch]?*
A spare key, please.	**Geben Sie mir bitte einen Ersatzschlüssel.** *Ghehben zee mere bit-eh eye-nen air-SAHTTS-SHL[UE]SS-ell.*
More hangers please.	**Geben Sie mir bitte ein paar zusätzliche Kleiderbügel.** *Ghehben zee mere bit-eh aihn par TSOO-sats-lee-[ch]e KLYE-dehr-b[ue]-ghell.*
I am allergic to down pillows.	**Ich bin allergisch gegen Daunenkissen.** *Ee[ch] bin ah-LERR-ghish gheghen DOW-nen-kissen.*
I'd like a wake-up call.	**Ich hätte gern einen Weckruf.** *Ee[ch] hat-teh ghern eye-nen VECK-roof.*

For full coverage of time-related terms, see p11.

Do you have alarm clocks?	**Haben Sie Wecker?** *Hah-ben zee VECK-ehr?*
Is there a safe in the room?	**Verfügt das Zimmer über einen Tresor?** *Fair-f[ue]ght dahs tsimmer [ue]h-ber eye-nen treh-SOHR?*
Does the room have a hair dryer?	**Gibt es auf dem Zimmer einen Haartrockner?** *Gheebt as ouf dehm tsimmer eye-nen HAAR-trocknehr?*

HOTEL ROOM TROUBLE

May I speak with the manager?	**Könnte ich bitte den Manager sprechen?** *K[oe]nn-teh ee[ch] bit-eh dehn MA-nager spre-[ch]en?*

The ___ does not work.	___ **funktioniert nicht.**
	___ *funk-tsee-oh-NEERT ni[ch]t.*
television	**Der Fernseher**
	Dehr FEHRN-sehh-her
telephone	**Das Telefon**
	Dahs tehleh-PHON
air conditioning	**Die Klimaanlage**
	Dee CLEE-mah-un-lahgheh
Internet access	**Der Internetzugang**
	Dehr IN-ternet-tsoo-gahng
cable TV	**Das Kabelfernsehen**
	Dahs KAH-bell-fehrn-sehhn
There is no hot water.	**Es kommt kein warmes Wasser.**
	As commt kyne varr-mes VAHSS-er.
The toilet is over-flowing!	**Die Toilette läuft über!**
	Dee toi-LET-teh loyft [ue]-ber!
This room is ___	**Dieses Zimmer ist ___**
	DEE-sess tsimmer isst ___
too noisy.	**zu laut.**
	tsoo lout.
too cold.	**zu kalt.**
	tsoo kahllt.
too warm.	**zu warm.**
	tsoo vaahrrm.

This room has _____

In diesem Zimmer gibt es _____
In DEE-semm tsimmer gheebt as _____

bugs.

Ungeziefer.
OOHN-gheh-tsee-fair.

mice.

Mäuse.
MOY-seh.

I'd like a different room.

Ich möchte ein anderes Zimmer.
Ee[ch] m[oe][ch]-te aihn UN-deh-res tsimmer.

Do you have a bigger room?

Haben Sie ein größeres Zimmer?
Hah-ben zee aihn GR[OE]-ceres tsimmer?

I locked myself out of my room.

Ich habe mich aus meinem Zimmer ausgesperrt.
Ee[ch] hah-be mi[ch] ous my-nem TSIMMER ous-gheh-shperrt.

Do you have any fans?

Haben Sie Ventilatoren?
Hah-ben zee venn-tee-lah-TOH-renn?

The sheets are not clean.

Die Bettwäsche ist schmutzig.
Dee BET-v[ae]sheh isst shmoottsig.

The towels are not clean.

Die Handtücher sind schmutzig.
Dee HAHND-t[ue]-[ch]er sinnd shmoottsig.

The room is not clean.

Das Zimmer ist schmutzig.
Dahs tsimmer isst shmoottsig.

The guests next door / above / below are being very loud.

Die Gäste nebenan / über dem Zimmer / unter dem Zimmer sind sehr laut.
Dee guess-teh neh-ben-UN / [UE]-ber dehm tsimmer / OOHN-ter dehm tsimmer sinnd sehr lout.

CHECKING OUT

I think this charge is a mistake.	**Ich glaube, diese Gebühr ist falsch.** *Ee[ch] GLAU-be, dee-se ghe-B[UE]HR isst fahllsh.*
Please explain this charge to me.	**Könnten Sie mir diese Gebühr bitte erklären?** *K[oe]nn-ten zee mere dee-se gheb[ue]hr bit-eh air-KL[AE]H-ren?*
Thank you, we enjoyed our stay.	**Vielen Dank, es war schön bei Ihnen.** *Feel-en dunk, as vaar SH[OE]HN by eehnen.*
The service was excellent.	**Der Service war ausgezeichnet.** *Dehr SER-vis vaar ous-gheh-TSAI[CH]-net.*
The staff is very professional and courteous.	**Das Personal ist sehr professionell und zuvorkommend.** *Dahs pair-soh-NAAHL isst sehr proh-fess-yo-NELL oonnd tsoo-VOHR-comm-end.*
Please call a cab for me.	**Rufen Sie mir bitte ein Taxi.** *Roo-fen zee mere bit-eh aihn TAHCK-zee.*
Would someone please get my bags?	**Könnte sich bitte jemand um mein Gepäck kümmern?** *K[oe]nn-te si[ch] bit-eh YEH-mahnd oohmm mine ghe-P[AE]CK k[ue]mm-ern?*

HAPPY CAMPING

I'd like a site for ____	**Ich hätte gern einen Platz für ____** *Ee[ch] hat-teh ghern eye-nen plahts f[ue]r ____*
a tent.	**ein Zelt.** *aihn TSELLT.*

a camper.	**einen Wohnwagen** *eye-nen VOHN-vaah-ghenn.*
Are there ____	**Gibt es hier ____** *Gheebt as heer ____*
bathrooms?	**Toiletten?** *toi-LET-ten?*
showers?	**Duschen?** *DOO-shenn?*
Is there running water?	**Gibt es fließend Wasser?** *Gheebt es fleecent vahsser?*
Is the water drinkable?	**Ist das Wasser trinkbar?** *Isst dahs vahsser TRINK-bahr?*
Where is the electrical hookup?	**Wo finde ich den Elektroanschluss?** *Voh fin-deh ee[ch] dehn eh-LECK-troh-unshlooss?*

CHAPTER FOUR

DINING

This chapter includes a menu reader and the language you need to communicate in a range of dining establishments and food markets.

FINDING A RESTAURANT

Would you recommend a good ___ restaurant?	**Können Sie mir ein gutes ___ Restaurant empfehlen?** *K[oe]nn-en zee mere aihn goo-tess ___ ress-toh-ROHNG empfehlen?*
local	**örtliches** *[oe]rrt-li[ch]-es*
Italian	**italienisches** *ee-tahl-yeh-nee-shess*
French	**französisches** *frahnn-ts[oe]h-see-shess*
Turkish	**türkisches** *t[ue]rr-kee-shess*
Spanish	**spanisches** *spah-nee-shess*
Chinese	**chinesisches** *[ch]ee-nehh-see-shess*
Japanese	**japanisches** *yah-pah-nee-shess*
Asian	**asiatisches** *ah-see-ah-tish-es*
pizza	**Pizzeria** *Pittseh-REE-ah*
steakhouse	**Steakhaus** *STEAK-house*
family	**Familien-** *fah-mee-lee-en-*

seafood	**Fisch-** *fish*
vegetarian	**vegetarisches** *veh-gheh-TAH-ree-shess*
buffet-style	**Selbstbedienungs-** *sellbst-beh-dee-noongs-*
Greek	**griechisches** *gree-[ch]ish-ess*
budget	**günstiges** *gh[ue]nns-tee-ghess*
Which is the best restaurant in town?	**Welches Restaurant ist das beste der Stadt?** *Vell-[ch]ess ress-toh-rohng isst dahs BESS-teh dehr shtahtt?*
Is there a late-night restaurant nearby?	**Gibt es in der Nähe ein Restaurant, das auch noch spät geöffnet hat?** *Gheebt as in dehr n[ae]h-heh aihn ress-toh-ROHNG, dahs ou[ch] noh[ch] SHP[AE]HT gheh-[oe]ff-net hut?*
Is there a restaurant that serves breakfast nearby?	**Gibt es in der Nähe ein Frühstückslokal?** *Gheebt as in dehr n[ae]h-heh aihn FR[UE]H-sht[ue]cks-loh-kahl?*
Is it very expensive?	**Ist es dort teuer?** *Isst as dohrrt TOY-ehr?*
Do I need a reservation?	**Benötige ich eine Reservierung?** *Beh-n[oe]h-tiggeh ee[ch] eye-neh reh-sehr-VEE-roong?*
Do I have to dress up?	**Muss ich mich herausputzen?** *Mooss ee[ch] mee[ch] heh-RAUS-put-senn?*
Do they serve lunch?	**Gibt es dort Mittagessen?** *Gheebt as dohrrt MIT-tahg-ess-en?*

What time do they open for dinner?	**Ab wann gibt es dort Abendessen?**
	Up vahnn gheebt as dohrrt AH-bent-ess-en?
For lunch?	**Mittagessen?**
	MIT-tahg-ess-en?
What time do they close?	**Wie lange ist dort geöffnet?**
	Vee lung-eh isst dohrrt gheh-[OE]FF-net?
Do you have a take out menu?	**Haben Sie Speisen zum Mitnehmen?**
	Hah-ben zee shpye-sen tsoom MIT-neh-men?
Do you have a bar?	**Haben Sie eine Bar?**
	Hah-ben zee eye-neh BAHR?
Is there a café nearby?	**Gibt es ein Café in der Nähe?**
	Gheebt as aihn kaff-EHH inn dehr n[ae]h-heh?

GETTING SEATED

Are you still serving?	**Haben Sie noch geöffnet?**
	Hah-ben zee noh[ch] gheh-[OE]FF-net?
How long is the wait?	**Wie lange muss ich warten? (sing.) / Wie lange müssen wir warten? (pl.)**
	Vee lung-eh mooss ee[ch] VAHRR-ten? / Vee lung-eh m[ue]ss-en veer VAHRR-ten?
Do you have a no-smoking section?	**Haben Sie einen Nichtraucherbereich?**
	Hah-ben zee eye-nen NI[CH]T-rauh-[ch]ehr-beh-rye[ch]?
A table for ____, please.	**Einen Tisch für ____ Personen, bitte.**
	Eye-nen TISH f[ue]hr ____ pehr-soh-nen, bit-eh.

For a full list of numbers, see p7.

Listen Up: Restaurant Lingo

Raucher oder Nichtraucher?	Smoking or nonsmoking?
RAUH-[ch]ehr oh-der NI[CH]T-rauh-[ch]ehr?	
Sie benötigen eine Krawatte und ein Jackett.	You'll need a tie and jacket.
Zee beh-n[oe]h-tiggen eye-neh krah-VAHTT-eh oonnd aihn shah-KETT.	
Es tut mir leid, aber kurze Hosen sind hier nicht erlaubt.	I'm sorry, no shorts are allowed.
As toot mere LYDE, ah-behr koorrt-seh HOH-senn sinnd hear ni[ch]t air-LAUBT.	
Kann ich Ihnen etwas zu trinken bringen?	May I bring you something to drink?
Khann ee[ch] eeh-nen at-vahs tsoo TRING-ken bring-en?	
Soll ich Ihnen die Weinkarte bringen?	Would you like to see a wine list?
Sohll ee[ch] eeh-nen dee VINE-kahrr-teh bring-en?	
Darf ich Ihnen unsere Spezialitäten vorstellen?	Would you like to hear our specials?
Dharrf ee[ch] eeh-nen oonn-seh-reh shpeh-tsee-yahl-ee-T[AE]H-ten fohr-shtell-en?	
Möchten Sie jetzt bestellen?	Are you ready to order?
M[oe][ch]-ten zee yetst beh-SHTELL-en?	
Es tut mir leid, aber Ihre Kreditkarte wurde nicht akzeptiert.	I'm sorry, but your credit card was declined.
As toot mere LYDE, ah-behr eeh-reh creh-DEET-kahrr-teh voorr-deh ni[ch]t ahcktsep-TEERT.	

Do you have a quiet table?	**Haben Sie einen ruhigen Tisch?** *Hah-ben zee eye-nen ROO-hee-ghenn tish?*
May we sit outside / inside please?	**Können wir draußen / drinnen sitzen?** *K[oe]nn-en veer DROW-ssen / DRINN-en sitt-sen?*
May we sit at the counter?	**Können wir an der Theke sitzen?** *K[oe]nn-en veer un dehr TEH-keh sitt-sen?*
The menu, please?	**Die Karte, bitte.** *Dee KAHRR-teh, bit-eh.*

ORDERING

Do you have a special tonight?	**Haben Sie heute Abend ein spezielles Angebot?** *Hah-ben zee hoy-teh ah-bend aihn shpeh-tsee-ell-es UN-gheh-boht?*
What do you recommend?	**Was können Sie empfehlen?** *Vahs k[oe]nn-en zee em-PFEH-len?*
May I see a wine list?	**Könnte ich bitte die Weinkarte haben?** *K[oe]nn-teh ee[ch] bit-eh dee VINE-kahrr-teh hah-ben?*
Do you serve wine by the glass?	**Servieren Sie Wein im Glas?** *Serr-veer-en zee vine im GLAHSS?*
May I see a drink list?	**Könnte ich bitte die Getränkekarte haben?** *K[oe]nn-teh ee[ch] bit-eh dee gheh-TR[AE]NG-keh-kahrr-teh hah-ben?*
I would like it cooked ____	**Ich hätte es gern ____** *Ee[ch] hat-eh as ghern ____*
rare.	**blutig.** *BLOO-tigg.*
medium rare.	**halb gar.** *hahlbb GHAHR.*

medium.	**medium.**
	MEH-dee-oomm.
medium well.	**halb durch.**
	hahlbb DOORR[CH].
well.	**gut durch.**
	goot DOORR[CH].
charred.	**verschmort.**
	fehr-SHMORRT.
Do you have a ____ menu?	**Haben Sie eine Karte mit ____ Speisen?**
	Hah-ben zee eye-neh kahrr-teh mit ____ shpye-sen?
diabetic	**diabetischen**
	dee-ah-BEH-tish-en
kosher	**kosheren**
	KOH-sheh-ren
vegetarian	**vegetarischen**
	veh-gheh-TAH-ree-shen
Do you have a children's menu?	**Haben Sie eine Karte für Kinder?**
	Hah-ben zee eye-neh kahrr-teh f[ue]hr KIN-dehr?
What is in this dish?	**Welche Zutaten enthält dieses Gericht?**
	Vell-[ch]eh TSOO-tah-ten ent-h[ae]llt dee-ses gheh-RI[CH]T?
How is it prepared?	**Wie wird es zubereitet?**
	Vee virrd ess TSOO-beh-rye-tet?
What kind of oil is that cooked in?	**In welchem Öl wird dieses Gericht zubereitet?**
	In vell-[ch]em [OE]HL virrd dee-ses gheh-ri[ch]t tsoo-beh-rye-tet?
Do you have any low-salt dishes?	**Haben Sie Gerichte mit wenig Salz?**
	Hah-ben zee ghe-ri[ch]-teh mit veh-nigg SAHLTTS?
On the side, please.	**Als Beilage, bitte.**
	Ahlls BYE-lah-gheh, bit-eh.

May I make a substitution?	**Kann ich die Zusammenstellung ändern?**
	Khann ee[ch] dee tsoo-SAHMM-en-shtell-oong [ae]nn-dehrn?
I'd like to try that.	**Das würde ich gern probieren.**
	Dahs v[ue]rr-deh ee[ch] ghern proh-BEE-ren.
Is that fresh?	**Ist das frisch?**
	Isst dahs FRISH?
Waiter!	**Bedienung!**
	Beh-DEE-noong!
Extra butter, please.	**Könnte ich bitte noch etwas Butter haben?**
	K[oe]nn-teh ee[ch] bit-eh noh[ch] at-vahs BOOTT-ehr hah-ben?
No butter, thanks.	**Keine Butter, danke.**
	Kye-neh BOOTT-ehr, dunk-eh.
No cream, thanks.	**Keine Sahne, danke.**
	Kye-neh SAH-neh, dunk-eh.
Dressing on the side, please.	**Dressing extra, bitte.**
	Dressing EKKS-trah, bit-eh.
No salt, please.	**Kein Salz, bitte.**
	Kyne SAHLTTS, bit-eh.
May I have some oil, please?	**Könnte ich bitte etwas Öl haben?**
	K[oe]nn-teh ee[ch] bit-eh at-vahs [OE]HL hah-ben?
More bread, please.	**Könnte ich bitte noch etwas Brot haben?**
	K[oe]nn-teh ee[ch] bit-eh noh[ch] at-vahs BROHT hah-ben?
I am lactose intolerant.	**Ich habe eine Laktoseunverträg-lichkeit.**
	Ee[ch] hah-beh eye-neh luck-TOH-seh-oon-fehr-tr[ae]g-li[ch]-kite.

Would you recommend something without milk?	**Könnten Sie mir bitte etwas ohne Milch empfehlen?** *K[oe]nn-ten zee mere bit-eh at-vahs oh-neh MILL[CH] em-pfeh-len?*
I am allergic to ____	**Ich bin allergisch gegen ____** *Ee[ch] bin ah-LERR-ghish gheh-ghenn ____*
seafood.	**Meeresfrüchte.** *mehh-res-fr[ue]ch-teh.*
shellfish.	**Schalentiere.** *shah-len-tee-reh.*
nuts.	**Nüsse.** *n[ue]ss-eh.*
peanuts.	**Erdnüsse.** *ehrrd-n[ue]ss-eh.*
Water ____, please.	**Wasser ____, bitte.** *Vahs-sehr ____, bit-eh.*
with ice	**mit Eis,** *mitt ICE*
without ice	**ohne Eis,** *ohh-ne ICE*
I'm sorry, I don't think this is what I ordered.	**Verzeihung, aber ich glaube, das habe ich nicht bestellt.** *Fehr-TSYE-oong, ah-behr ee[ch] GLAU-beh, dahs hah-beh ee[ch] ni[ch]t beh-SHTELLT.*
My meat is a little over / under cooked.	**Mein Fleisch ist etwas zu stark / zu wenig durch.** *Mine flye-sh isst at-vahs tsoo SHTARRK / tsoo VEH-nigg duhrr[ch].*
My vegetables are a little over / under cooked.	**Mein Gemüse wurde etwas zu lang / zu kurz gekocht.** *Mine gheh-m[ue]h-seh wurde at-vahs tsoo LUNG / tsoo KOORRTS gheh-ko[ch]t.*

DINING

There's a bug in my food!	**Da ist ein Käfer in meinem Essen!**
	Dah isst aihn K[AE]H-fehr in my-nem ess-en!
May I have a refill?	**Würden Sie bitte nachschenken?**
	V[ue]rr-den zee bit-eh NAH[CH]-sheng-ken?
A dessert menu, please.	**Die Dessertkarte, bitte.**
	Dee dess-SEHR-kahrr-teh, bit-eh.

DRINKS

alcoholic	**Alkoholisch**
	ahll-koh-HOH-lish
neat / straight	**pur**
	poor
on the rocks	**auf Eis**
	ouf ICE
with (seltzer or soda) water	**mit (Selters- oder Soda-) Wasser**
	mitt (SELL-terrs oh-der SOH-dah) Vahs-sehr
beer	**Bier**
	beer
dark beer	**dunkles Bier**
	DOONNK-less beer
light beer	**helles Bier**
	HELL-ess bier
Kölsch	**Kölsch**
	K[OE]LL-sh
Weissbier	**Weißbier**
	VICE-beer
pilsner	**Pils**
	pillss
bock beer	**Bockbier**
	BOCK-beer
bottle	**Flasche**
	FLUSH-eh
glass	**Glas**
	glahss

wine	**Wein**
	vine
house wine	**Hauswein**
	HOUSE-vine
sweet wine	**lieblicher Wein**
	LEEB-li[ch]-ehr vine
dry white wine	**trockener Weißwein**
	trokken-er VICE-vine
Gewürztraminer	**Gewürztraminer**
	Geh-V[UE]RRTS-trah-mee-nehr
Riesling	**Riesling**
	REES-ling
rosé	**Rosé**
	roh-SEHH
Scotch	**Scotch**
	Scotch
red wine	**Rotwein**
	ROHT-vine
Whiskey	**Whiskey**
	Whiskey
sparkling sweet wine	**Sekt**
	SEKKT
liqueur	**Likör**
	lee-K[OE]HR
brandy	**Brandy**
	BRAN-dee
cognac	**Kognak**
	CON-yukk
Kirschwasser	**Kirschwasser**
(cherry-flavored liqueur)	*KEERRSH-vahs-sehr*
gin	**Gin**
	jinn
vodka	**Wodka**
	VODD-kah
rum	**Rum**
	roomm

nonalcoholic	**alkoholfrei**
	ahll-koh-HOHL-frye
hot chocolate	**heiße Schokolade**
	hye-sseh shoh-koh-LAH-deh
lemonade	**Limonade**
	lee-moh-NAH-deh
radler / radlermass	**Radler (0,5 L) / Radlermaß (1 L)**
(beer mixed with lemonade	*RAHD-lehr / RAHD-lehr-mahss*
or soda)	
Apfelmost (hard cider)	**Apfelmost**
	UP-fell-mohsst
milkshake	**Milchshake**
	MILL[CH]-shake
milk	**Milch**
	mill[ch]
tea	**Tee**
	tehh
coffee	**Kaffee**
	kah-FEHH
cappuccino	**Cappuccino**
	kappoo-TSHEE-noh
espresso	**Espresso**
	ess-PRRESS-oh
iced coffee	**Eiskaffee**
	ICE-kahff-eh
fruit juice	**Fruchtsaft**
	FROO[CH]T-sufft

For a full list of fruits, see p91.

SETTLING UP

I'm stuffed.	**Ich bin voll.**
	Ee[ch] binn FOLL.
The meal was excellent.	**Das Essen war ausgezeichnet.**
	Dahs ess-en vaar ous-gheh-TSAI[CH]-net.

There's a problem with my bill.	**Es gibt da ein Problem mit meiner Rechnung.**
	As gheebt dah aihn proh-blehm mit minor RE[CH]-noong.
Is the tip included?	**Ist das inklusive Trinkgeld?**
	Isst dahs in-kloo-see-veh TRINK-gelld?
My compliments to the chef!	**Mein Kompliment an den Chefkoch!**
	Mine komm-plee-MEANT un dehn CHEFF-koh[ch]!
Check, please.	**Zahlen, bitte.**
	TSAH-len, bit-eh.

MENU READER

Each German-speaking country has its own regional and national specialties, but we've tried to make our list of classic dishes as broad as possible.

BREAKFAST

Eier: Eggs
EYE-ehr

Bread (Note: There are many kinds of bread in Germany. Following are some of the most common and delicious varieties.)

> **Roggenbrot:** rye bread
> **Toastbrot:** toast bread
> **Vollkornbrot:** whole-grain bread
> **Weizenbrot:** wheat bread
> **Weissbrot:** white bread
> **Mehrkornbrot:** multigrain bread
> **Roggenmischbrot:** rye-wheat bread
> **Zwiebelbrot:** onion bread
> **Semmel, Brötchen:** bread rolls

Sausage (Sausages can be bought at outdoor stalls throughout the year. They are eaten with a roll and some mustard.)
Weißwurst: Weisswurst
VICE-voorrst
Blutwurst: Blutwurst
BLOOT-voorrst
Kaffee: Coffee
KAHFF-eh
Sahne: Cream
SAH-ne
Butter: Butter
BOOTT-ehr
Zucker: Sugar
TSOOKK-ehr
Salz: Salt
sahllts
Pfeffer: Pepper
PFEHFF-ehr
Jogurt: Yogurt
YOH-ghoorrt
Quark: Quark (a creamy, savory dish eaten on bread)
kwarrk
Nutella: Nutella (a chocolate-hazelnut spread)
noo-TELL-ah

LUNCH / DINNER

German / Swiss / Austrian specialties

Following are special dishes from different German-speaking regions and countries. Although many are available in most regions in one form or another, the names can vary. The region or country is indicated in parentheses after the name of the dish.

Pfannkuchen: potato pancakes
PFAHNN-coo-[ch]en
Sauerbraten: marinated beef
SOUER-brah-ten

Rösti: fried potato dish (Switzerland)
R[OE]SS-tee
Wiener Schnitzel: breaded veal cutlets
vee-nair SHNITT-sell
Spätzle: heavy pasta served in place of potatoes (Southern Germany)
SHPATS-leh
Knödel: dumplings
KHN[OE]H-dell
Hasenpfeffer: rabbit stew
HAH-sen-pfeff-ehr
Jägerschnitzel: type of cutlet with mushrooms and peppers
Y[AE]H-ghair-shnitt-sell
Maultaschen: Swabian ravioli
MAUHL-tahshen
Nockerln: dumplings in Austria and Bavaria
NOCK-errln
Ochsenschwanzsuppe: Oxtail soup
OKKS-en-shvahnnts-soopp-eh
Schweinshaxe: pork hock
SHVINES-hahkks-eh
Sauerkraut
SOUER-kraut
Spanferkel: whole-roasted suckling pig
SHPAHN-fehrr-kell
Rote Grütze: red fruit pudding
roh-teh GR[UE]TT-seh
Menü: daily special
Meh-N[UE]H
Tagesgericht: dish of the day
TAH-ghess-gheh-ri[ch]t

DESSERT

Sacher Torte: Sacher Torte
SAH[CH]-ehr torr-teh

Käsekuchen: Cheese cake
K[AE]H-seh-coo-[ch]en

Apfelstrudel: Apple strudel
UP-fell-shtroo-dell

Schokolade: Chocolate
shoh-koh-LAH-deh

Stollen: Stollen (typically served at Christmas)
SHTOLL-en

Marzipan: Marzipan
MAHRR-tsee-pahn

Eiscreme: Ice cream
ICE-krehm

Kekse: Cookies / biscuits
KEHK-seh

MEAT

Rindfleisch: Beef
RINND-flye-sh

Schweinefleisch: Pork
SHVINE-eh-flye-sh

Würstchen: Sausage
V[UE]RRST-[ch]enn

Hähnchen: Chicken
H[AE]HN-[ch]en

Kalbfleisch: Veal
KAHLLB-flye-sh

Lammfleisch: Lamb
LAHMM-flye-sh

Hasenfleisch: Rabbit
HAH-senn-flye-sh

FISH AND SEAFOOD

Tunfisch: Tuna
TOON-fish

Lachs: Salmon
lahkks
Kabeljau: Cod
KAH-bell-yow
Hering: Herring
HEH-rring
Forelle: Trout
foh-RELL-eh
Buntbarsch: Tilapia
BOONNTT-bahrrsh
Karpfen: Carp
CAHRR-pfenn
Schwertfisch: Swordfish
SHVEHRRT-fish
Heilbutt: Halibut
HYLE-boott
Muscheln: Mussels
MOOSH-elln

PASTA
Spaghetti: Spaghetti
shpah-GET-ee
Pizza: Pizza
PIT-sah
Döner Kebab: meat sandwich with lettuce, onions and a cream sauce; invented by Turkish immigrants to Germany in Berlin in 1971.
d[oe]h-nehr KEH-bahpp
Currywurst: sausage seasoned with curry powder, usually served with French fries
CURRY-voorrsst

CHEESE

Blauschimmelkäse: Blue cheese
BLAUH-shimmel-k[ae]h-seh

Hüttenkäse: Cottage cheese
H[UE]TT-en-k[ae]h-seh

Frischkäse: Cream cheese
FRISH-k[ae]h-seh

Schweizer Käse: Swiss cheese
SHVYE-tsair k[ae]h-seh

Gorgonzola: Gorgonzola
gore-ghonn-TSOH-lah

Ziegenkäse: Goat cheese
TSEE-ghenn-k[ae]h-seh

UTENSILS

Gabel: Fork
GHAH-bell

Messer: Knife
MESS-ehr

Löffel: Spoon
L[OE]FF-ell

Suppenlöffel: Soup spoon
SOOPP-en-l[oe]ff-ell

Teelöffel: Teaspoon
TEHH-l[oe]ff-ell

Teller: Plate
TELL-ehr

Schüssel: Bowl
SH[UE]SS-ell

Topf: Pot
toppf

Pfanne: Pan
PFAHNN-eh

Serviette: Napkin
serr-vee-AT-eh

BUYING GROCERIES

Groceries can be purchased at supermarkets, neighborhood stores, or farmers' markets. Most cities and towns have farmers' markets that sell fruits, vegetables, cheeses, and other goods.

AT THE SUPERMARKET

Which aisle has ____	**In welchem Regal finde ich ____** *In vell-[ch]em reh-GAHL fin-deh* *ee[ch] ____*
spices?	**Gewürze?** *geh-V[UE]RR-tseh?*
toiletries?	**Hygieneartikel?** *h[ue]-GYEH-neh-arr-tee-kell?*
paper plates and napkins?	**Papierteller und Servietten?** *pah-PEER-tell-ehr oonnd* *serr-vee-AT-ten?*
canned goods?	**Konserven?** *con-SERR-ven?*
snack food?	**Snacks?** *snacks?*
baby food?	**Babynahrung?** *BEH-bee-nah-roong?*
water?	**Wasser?** *VAHS-ser?*
juice?	**Säfte?** *S[AE]FF-teh?*
bread?	**Brot?** *broht?*
cheese?	**Käse?** *K[AE]H-seh?*
fruit?	**Obst?** *Ohbsst?*
cookies?	**Kekse?** *KEHK-seh?*

AT THE BUTCHER SHOP

Is the meat fresh?	**Ist das Fleisch frisch?**
	Isst dahs flye-sh FRISH?
Do you sell fresh ____	**Verkaufen Sie frisches ____**
	Fehr-cow-fen zee frish-ess ____
beef?	**Rindfleisch?**
	RINND-flye-sh?
pork?	**Schweinefleisch?**
	SHVINE-eh-flye-sh?
lamb?	**Lammfleisch?**
	LAHMM-flye-sh?
I would like a cut of ____	**Ich hätte gern ____**
	Ee[ch] HAT-eh gern ____
tenderloin.	**ein Filetstück.**
	aihn fee-LEHH-sht[ue]ck.
T-bone.	**ein T-Bone-Steak.**
	aihn TEE-bone-steak.
brisket.	**ein Bruststück.**
	aihn BROOSTT-sht[ue]ck.
rump roast.	**ein Rumpsteak.**
	aihn ROOMMP-steak.
chops.	**Koteletts.**
	kott-LETTS.
filet.	**ein Filet.**
	aihn fee-LEHH.
Thin / Thick cuts please.	**Dünne / Dicke Scheiben, bitte.**
	D[UE]NN-eh / DICK-eh shy-ben, bit-eh.
Please trim the fat.	**Entfernen Sie bitte das Fett.**
	Ent-fehr-nen zee bit-eh dahs FETT.
Do you have any sausage?	**Haben Sie Würstchen?**
	Hah-ben zee V[UE]RRST-[ch]enn?
Is the ____ fresh?	**____ frisch?**
	____ FRISH?

fish	**Ist der Fisch** *Isst dehr fish*
seafood	**Sind die Meeresfrüchte** *Sinnd dee mehh-res-fr[ue]ch-teh*
shrimp	**Sind die Garnelen** *Sinnd dee gharr-neh-len*
trout	**Ist die Forelle** *Isst dee foh-rell-eh*
flounder	**Ist die Flunder** *Isst dee floonn-dehr*
clams	**Sind die Muscheln** *Sinnd dee moosh-elln*
oysters	**Sind die Austern** *Sinnd dee ous-terrn*
May I smell it?	**Dürfte ich bitte daran riechen?** *D[ue]rf-teh ee[ch] bit-eh dah-rahn REE-[ch]en?*
Would you please ____	**Könnten Sie ____** *K[oe]nn-ten zee ____*
filet it?	**das bitte filetieren?** *dahs bit-eh fee-leh-TEE-ren?*
debone it?	**das bitte entbeinen?** *dahs bit-eh ent-BYE-nen?*
remove the head and tail?	**bitte Kopf und Schwanz entfernen?** *bit-eh copf oonnd SHVAHNNTS ent-fehr-nen?*

AT THE PRODUCE STAND / MARKET

Fruits

banana	**Banane** *bah-NAH-neh*
apple	**Apfel** *UP-fell*

grapes (green, red)	**Trauben** *TRAUH-ben*
orange	**Orange** *oh-RUN-sheh*
lime	**Limette** *lee-METT-eh*
lemon	**Zitrone** *tsee-TROH-neh*
mango	**Mango** *MAHNG-goh*
melon	**Melone** *meh-LOH-neh*
cantaloupe	**Cantaloupe-Melone** *khann-tah-LOOP-meh-loh-neh*
watermelon	**Wassermelone** *VAHS-sehr-meh-loh-neh*
honeydew	**Honigmelone** *HOH-nigg-meh-loh-neh*
cranberry	**Cranberry** *CRAN-berry*
cherry	**Kirsche** *KEERR-sheh*
peach	**Pfirsich** *PFIRR-si[ch]*
apricot	**Aprikose** *up-ree-KOH-seh*
strawberry	**Erdbeere** *EHRRD-beh-reh*
blueberry	**Heidelbeere** *HYE-dell-beh-reh*
kiwi	**Kiwi** *KEE-vee*
pineapple	**Ananas** *ANNAH-nahss*

blackberries	**Brombeeren** *BROM-beh-ren*
grapefruit	**Grapefruit** *GRAPE-fruit*
gooseberry	**Stachelbeere** *SHTAH[CH]-ell-beh-reh*
papaya	**Papaya** *pah-PAHY-yah*
tamarind	**Tamarinde** *tah-mah-RINN-deh*
tangerine	**Mandarine** *mahnn-dah-REE-neh*
plum	**Pflaume** *PFLAUH-meh*
pear	**Birne** *BIRR-neh*
Vegetables	
plantain	**Kochbanane** *KOH[CH]-bah-nah-neh*
regular	**normal** *norr-MAHL*
ripe	**reif** *rye-ff*
lettuce	**Kopfsalat** *COPF-sah-laht*
spinach	**Spinat** *spee-NAHHT*
avocado	**Avocado** *ah-voh-KAH-doh*
artichoke	**Artischocke** *arr-tee-SHOCK-eh*
olives	**Oliven** *oh-LEE-ven*
beans	**Bohnen** *BOH-nen*

DINING

green beans	**grüne Bohnen**
	gr[ue]h-neh BOH-nen
tomato	**Tomate**
	toh-MAH-teh
potato	**Kartoffel**
	karr-TOFF-ell
peppers	**Paprika**
	PAHPP-ree-kah
hot	**scharf**
	shahrrff
mild	**mild**
	milld
jalapeno	**Peperoni**
	pepp-eh-ROH-nee
onion	**Zwiebel**
	TSVEE-bell
celery	**Sellerie**
	SELL-eh-ree
broccoli	**Brokkoli**
	BROCK-oh-lee
cauliflower	**Blumenkohl**
	BLOOH-menn-kohl
carrot	**Karrotte**
	kah-ROTT-eh
corn	**Mais**
	mice
cucumber	**Gurke**
	GHOORR-keh
bean sprouts	**Sojasprossen**
	SOH-yah-shpross-en
sweet corn	**Mais**
	mice
eggplant	**Aubergine**
	oh-behr-SHEE-neh

sorrel	**Ampfer**
	UM-pfehr
yam	**Süßkartoffel**
	S[UE]HS-kahr-toff-ell
squash	**Kürbis**
	KYRR-biss

Fresh Herbs & Spices

cilantro / coriander	**Koriander**
	koh-ree-UNDER
black pepper	**schwarzer Pfeffer**
	shvahrrz-ehr PFEFF-ehr
salt	**Salz**
	sahltts
basil	**Basilikum**
	bah-SEE-lee-koom
parsley	**Petersilie**
	peh-tehr-SEAL-yeh
oregano	**Oregano**
	oh-REH-ghah-noh
sage	**Salbei**
	SAHLL-bye
thyme	**Thymian**
	T[UE]H-mee-ahn
cumin	**Kreuzkümmel**
	KRROYTS-k[ue]m-mell
paprika	**Paprika**
	PAHPP-ree-kah
garlic	**Knoblauch**
	KNOHB-lauh[ch]
clove	**Nelke**
	NELL-keh
allspice	**Piment**
	pee-MEANT
saffron	**Safran**
	SAHFF-rahn

DINING

rosemary	**Rosmarin**
	ROHS-mah-reen
anise	**Anis**
	AH-niss
sugar	**Zucker**
	TSOOKK-ehr
marjoram	**Majoran**
	MAH-yoh-rahn
dill	**Dill**
	dill
caraway	**Kümmel**
	K[UE]M-mell
bay leaf	**Lorbeer**
	LOHRR-behr
cacao	**Kakao**
	kah-COW
dried	**getrocknet**
	gheh-TROCK-net
fresh	**frisch**
	frish
seed	**Samen**
	SAH-men

AT THE DELI

What kind of salad is that?	**Was für ein Salat ist das?**
	Vahs f[ue]hr aihn sah-LAHT isst dahs?
What type of cheese is that?	**Was für ein Käse ist das?**
	Vahs f[ue]hr aihn K[AE]H-seh isst dahs?
What type of bread is that?	**Was für ein Brot ist das?**
	Vahs f[ue]hr aihn BROHT isst dahs?
Some of that, please.	**Geben Sie mir etwas davon, bitte.**
	Gheh-ben zee mere at-vahs DAH-fonn, bit-eh.

Is the salad fresh?	**Ist der Salat frisch?**
	Isst dehr sah-laht FRISH?
I'd like ____	**Ich hätte gern ____**
	Ee[ch] hat-eh ghern ____
a sandwich.	**ein Sandwich.**
	aihn SAND-which.
a salad.	**einen Salat.**
	eye-nen sah-LAHT.
tuna salad.	**einen Tunfischsalat.**
	eye-nen TOON-fish-sah-laht.
chicken salad.	**einen Geflügelsalat.**
	eye-nen gheh-FL[UE]H-ghell-sah-laht.
roast beef.	**ein Roastbeef.**
	aihn ROAST-beef.
ham.	**einen Schinken.**
	eye-nen SHING-ken.
that cheese.	**diesen Käse.**
	dee-sen K[AE]H-seh.
cole slaw.	**einen Krautsalat.**
	eye-nen KRAUT-sah-laht.
a package of tofu.	**eine Packung Tofu.**
	eye-neh pahkk-oong TOH-foo.
mustard.	**Senf.**
	sennff.
mayonaisse.	**Majonäse.**
	mah-yoh-N[AE]H-seh.
a pickle.	**eine Essiggurke.**
	eye-neh ESS-igg-ghoorr-keh.
Is that smoked?	**Ist das geräuchert?**
	Isst dahs gheh-ROY-[ch]errt?
a pound (0,5 kg)	**ein Pfund**
	ain PFOONND

a quarter-pound (0,125 kg)	**ein Viertelpfund** *ain FEER-tell-pfoonnd*
a half-pound (0,25 kg)	**ein halbes Pfund** *ain HAHLL-bess pfoonnd*

CHAPTER FIVE
SOCIALIZING

Whether you're meeting people in a bar or a park, you'll find the language you need, in this chapter, to make new friends.

GREETINGS

Hello.	**Hallo.**
	Hah-LOH.
How are you?	**Wie geht es Ihnen?**
	Vee GHEHHT as eehnen?
Fine, thanks.	**Gut, danke.**
	Goot, DUNK-eh.
And you?	**Und Ihnen?**
	Oonnd EEH-nen?
I'm exhausted from the trip.	**Ich bin erschöpft von der Reise.**
	Ee[ch] bin air-SH[OE]PFT fonn dehr RYE-seh.
I have a headache.	**Ich habe Kopfschmerzen.**
	Ee[ch] hah-beh COPF-shmairtsenn.
I'm terrible.	**Ich fühle mich schlecht.**
	Ee[ch] f[ue]hl-eh mi[ch] SHLE[CH]T.
I have a cold.	**Ich habe eine Erkältung.**
	Ee[ch] hah-beh eye-ne air-KELL-toong.
Good morning.	**Guten Morgen.**
	Goo-ten MOR-ghenn.
Good evening.	**Guten Abend.**
	Goo-ten AHH-bend.
Good afternoon.	**Guten Tag.**
	Goo-ten TAHHG.
Good night.	**Gute Nacht.**
	Goo-teh NA[CH]T.

Listen Up: Common Greetings

Freut mich. *FROYT mee[ch].*	It's a pleasure.
Sehr erfreut. *Sehhr ehr-FROYT.*	Delighted.
Zu Ihren Diensten. / Ganz wie Sie wünschen. *Tsooh eehren DEENS-ten. / Gahnnts vee zee V[UE]N-shenn.*	At your service. / As you wish.
Guten Tag. *Goo-ten TAHGG.*	Good day.
Hallo. *Hah-LOH.*	Hello.
Wie geht's? *Vee GHETS?*	How's it going?
Was gibt's? *Vahs GHEEBTS?*	What's up?
Was ist los? *Vahs isst LOHHS?*	What's going on?
Tschüss! *Tsh[ue]ss!*	Bye!
Auf Wiedersehen. *Ouf VEE-dehr-seh-hen.*	Goodbye.
Bis später. *Biss SHP[AE]-tehr.*	See you later.

OVERCOMING THE LANGUAGE BARRIER

I don't understand.	**Ich verstehe Sie nicht.**
	Ee[ch] fair-STEH-heh zee ni[ch]t.
Please speak more slowly.	**Könnten Sie bitte etwas langsamer sprechen?**
	K[oe]nn-ten zee bit-eh atvahs LAHNG-summer shpre-[ch]en?
Please speak louder.	**Könnten Sie bitte etwas lauter sprechen?**
	K[oe]nn-ten zee bit-eh atvahs LOU-tehr shpre-[ch]en?

Curse Words

Here are some common curse words used across German-speaking countries.

Scheiße	shit
SHYE-sseh	
Drecksau	son of a bitch (literally, dirty sow)
DREKK-saoo	
Vollidiot	jerk
FOLL-eedeeoht	
Verdammt!	damn
Fehr-DAHMMT!	
Arsch	ass
arrsh	
durchgeknallt	screwed up
DUHR[CH]-gheh-knallt	
Arschloch	bastard
ARRSH-lo[ch]	
abgewichst	fucked up
UP-gheh-vixt	
ficken	to fuck
fikken	

See p20, 21 for conjugation.

Do you speak English?	**Sprechen Sie Englisch?** *Shpre-[ch]en zee ENG-lish?*
I speak ____ better than German.	**Ich spreche besser ____ als Deutsch.** *Ee[ch] shpre-[ch]eh bess-er ____ ahlls DOYTSH.*
Please spell that.	**Könnten Sie das bitte buchsta- bieren?** *K[oe]nn-ten zee dahs bit-eh bu[ch]-shtah-BEE-ren?*
Please repeat that?	**Könnten Sie das bitte wiederho- len?** *K[oe]nn-ten zee dahs bit-eh vee- dair-HOH-len?*
How do you say ____?	**Wie sagt man ____?** *Vee sahggt man ____?*
Would you show me that in this dictionary?	**Könnten Sie mir das bitte in die- sem Wörterbuch zeigen?** *K[oe]nn-ten zee mere dahs bit-eh in dee-sem V[OE]R-tehr-boo[ch] tsai-ghen?*

GETTING PERSONAL

People in German-speaking countries are generally friendly, but more formal than Americans. Remember to use the *Sie* form of address until given permission to employ the more familiar *Du*.

INTRODUCTIONS

What is your name?	**Wie heißen Sie?** *Vee HYE-ssenn zee?*
My name is ____.	**Ich heiße ____.** *Ee[ch] HYE-sseh ____.*
I'm very pleased to meet you.	**Freut mich, Sie kennen zu lernen.** *Freud mi[ch], zee CANON tsoo lehr-nen.*

May I introduce my ____	**Darf ich Sie meinem (male) / meiner (female) / meinen (plural) ____ bekannt machen?** *Dahrrff ee[ch] zee mitt my-nem / minor/my-nen ____ beh-KAHNNT ma[ch]en?*
How is your ____	**Wie geht es Ihrem (male) / Ihrer (female) / Ihren (plural) ____** *Vee ghehht as eehrehr (eeh-rem / eeh-ren) ____*
wife?	**Frau?** *frow?*
husband?	**Mann?** *mahnn?*
child?	**Kind?** *kin-d?*
friends?	**Freunden?** *FROYN-denn?*
boyfriend / girlfriend?	**Freund / Freundin?** *froynd / froyn-din?*
family?	**Familie?** *fah-MEE-lee-eh?*
mother?	**Mutter?** *MOOT-tehr?*
father?	**Vater?** *FAH-tehr?*
brother / sister?	**Bruder / Schwester?** *broo-dehr / shvesstehr?*
friend?	**Freund / Freundin?** *froynd / froyn-din?*
neighbor?	**Nachbarn / Nachbarin?** *nah[ch]-bar / nah[ch]-bah-rinn?*
boss?	**Chef?** *sheff?*
cousin?	**Cousin / Cousine?** *coo-SAH / coo-SEE-neh?*

aunt / uncle?	**Tante / Onkel?**
	tahnn-teh / ong-kell?
fiancée / fiancé?	**Verlobten?**
	fehr-LOHB-ten?
partner?	**Partner / Partnerin?**
	PARRT-ner / PARRT-neh-rin?
niece / nephew?	**Nichte / Neffen?**
	NI[CH]-teh / NEFF-en?
parents?	**Eltern?**
	ELL-tern?
grandparents?	**Großeltern?**
	GROHS-ell-tern?
Are you married / single?	**Sind Sie verheiratet / ledig?**
	Sinnd zee fehr-HAI-rah-tet / LEH-dig?
I'm married.	**Ich bin verheiratet.**
	Ee[ch] bin fehr-HAI-rah-tet.
I'm single.	**Ich bin ledig.**
	Ee[ch] bin LEH-dig.
I'm divorced.	**Ich bin geschieden.**
	Ee[ch] bin gheh-SHEE-den.
I'm a widow / widower.	**Ich bin Witwe / Witwer.**
	Ee[ch] bin VIT-veh / VIT-vehr.
We're separated.	**Wir leben getrennt.**
	Veer leh-ben gheh-TRENNT.
I live with my boyfriend / girlfriend.	**Ich wohne mit meinem Freund / meiner Freundin zusammen.**
	Ee[ch] VOH-neh mit my-nem FROYND / minor FROYN-din tsoo-sahmmen.
How old are you?	**Wie alt sind Sie?**
	Vee AHLLT sinnd zee?
How old are your children?	**Wie alt sind Ihre Kinder?**
	Vee ahllt sinnd eehreh KIN-dehr?

Wow! That's very young.	**Wow! Noch so jung?**
	Wow! Noh[ch] SOH yoonng?
No you're not! You're much younger.	**Das kann nicht stimmen! Sie sind doch viel jünger.**
	Dahs kahnn ni[ch]t shtimmen! Zee sinnd doh[ch] FEEL y[ue]hngh-ehr.
Your wife / daughter is beautiful.	**Sie haben eine hübsche Frau / Tochter.**
	Zee hah-ben eye-neh H[UE]B-sheh frow / to[ch]-tehr.
Your husband / son is handsome.	**Sie haben einen gutaussehenden Mann / Sohn.**
	Zee hah-ben eye-nen GOOT-ous-seh-hen-denn mahnn / sohn.
What a beautiful baby!	**Was für ein bezauberndes Baby!**
	Vahs f[ue]hr aihn beh-TSOW-behrn-dess baby!
Are you here on business?	**Sind Sie geschäftlich hier?**
	Sinnd zee ge-SHAFT-li[ch] heer?
I am vacationing.	**Ich mache Urlaub.**
	Ee[ch] ma[ch]-eh OOHR-loub.
I'm attending a conference.	**Ich nehme an einer Konferenz teil.**
	Ee[ch] neh-meh un eye-nehr kon-feh-RENTS tile.
How long are you staying?	**Wie lange bleiben Sie?**
	Vee lahng-he BLYE-ben zee?
What are you studying?	**Was studieren Sie?**
	Vahs shtoo-DEE-ren zee?
I'm a student.	**Ich bin Student.**
	Ee[ch] bin shtoo-DENT.
Where are you from?	**Woher kommen Sie?**
	Voh-hair COM-mehnn zee?

PERSONAL DESCRIPTIONS

blond(e)	**blond**	*blonnd*
brunette	**brünett**	*br[ue]h-nett*
redhead	**rothaarig**	*ROHT-haah-rig*
straight hair	**glattes Haar**	*GLAHT-tes haahr*
curly hair	**gelocktes Haar**	*gheh-LOCK-tess haahr*
kinky hair	**krauses Haar**	*KROUH-sess haahr*
long hair	**lange Haare**	*LAHNG-he haah-reh*
short hair	**kurze Haare**	*KUHRT-seh haah-reh*
tanned	**braungebrannt**	*brown-gheh-brahnnt*
pale	**blass**	*blahss*
mocha-skinned	**dunkelhäutig**	*DOONG-kell-hoy-tig*
black	**schwarz**	*shvahrrz*

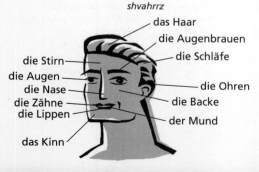

das Haar

die Augenbrauen

die Schläfe

die Stirn

die Augen

die Nase

die Zähne

die Lippen

die Ohren

die Backe

der Mund

das Kinn

white	**weiß**	*vice*
Asian	**asiatisch**	*ah-see-AH-tish*
African-American	**afro-amerikanisch**	*ah-froh-ah-merry-KAH-nish*
caucasian	**weiß**	*vice*
tall	**groß**	*grohss*
short	**klein**	*klyne*
thin	**dünn**	*d[ue]nn*
fat	**dick**	*dick*
blue eyes	**blaue Augen**	*blou-eh ou-ghenn*
brown eyes	**braune Augen**	*brown-eh ou-ghenn*
green eyes	**grüne Augen**	*gr[ue]h-neh ou-ghenn*
hazel eyes	**braune Augen**	*brown-eh ou-ghenn*
eyebrows	**Augenbrauen**	*OU-ghenn-brown*
eyelashes	**Wimpern**	*whimpern*
freckles	**Sommersprossen**	*SOHMMER-shprossen*
moles	**Muttermale**	*MUHTT-ehr-mah-leh*
face	**Gesicht**	*gheh-SI[CH]T*

Listen Up: Nationalities

Ich bin Deutscher (m) / Deutsche (f).   I'm German.
Ee[ch] bin DOY-tsher / DOY-tsheh.

Ich bin Österreicher (m) / Österreicherin (f).   I'm Austrian.
Ee[ch] bin [OE]HS-tehr-rye-[ch]ehr /
[OE]HS-tehr-rye-[ch]ehr-in.

Ich bin Türke (m) / Türkin (f).   I'm Turkish.
Ee[ch] bin T[UE]RR-keh / T[UE]RR-kin.

Ich bin Schweizer (m) / Schweizerin (f).   I'm Swiss.
Ee[ch] bin SHVYE-tsehr / SHVYE-tsehr-in.

Ich bin Italiener (m) / Italienerin (f).   I'm Italian.
Ee[ch] bin eetal-YEH-nehr / eetal-YEH-
nehr-in.

Ich bin Franzose (m) / Französin (f).   I'm French.
Ee[ch] bin frahnn-TSOH-seh / frahnn-
TS[OE]H-sinn.

Ich bin Pole (m) / Polin (f).   I'm Polish.
Ee[ch] bin POH-leh / POH-lin.

Ich bin Tscheche (m) / Tschechin (f).   I'm Czech.
Ee[ch] bin TSHE[CH]-eh / TSHE[CH]-in.

Ich bin Spanier (m) / Spanierin (f).   I'm Spanish.
Ee[ch] bin SHPAH-nee-her / SHPAH-nee-
her-in.

Ich bin Portugiese (m) / Portugiesin (f).   I'm Portuguese.
Ee[ch] bin porr-too-GHEE-seh / porr-too-
GHEE-sin.

Ich bin Grieche (m) / Griechin (f).   I'm Greek.
Ee[ch] bin GREE-[ch]eh / GREE-[ch]inn.

Ich bin Niederländer (m) / Niederländerin (f).   I'm Dutch.
Ee[ch] bin NEE-dair-lenn-dehr / NEE-dair-
lenn-dehr-in.

Ich bin Belgier (m) / Belgierin (f).   I'm Belgian.
Ee[ch] bin BELL-ghee-her / BELL-ghee-her-in.

Ich bin Däne (m) / Dänin (f).   I'm Danish.
Ee[ch] bin D[AE]H-neh / D[AE]H-nin.

Ich bin Vietnamese (m) / Vietnamesin (f). *Ee[ch] bin vee-at-nah-MEH-seh / vee-at-nah-MEH-sin*	I'm Vietnamese.
Ich bin Nordafrikaner (m) / Nordafrikanerin (f). *Ee[ch] bin norrd-uff-ree-KAH-nehr / norrd-uff-ree-KAH-nehr-in*	I'm North African.
Ich bin Iraner (m) / Ich bin Iranerin (f). *Ee[ch] bin eeh-RAH-nehr / eeh-RAH-nehr-in.*	I'm Iranian.
Ich bin Japaner (m) / Japanerin (f). *Ee[ch] bin yah-PAH-nehr / yah-PAH-nehr.*	I'm Japanese.
Ich bin Schwede (m) / Schwedin (f). *Ee[ch] bin SHVEH-deh / SHVEH-dinn.*	I'm Swedish.
Ich bin Norweger (m) / Norwegerin (f). *Ee[ch] bin NORR-veh-gher / NORR-veh-gher-in.*	I'm Norwegian.
Ich bin Amerikaner (m) / Amerikanerin (f). *Ee[ch] bin ah-meh-rhee-KAH-nehr / ah-meh-rhee-KAH-nehr-in.*	I'm American.
Ich bin Russe (m) / Russin (f). *Ee[ch] bin RUUSS-eh / RUSS-in.*	I'm Russian.

For a full list of nationalities, see English / German dictionary.

DISPOSITIONS AND MOODS

sad	**traurig** *TROU-rig*
happy	**fröhlich** *FR[OE]H-li[ch]*
angry	**verärgert** *fehr-AIR-ghert*
tired	**müde** *M[UE]H-deh*
anxious	**besorgt** *beh-SORGHT*
confused	**verwirrt** *fehr-VIRRT*
enthusiastic	**begeistert** *beh-GYSE-tehrt*

PROFESSIONS

What do you do for a living?	**Was machen Sie beruflich?**
	Vaahs mah[ch]en zee beh-ROOF-li[ch]?
Here is my business card.	**Hier ist meine Karte.**
	Heer isst my-neh KAHRR-teh.
I am ____	**Ich bin ____**
	ee[ch] bin ____
a doctor.	**Arzt / Ärztin.**
	artst / airts-tin.
an engineer.	**Ingenieur / -in.**
	in-genn- / IEUR / -in.
a lawyer.	**Anwalt / Anwältin.**
	UN-wallt / un-VELL-tin.
a salesperson.	**Verkäufer / -in.**
	fehr-KOY-fehr / -in.
a writer.	**Autor / Autorin.**
	OU-tohr / ou-TOH-rin.
an editor.	**Redakteur / -in.**
	reh-duck-T[OE]HR / -in.
a designer.	**Designer / -in.**
	designer / -in.
an educator.	**Erzieher / -in.**
	air-TSEE-hair / -in.
an artist.	**Künstler / -in.**
	K[UE]NNST-lair / -in.
a craftsperson.	**Handwerker / -in.**
	HAHNND-verr-kerr / -in.
a homemaker.	**Hausfrau / Hausmann.**
	HOUSE-frow / HOUSE-mahnn.
an accountant.	**Buchhalter / -in.**
	BOOH[CH]-hall-tehr / -in.
a nurse.	**Krankenpfleger / -in.**
	KRAHNG-ken-pfleh-gher / -in.
a musician.	**Musiker / -in.**
	MOO-sicker / -in.

a military professional.	**beim Militär.** *byme milli-TEHR.*
a government employee.	**Regierungsangestellter.** *reh-GHEE-roongs-un-gheh-shtell-tehr.*

DOING BUSINESS

I'd like an appointment.	**Ich hätte gern einen Termin.** *Ee[ch] HAT-eh ghern eye-nen tair-MEAN.*
I'm here to see ____.	**Ich habe einen Termin bei ____.** *Ee[ch] hah-beh eye-nen tair-MEAN bye ____.*
May I photocopy this?	**Kann ich das bitte kopieren?** *Khann ee[ch] dahs bit-eh koh-PEE-ren?*
May I use a computer here?	**Kann ich hier einen Computer benutzen?** *Khann ee[ch] heer eye-nen compu-ter beh-NOOTT-sen?*
What's the password?	**Wie lautet das Kennwort?** *Vee loutet dahs KENN-vohrt?*
May I access the Internet?	**Dürfte ich bitte auf das Internet zugreifen?** *D[ue]rf-teh ee[ch] bit-eh ouf dahs internet TSOO-grye-fenn?*
May I send a fax?	**Dürfte ich bitte das Faxgerät benutzen?** *D[ue]rf-teh ee[ch] bit-eh dahs FAHXX-gheh-r[ae]ht beh-NOOTT-sen?*
May I use the phone?	**Dürfte ich bitte das Telefon benutzen?** *D[ue]rf-teh ee[ch] bit-eh dahs teh-leh-PHON beh-NOOTT-sen?*

PARTING WAYS

Keep in touch.

Lassen Sie uns in Verbindung bleiben.
Lahssen zee oons in fair-BIN-doong blye-ben.

Please write or email.

Schicken Sie mir einen Brief oder eine E-Mail.
CHIC-en zee mere eye-nen BRIEF oh-dehr eye-neh E-mail.

Here's my phone number.

Hier ist meine Telefonnummer.
Heer isst my-neh tehleh-PHON-noommer.

Call me.

Rufen Sie mich an.
Roo-fenn zee mi[ch] UN.

May I have your phone number / e-mail please?

Könnten Sie mir bitte Ihre Telefonnummer / E-Mail-Adresse geben?
K[oe]nn-ten zee mere bit-eh eeh-reh tehleh-PHON-noommer / E-mail-ah-dress-eh gheh-ben?

May I have your card?

Geben Sie mir Ihre Visitenkarte?
Gheh-ben zee mere eehre vee-SEE-ten-kahrr-teh?

Give me your address and I'll write you.

Wenn Sie mir Ihre Adresse geben, schreibe ich Ihnen.
Venn zee mere eehre ah-DRESS-eh ghehben, shryebeh ee[ch] eehnen.

TOPICS OF CONVERSATION

As in the United States or Europe, the weather and current affairs are common conversation topics.

THE WEATHER

It's so ____   **Es ist so ____**
As isst soh ____

Is it always so ____   **Ist es immer so ____**
Isst as IM-mehr soh ____

sunny?   **sonnig?**
sonic?

rainy?   **regnerisch?**
REHG-nehrish?

cloudy?   **bewölkt?**
beh-W[OE]LLKT?

humid?   **feucht?**
foy[ch]t?

warm?   **warm?**
vahrrm?

cool?   **kalt?**
kahllt?

windy?   **windig?**
VINN-digg?

Do you know the weather forecast for tomorrow?   **Wissen Sie, wie morgen das Wetter wird?**
Vissen zee, vee MOR-ghen dahs vetter virrd?

THE ISSUES

What do you think about ____   **Was denken Sie über ____**
Vahs dengh-kenn zee [ue]ber ____

democracy?   **Demokratie?**
deh-moh-krah-TEE?

socialism?   **Sozialismus?**
soh-tsee-ah-LISS-mooss?

American Democrats?   **die Demokraten in Amerika?**
dee deh-moh-KRAH-ten in ah-MEH-ree-kah?

American Republicans?	**die Republikaner in Amerika?**
	dee reh-puh-blee-KAH-nehr in ah-MEH-ree-kah?
monarchy?	**die Monarchie?**
	dee moh-nahr-[CH]EE?
the environment?	**die Umwelt?**
	dee OOHM-vellt?
climate change?	**den Klimawandel?**
	dehn KLEEH-mah-wunn-dell?
the economy?	**die Wirtschaft?**
	dee VIRRT-shafft?
What political party do you belong to?	**Welcher Partei gehören Sie an?**
	Vell-[ch]er pahrr-TYE gheh-h[oe]ren zee un?
What did you think of the election in ____?	**Was halten Sie von den Wahlen in ____?**
	Vahs hull-ten zee vonn dehn vah-len in ____?
What do you think of the war in ____?	**Was denken Sie über den Krieg in ____?**
	Vahs dengh-kenn zee [ue]ber dehn kreegg in ____?

RELIGION

Do you go to church / temple / mosque?	**Gehen Sie in die Kirche / den Tempel / die Moschee?**
	Ghe-hen zee in dee KIRR-[ch]eh / dehn TEM-pell / dee moh-SHEHH?
Are you religious?	**Sind Sie religiös?**
	Sinnd zee reli-GY[OE]SS?
I'm ____ / I was raised ____	**Ich bin ____ / Ich wurde ____ erzogen.**
	Ee[ch] bin ____ / Ee[ch] vurr-deh ____ ehr-TSOH-ghenn.

Protestant.	**protestantisch.**
	proh-tess-TANN-tish.
Catholic.	**katholisch.**
	kah-TOH-lish.
Jewish.	**jüdisch.**
	Y[UE]H-dish.
Muslim.	**muslimisch.**
	mooss-LEE-mish.
Buddhist.	**buddhistisch.**
	boo-DISS-tish.
Greek Orthodox.	**griechisch-orthodox.**
	GREE-[ch]ish-ortodox.
Hindu.	**hinduistisch.**
	hin-doo-ISS-tish.
agnostic.	**agnostisch.**
	ahgg-NOSS-tish.
atheist.	**atheistisch.**
	ah-teh-ISS-tish.

I'm spiritual but I don't attend services.
Ich bin gläubig, gehe aber nicht zu Gottesdiensten.
Ee[ch] bin GLOY-big, gheh-he ah-behr ni[ch]t tsoo GOT-tess-deensten.

I don't believe in that.
Ich bin nicht gläubig.
Ee[ch] bin ni[ch]t GLOY-big.

That's against my beliefs.
Das ist gegen meinen Glauben.
Dahs isst GHEH-gen my-nen GLOU-ben.

I'd rather not talk about it.
Darüber möchte ich eigentlich nicht sprechen.
DAH-r[ue]h-behr m[oe][ch]-te ee[ch] eye-ghent-li[ch] ni[ch]t sprechen.

GETTING TO KNOW SOMEONE

Following are some conversation starters.

MUSICAL TASTES

What kind of music do you like?	**Welche Art von Musik mögen Sie?** *Vell-[ch]eh ahrt fonn moo-SEEK m[oe]-ghenn zee?*
I like _____	**Ich mag _____** *Ee[ch] mahgg _____*
rock 'n' roll.	**Rock'n'Roll.** *Rock'n'Roll.*
hip hop.	**Hiphop.** *Hip hop.*
techno.	**Techno.** *Tekkno.*
Soul.	**Soul.** *soul.*
classical.	**Klassik.** *KLASSick.*
jazz.	**Jazz.** *Jazz.*
country and western.	**Country-Musik.** *Country-moo-SEEK.*
reggae.	**Reggae.** *Reggae.*
calypso.	**Calypso.** *Kah-LYPP-soh.*
opera.	**Opern.** *OH-pehrrn.*
show-tunes / musicals.	**Shows / Musicals.** *Shows / Musicals.*
New Age.	**New Age.** *New Age.*
pop.	**Pop.** *Pop.*

HOBBIES

What do you like to do in your spare time?	**Was machen Sie in Ihrer Freizeit?** *Vahs mah-[ch]en zee inn eehrer FRYE-tsait?*
I like _____	**Ich _____** *Ee[ch] _____*
playing guitar.	**spiele gern Gitarre.** *spee-leh ghern ghee-TARR-eh.*
piano.	**spiele gern Klavier.** *spee-leh ghern klah-VEER.*

For other instruments, see the English / German dictionary.

painting.	**male gern.** *MAH-leh ghern.*
drawing.	**zeichne gern.** *TSAI[CH]-neh ghern.*
dancing.	**tanze gern.** *TAHNN-tseh ghern.*
reading.	**lese gern.** *LEH-seh ghern.*
watching TV.	**sehe gern fern.** *seh-heh ghern FEHRN.*
shopping.	**gehe gern einkaufen.** *ghe-heh ghern AIHN-cow-fenn.*
going to the movies.	**gehe gern ins Kino.** *geh-heh ghern inns KEE-noh.*
hiking.	**gehe gern wandern.** *geh-heh ghern VANN-dehrn.*
camping.	**gehe gern campen.** *geh-heh ghern KAM-penn.*
hanging out.	**treffe mich gern mit Freunden.** *treff-eh mee[ch] ghern mitt FROYN-denn.*
traveling.	**reise gern.** *RYE-seh ghern.*

eating out.	**esse gern auswärts.**
	ESS-eh ghern OUS-v[ae]rts.
cooking.	**koche gern.**
	KO[CH]-eh ghern.
sewing.	**nähe gern.**
	N[AE]H-heh ghern.
sports.	**interessiere mich für Sport.**
	interess-EE-reh mi[ch] f[ue]hr SHPOHRRT.

Do you like to dance?	**Möchten Sie tanzen?**
	M[oe][ch]-ten zee TAHNN-tsenn?
Would you like to go out?	**Würden Sie gern ausgehen?**
	V[ue]rr-denn zee ghern OUS-gheh-hen?
May I buy you dinner sometime?	**Darf ich Sie vielleicht mal zum Essen einladen?**
	Daahrf ee[ch] zee feel-lai[ch]t mahl tsoomm ESS-en aihn-lah-denn?
What kind of food do you like?	**Welche Art von Essen mögen Sie?**
	Vell-[ch]eh ahrt fonn essen M[OE]-ghenn zee?

For a full list of food types, see Dining in Chapter 4.

Would you like to go ____	**Würden Sie gern ____**
	V[ue]rr-denn zee ghern ____
to a movie?	**ins Kino gehen?**
	inns KEE-noh ghe-hen?
to a concert?	**zu einem Konzert gehen?**
	tsooh eye-nem konn-TSEHRRT ghe-hen?
to the zoo?	**in den Zoo gehen?**
	inn dehn TSOHH ghe-hen?
to the beach?	**an den Strand gehen?**
	un dehn SHTRAHND ghe-hen?
to a museum?	**ein Museum besuchen?**
	aihn moo-SEHH-oom beh-SOO-[ch]enn?

for a walk in the park?	**im Park spazieren gehen?** *imm PARRK shpah-TSEE-ren gheh-hen?*
dancing?	**tanzen gehen?** *TAHNN-tseh gheh-hen?*
Would you like to get ____	**Hätten Sie Lust auf ____** *Hat-ten zee LOOSST ouf ____*
lunch?	**ein Mittagessen?** *aihn MIT-tahg-essen?*
coffee?	**einen Kaffee?** *eye-nen kah-FEHH?*
dinner?	**ein Abendessen?** *aihn AH-bend-essen?*
What kind of books do you like to read?	**Welche Art von Büchern lesen Sie gern?** *Vell-[ch]eh ahrt fonn B[UE]-[ch]ern leh-senn zee ghern?*
I like ____	**Ich mag ____** *Ee[ch] mahgg ____*
mysteries.	**Mystery-Romane.** *Mystery-roh-MAH-neh.*
Westerns.	**Westernromane.** *Western-roh-MAH-neh.*
dramas.	**Dramen.** *DRAH-men.*
novels.	**Romane.** *roh-MAH-neh.*
biographies.	**Biografien.** *bee-oh-gra-FEE-hen.*
auto-biographies.	**Autobiografien.** *ou-toh-bee-oh-gra-FEE-hen.*
romance.	**Liebesgeschichten.** *LEE-bess-gheh-shi[ch]-ten.*
history.	**historische Romane.** *his-TOH-ree-sheh roh-MAH-neh.*

For dating terms, see Nightlife in Chapter 10.

CHAPTER SIX

MONEY & COMMUNICATIONS

This chapter covers money, the mail, phone, Internet service, and other tools you need to connect with the outside world.

MONEY

Do you accept ____	**Akzeptieren Sie ____** *Ahcktsep-TEEREN zee ____*
Visa / MasterCard / Discover / American Express / Diners' Club?	**Visa / MasterCard / Discover / American Express / Diners' Club?**
credit cards?	**Kreditkarten?** *Creh-DEET-kahrr-ten?*
bills?	**Scheine?** *SHY-neh?*
coins?	**Münzen?** *M[UE]NN-tsen?*
checks?	**Schecks?** *Shecks?*
travelers checks?	**Reiseschecks?** *RYE-seh-shecks?*
money transfer?	**Überweisungen?** *[Ue]h-behr-VYE-soong-en?*
May I wire transfer funds here?	**Kann ich hier Überweisungen vornehmen?** *Khann ee[ch] hear [Ue]h-behr-VYE-soong-en FOHR-neh-men?*
Would you please tell me where to find ____	**Wo finde ich hier ____** *Voh FIN-deh ee[ch] hear ____*
a bank?	**eine Bank?** *eye-neh BAHNNK?*
a credit bureau?	**ein Kreditinstitut?** *aihn creh-DEET-ins-tee-toot?*

an ATM?	**einen Geldautomaten?** *eye-nen GELLD-auh-toh-MAH-ten?*
a currency exchange?	**eine Geldwechselstube?** *eye-neh GELLD-wheccksel-shtoobeh?*
A receipt, please.	**Geben Sie mir bitte eine Quittung.** *Gheh-ben zee mere bit-eh eye-neh QUIT-toong.*
Would you tell me ___	**Sagen Sie mir bitte ___** *Sah-ghenn zee mere bit-eh ___*
the exchange rate for dollars to ___?	**den Wechselkurs von Dollar in ___?** *dehn VECK-sell-koorrs fonn dollar in ___?*
the exchange rate for pounds to ___?	**den Wechselkurs von Pfund in ___?** *dehn veck-sell-koorrs fonn PFOONND in ___?*
Is there a service charge?	**Gibt es eine Servicegebühr?** *Gheebt as eye-ne SIR-viss-ghe-b[ue]hr?*
May I have a cash advance on my credit card?	**Könnte ich bitte eine Barauszahlung über meine Kreditkarte bekommen?** *K[oe]nn-teh ee[ch] bit-eh eye-neh BAHR-ous-tsah-loonng [ue]h-behr my-neh creh-DEET-kahrr-teh beh-com-men?*
Will you accept a credit card?	**Akzeptieren Sie eine Kreditkarte?** *Ahcktsep-teeren zee eye-neh creh-DEET-kahrr-teh?*
May I have smaller bills, please.	**Könnte ich bitte kleinere Scheine bekommen?** *K[oe]nn-teh ee[ch] bit-eh klye-neh-reh SHY-neh beh-com-men?*

Listen Up: Bank Lingo

Unterschreiben Sie bitte hier.	Please sign here.
Oonn-tehr-shrye-ben zee bit-eh HEAR.	
Hier ist Ihre Quittung.	Here is your receipt.
Hear isst eeh-reh QUIT-toong.	
Zeigen Sie mir bitte Ihren Ausweis.	May I see your ID, please?
Tsye-ghenn zee mere bit-eh eeh-ren OUS-vise.	
Wir akzeptieren Reiseschecks.	We accept travelers checks.
Veer ahcktsep-teeren RYE-seh-shecks.	
Nur gegen bar.	Cash only.
Noor gheh-ghen BAR.	

Can you make change?	**Können Sie wechseln?**
	K[oe]nn-en zee VECK-selln?
I only have bills.	**Ich habe nur Scheine.**
	Ee[ch] hah-beh noor SHY-neh.
Some coins, please.	**Geben Sie mir bitte ein paar Münzen.**
	Gheh-ben zee mere bit-eh aihn paahr M[UE]NN-tsen.

PHONE SERVICE

Where can I buy or rent a cell phone?	**Wo kann ich ein Mobiltelefon kaufen oder mieten?**
	Voh khann ee[ch] aihn moh-BEEL-tehleh-fohn COW-fenn oh-dehr MEE-ten?

ATM Machine

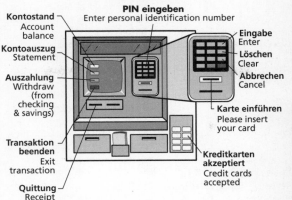

PIN eingeben
Enter personal identification number

Kontostand
Account balance

Kontoauszug
Statement

Auszahlung
Withdraw (from checking & savings)

Transaktion beenden
Exit transaction

Quittung
Receipt

Eingabe
Enter

Löschen
Clear

Abbrechen
Cancel

Karte einführen
Please insert your card

Kreditkarten akzeptiert
Credit cards accepted

What rate plans do you have?

Welche Tarife bieten Sie an?
Vell-[ch]eh tah-REEF-eh beaten zee un?

Is this good throughout the country?

Funktioniert das im ganzen Land?
Foonk-tsee-yoh-neert dahs im GHAHNN-tsenn lahnnd?

May I have a prepaid phone?

Könnte ich bitte ein Prepaid-Telefon haben?
K[oe]nn-teh ee[ch] bit-eh aihn PRE-paid-tehleh-fohn hah-ben?

Where can I buy a phone card?

Wo kann ich eine Telefonkarte kaufen?
Voh khann ee[ch] eye-neh tehleh-FOHN-kahrr-teh cow-fehn?

May I add more minutes to my phone card?

Kann ich meine Telefonkarte auf-laden?
Khann ee[ch] my-neh tehleh-FOHN-kahrr-teh ouf-lah-denn?

MAKING A CALL

May I dial direct?	**Kann ich direkt wählen?**
	Khann ee[ch] dee-RECKT v[ae]h-lenn?
Operator please.	**Die Vermittlung, bitte.**
	Dee Fehr-MITT-loong, bit-eh.
I'd like to make an international call.	**Ich möchte ein Auslandsgespräch führen.**
	Ee[ch] m[oe][ch]-te aihn OUS-lahnds-gheh-shpr[ae][ch] f[ue]h-ren.
I'd like to make a collect call.	**Ich möchte ein R-Gespräch führen.**
	Ee[ch] m[oe][ch]-te aihn ERR-gheh-shpr[ae][ch] f[ue]h-ren.
I'd like to use a calling card.	**Ich möchte eine Telefonkarte verwenden.**
	Ee[ch] m[oe][ch]-te eye-neh teh-leh-FOHN-kahrr-teh fehr-venn-denn.
Bill my credit card.	**Belasten Sie meine Kreditkarte.**
	Beh-LUSS-ten zee my-neh creh-DEET-kahrr-teh.
May I bill the charges to my room?	**Kann ich die Kosten über mein Zimmer abrechnen?**
	Khann ee[ch] dee coss-ten [ue]h-behr mine TSIMMER up-re[ch]-nen?
May I bill the charges to my home phone?	**Kann ich die Kosten über meine Telefonrechnung abrechnen?**
	Khann ee[ch] dee coss-ten [ue]h-behr my-neh tehleh-FOHN-re[ch]-noonng up-re[ch]-nen?
Information, please.	**Die Auskunft, bitte.**
	Dee OUS-koonnft, bit-eh.

Listen Up: Telephone Lingo

Hallo?
HAH-loh?

Hello?

Welche Nummer?
Vell-[ch]eh NOOMMER?

What number?

**Es tut mir leid, die
Leitung ist besetzt.**
*As toot mere lyde, dee
lye-toong isst beh-
SETTST.*

I'm sorry, the line
is busy.

**Legen Sie bitte auf,
und wählen Sie erneut.**
*Leh-ghen zee bit-eh
OUF, oonnd v[ae]h-len
zee air-NOYT.*

Please, hang up and redial.

**Leider nimmt niemand
ab.**
*Lye-dehr nimmt nee-
mahnd UP.*

I'm sorry, nobody is answering.

**Auf Ihrer Karte sind
noch zehn Minuten
übrig.**
*Ouf eeh-rehr kahrr-teh
sinnd noh[ch] TSEHN
mee-nooh-ten [ue]h-
brigg.*

Your card has ten minutes left.

I'd like the number for ___.	**Ich hätte gern die Nummer von ___.**
	Ee[ch] hat-eh ghern dee noommer fonn ___.
I just got disconnected.	**Die Verbindung wurde gerade unterbrochen.**
	Dee fehr-BIN-doonng vuhr-deh gheh-rah-deh oontehr-BRO[CH]-enn.
The line is busy.	**Die Leitung ist belegt.**
	Dee lye-toonng isst beh-LEHGT.
I lost the connection.	**Die Verbindung wurde unterbrochen.**
	Dee fehr-BIN-doonng vuhr-deh oontehr-BRO[CH]-enn.

INTERNET ACCESS

Where is an Internet café?	**Wo finde ich ein Internetcafé?**
	Voh fin-deh ee[ch] aihn INternet-kaff-ehh?
Is there a wireless hub nearby?	**Gibt es in der Nähe einen Wireless-Hub?**
	Gheebt as in der n[ae]h-heh eye-nen WIREless-hub?

How much do you charge per minute / hour?	**Wie viel kostet das pro Minute / Stunde?**
	Vee-feel coss-tet dahs proh mee-NOO-teh / SHTOONN-deh?
Can I print here?	**Kann ich hier etwas ausdrucken?**
	Khann ee[ch] hear at-vahs OUS-drookk-kenn?
Can I burn a CD?	**Kann ich eine CD brennen?**
	Khann ee[ch] eye-neh tseh-DEH brenn-en?
Would you please help me change the language preference to English?	**Könnten Sie mir bitte die Sprache auf Englisch umstellen?**
	K[oe]nn-ten zee mere bit-eh dee shprah-[ch]eh ouf ENG-lish oomm-shtell-en?
May I scan something?	**Kann ich etwas einscannen?**
	Khann ee[ch] at-vahs AIHN-scan-nen?
Can I upload photos?	**Kann ich Fotos hochladen?**
	Khann ee[ch] FOH-tohs ho[ch]-lah-denn?
Do you have a USB port so I can download music?	**Gibt es hier einen USB-Anschluss, damit ich Musik herunterladen kann?**
	Gheebt as hear eye-nen ooh-ess-BEH-un-shlooss, dah-mitt ee[ch] moo-SEEK hehrunn-tehr lah-denn khann?
Do you have a machine compatible with iTunes?	**Haben Sie einen iTunes-kompati-blen Computer?**
	Hah-ben zee eye-nen iTUNES-comm-pah-teeblen computer?

COMMUNICATIONS

Do you have a Mac?	**Haben Sie einen Mac?**
	Hah-ben zee eye-nen MAC?
Do you have a PC?	**Haben Sie einen PC?**
	Hah-ben zee eye-nen peh-TSEH?
Do you have a newer version of this software?	**Haben Sie eine neuere Version dieser Software?**
	Hah-ben zee eye-neh noy-eh-reh verr-SYOHN dee-sehr software?
Do you have broadband?	**Haben Sie einen Breitbandzugang?**
	Hah-ben zee eye-nen BRITE-bund-tsoo-gung?
How fast is your connection speed here?	**Wie hoch ist hier die Verbindungsgeschwindigkeit?**
	Vee hoh[ch] isst hear dee fehr-BIN-doonngs-ghe-shvinn-digg-kite?

GETTING MAIL

Where is the post office?	**Wo finde ich das Postamt?**
	Voh fin-deh ee[ch] dahs POSST-ahmmt?
May I send an international package?	**Kann ich ein Paket ins Ausland versenden?**
	Khann ee[ch] aihn pah-KEHHT inns OUS-lahnd fehr-senn-den?
Do I need a customs form?	**Benötige ich ein Zollformular?**
	Beh-n[oe]h-tiggeh ee[ch] aihn TSOLL-forr-moo-lahr?
Do you sell insurance for packages?	**Bieten Sie Paketversicherungen an?**
	Beaten zee pah-KEHHT-fehr-si[ch]e-roong-en un?

Please, mark it fragile.	**Kennzeichnen Sie das Paket bitte als zerbrechlich.** *Kenn-tsye[ch]-nen zee dahs pah-kehht bit-eh ahlls tsaihr-BRE[CH]-li[ch].*
Please, handle with care.	**Behandeln Sie es bitte vorsichtig.** *Beh-hun-delln zee as bit-eh FOHR-si[ch]-tigg.*
Do you have twine?	**Haben Sie Paketschnur?** *Hah-ben zee pah-KEHHT-shnoor?*
Where is a DHL office?	**Wo finde ich eine DHL-Niederlassung?** *Voh fin-deh ee[ch] eye-neh deh-hah-ELL nee-dehr-lass-oong?*
Do you sell stamps?	**Verkaufen Sie Briefmarken?** *Fehr-cow-fenn zee BREEF-marr-ken?*
Do you sell postcards?	**Verkaufen Sie Postkarten?** *Fehr-cow-fenn zee POSST-kahrr-ten?*
May I send that first class?	**Kann ich das erster Klasse versenden?** *Khann ee[ch] dahs airs-tehr KLASS-eh fehr-senn-den?*
How much to send that express / air mail?	**Wie viel kostet der Expressversand / Luftpostversand?** *Vee feel coss-tet dehr ex-PRESS-fehr-sannd / LOOFFT-pohsst-fehr-sannd?*
Do you offer overnight delivery?	**Bieten Sie einen Übernachtversand an?** *Beaten zee eye-nen [ue]h-behr-NAH[CH]T-fehr-sannd un?*

Listen Up: Postal Lingo

Der Nächste, bitte! *Dehr N[AE][CH]S-teh, bit-eh!*	Next!
Stellen Sie das bitte hier ab. *Shtell-en zee dahs bit-eh HEAR up.*	Please, set it here.
Welche Klasse? *Vell-[ch]eh KLAHSS-eh?*	Which class?
Welchen Service möchten Sie? *Vell-[ch]en SIR-viss m[oe][ch]-ten zee?*	What kind of service would you like?
Was kann ich für Sie tun? *Vahss kann ee[ch] f[ue]hr zee TOON?*	How can I help you?
Abgabeschalter *UP-ghah-beh-shull-tehr*	dropoff window
Abholschalter *UP-hohl-shull-tehr*	pickup window

How long will it take to reach the United States?	**Wie lange dauert der Versand in die USA?** *Vee lung-eh dowert dehr fehr-sannd inn dee ohh ess AH?*
I'd like to buy an envelope.	**Ich möchte ein Kuvert kaufen.** *Ee[ch] m[oe][ch]-teh aihn coo-VEHR cow-fen.*

May I send it airmail?

Kann ich das per Luftpost senden?
Khann ee[ch] dahs pair LOOFFT-posst senn-den?

I'd like to send it certified / registered mail.

Ich möchte das als Einschreiben senden.
Ee[ch] m[oe][ch]-teh dahs ahlls AIHN-shrye-ben senn-den.

CHAPTER SEVEN

CULTURE

CINEMA

Is there a movie theater nearby?	**Gibt es hier in der Nähe ein Kino?** *Gheebt as hear in dehr n[ae]h-heh aihn KEE-noh?*
What's playing tonight?	**Was läuft heute Abend?** *Vahhs LOYFT hoy-teh ah-bend?*
Is that in English or German?	**Ist das auf Englisch oder auf Deutsch?** *Isst dahs ouf ENG-lish oh-dehr ouf doytsh?*
Are there English subtitles?	**Gibt es englische Untertitel?** *Gheebt as eng-lisheh OONN-tehr-tee-tell?*
Is the theater air conditioned?	**Ist das Kino klimatisiert?** *Isst dahs kee-noh klee-mah-tee-SEERT?*
How much is a ticket?	**Wie viel kostet eine Karte?** *Vee feel coss-tet eye-neh KAHRR-teh?*
Do you have a ____ discount?	**Gibt es einen Rabatt für ____?** *Gheebt as eye-nen rah-BAHTT f[ue]hr ____?*
senior	**Senioren** *sehn-YOH-ren*
student	**Studenten** *shtoo-DENN-ten*
children's	**Kinder** *KIN-dehr*
What time is the movie showing?	**Wann läuft der Film?** *Vahnn LOYFT dehr fillm?*

How long is the movie?	**Wie lang dauert der Film?**
	Vee lahng DOW-ert dehr fillm?
May I buy tickets in advance?	**Kann ich schon vorher Karten kaufen?**
	Khann ee[ch] shohn FOHR-hair kahrr-ten cow-fen?
Is it sold out?	**Ist die Vorstellung ausverkauft?**
	Isst dee fohr-shtelloong OUS-fehr-cowft?
When does it begin?	**Wann beginnt die Vorstellung?**
	Vahnn beh-GHINNT dee fohr-shtel-loong?

PERFORMANCES

Do you have ballroom dancing?	**Gibt es hier Gesellschaftstanz?**
	Gheebt as hear gheh-SELL-shahfts-tunnts?
Are there any plays showing right now?	**Finden derzeit irgendwelche Aufführungen statt?**
	Fin-den dehr-tsyte irr-ghennd-vell-[ch]eh OUF-f[ue]h-roong-en shtahtt?
Is there a dinner theater?	**Gibt es hier ein Theater mit angeschlossener Gastronomie?**
	Gheebt as hear aihn teh-AH-tehr mitt un-gheh-shloss-ehn-er gahss-troh-noh-MEE?
Where can I buy tickets?	**Wo kann ich Karten kaufen?**
	Voh khann ee[ch] KAHRR-ten cow-fen?
Are there student discounts?	**Gibt es einen Studentenrabatt?**
	Gheebt as eye-nen shtoo-DENN-ten-rah-bahtt?
I need ____ seats.	**Ich benötige ____ Plätze.**
	Ee[ch] beh-n[oe]-tiggeh ____ PL[AE]TT-seh.

For a full list of numbers, see p7.

Listen Up: Box Office Lingo

Was möchten Sie gern sehen?
Vahs m[oe][ch]-ten zee ghern SEHH-hen?

What would you like to see?

Wie viele?
Vee FEE-leh?

How many?

Für zwei Erwachsene?
F[ue]hr tsvaih air-VUCK-seh-neh?

For two adults?

Mit Butter? Gesalzen?
Mitt BOOTT-ehr? Ghe-SAHLL-tsenn?

With butter? Salt?

Darf's sonst noch was sein?
Dharrfs SONNST noh[ch] vahs syne?

Would you like anything else?

An aisle seat.	**Einen Gangplatz, bitte.** *Eye-nen GAHNG-plahts, bit-eh.*
Orchestra seat, please.	**Einen Orchesterplatz, bitte.** *Eye-nen orr-KESS-tehr-plahts, bit-eh.*
What time does the play start?	**Wann beginnt die Vorstellung?** *Vahnn beh-GHINNT dee fohr-shtel-loong?*
Is there an intermission?	**Gibt es eine Pause?** *Gheebt as eye-neh POW-seh?*
Do you have an opera house?	**Gibt es hier ein Opernhaus?** *Gheebt as hear aihn OH-pehrrn-house?*
Is there a local symphony?	**Gibt es hier ein örtliches Symphonieorchester?** *Gheebt as hear aihn [oe]rrt-li[ch]-ess sym-foh-NEE-orr-kess-tehr?*

May I purchase tickets over the phone?

Kann ich die Karten telefonisch bestellen?
Khann ee[ch] dee kahrr-ten teh-leh-FOH-nish beh-shtellen?

What time is the box office open?

Welche Öffnungszeiten hat der Kartenschalter?
Vell-[ch]eh [OE]FF-noongs-tsye-ten hut dehr kahrr-ten-shahlll-tehr?

I need space for a wheelchair, please.

Ich benötige einen Platz für einen Rollstuhl.
Ee[ch] beh-n[oe]-tiggeh eye-nen plahts f[ue]hr eye-nen ROLL-shtool.

Do you have private boxes available?

Verfügen Sie über Privatlogen?
Fehr-f[ue]h-ghenn zee [ue]h-behr pree-VAHT-loh-shen?

Is there a church that gives concerts?

Gibt es hier eine Kirche, in der Konzerte gegeben werden?
Gheebt as hear eye-neh kirr-[ch]eh, inn dehr con-TSERR-teh gheh-gheh-ben vehr-denn?

A program, please.

Ein Programm, bitte.
Aihn proh-GRAHMM, bit-eh.

Please show us to our seats.

Zeigen Sie uns bitte unsere Plätze.
Tsye-ghenn zee oonns bit-eh oonn-seh-reh PL[AE]TT-seh.

MUSEUMS, GALLERIES & SIGHTS

Do you have a museum guide?

Haben Sie einen Museumsführer?
Hah-ben zee eye-nen moo-SEHH-ooms-f[ue]h-rehr?

Do you have guided tours?

Bieten Sie Fremdenführungen an?
Beaten zee FREMM-denn-f[ue]h-roongen un?

CULTURE

What are the museum hours?	**Wann hat das Museum geöffnet?**
	Vahnn hut dahs moo-sehh-oom gheh-[OE]FF-net?
Do I need an appointment?	**Benötige ich einen Termin?**
	Beh-n[oe]-tiggeh ee[ch] eye-nen tehr-MEEN?
What is the admission fee?	**Wie hoch ist der Eintrittspreis?**
	Vee hoh[ch] isst dehr AIHN-tritts-pryes?
Do you have ____	**Haben Sie ____?**
	Hah-ben zee ____?
student discounts?	**Studentenrabatte?**
	shtoo-DENN-ten-rah-bahtt-eh?
senior discounts?	**Seniorenrabatte?**
	senn-YOH-ren-rah-bahtt-eh?
Do you have services for the hearing impaired?	**Haben Sie Angebote für Hörgeschädigte?**
	Hah-ben zee UN-gheh-boh-teh f[ue]r H[OE]R-gheh-sh[ae]h-digg-teh?
Do you have audio tours in English?	**Werden Audioführungen in englischer Sprache angeboten?**
	Vehr-denn OW-dee-ohh-f[ue]h-roongen in eng-lisher SHPRAH-[ch]eh un-gheh-boh-ten?

CHAPTER EIGHT

SHOPPING

This chapter covers the phrases you'll need to shop in a variety of settings, from the mall to the town square artisan market. We also threw in the terminology you'll need to visit the barber or hairdresser.

For coverage of food and grocery shopping, see p89.

GENERAL SHOPPING TERMS

Please tell me _____	**Könnten Sie mir bitte sagen, _____** *K[oe]nn-ten zee mere bit-eh SAH-ghenn, _____*
how to get to a mall?	**wie ich zu einem Einkaufszentrum komme?** *ee[ch] tsoo eye-nem AIHN-cowfs-tsenn-troom kom-meh?*
the best place for shopping?	**wo man hier am besten Shoppen kann?** *voh mahn hear um bess-ten SHOPPEN khann?*
how to get downtown?	**wie ich in die Stadt komme?** *vee ee[ch] inn dee SHTAHTT kom-meh?*
Where can I find a _____	**Wo finde ich _____** *Voh fin-deh ee[ch] _____*
shoe store?	**ein Schuhgeschäft?** *aihn SHOO-gheh-sh[ae]fft?*
men's / women's / children's clothing store?	**ein Bekleidungsgeschäft für Herren / Damen / Kinder?** *aihn beh-KLYE-doongs-gheh-sh[ae]fft f[ue]hr HERR-en / DAH-menn / KIN-dehr?*

designer fashion shop?	**ein Geschäft mit Designermode?** *aihn gheh-SH[AE]FFT mitt designer-moh-deh?*
vintage clothing store?	**ein Second-Hand-Geschäft?** *aihn second-HAND-gheh-sh[ae]fft?*
jewelry store?	**einen Juwelier?** *eye-nen you-vehll-LEER?*
bookstore?	**eine Buchhandlung?** *eye-neh BOO[CH]-hahnd loong?*
toy store?	**ein Spielwarengeschäft?** *aihn SHPEEL-vah-ren-gheh-sh[ae]fft?*
stationery store?	**eine Schreibwarenhandlung?** *eye-neh SHRYEB-vah-ren-hahndloong?*
antique shop?	**einen Antiquitätenhändler?** *eye-nen ahnnti-quee-T[AE]H-ten-hen-dlehr?*
cigar shop?	**einen Tabakladen?** *eye-nen TAH-buck-lah-denn?*
souvenir shop?	**ein Souvenirgeschäft?** *aihn souveNIR-gheh-sh[ae]fft?*
Where can I find a flea market?	**Wo finde ich einen Flohmarkt?** *Voh finn-deh ee[ch] eye-nen FLOHH-marrkt?*

CLOTHES SHOPPING

I'd like to buy ____	**Ich möchte ____ kaufen.** *Ee[ch] m[oe][ch]-teh ____ cow-fen.*
men's shirts.	**Herrenhemden** *HERR-en-hem-denn*

women's shoes.	**Damenschuhe**
	DAH-menn-shoo-heh
children's clothes.	**Kinderbekleidung**
	KIN-dehr-beh-klye-doong
toys.	**Spielwaren**
	SHPEEL-vah-ren

For a full list of numbers, see p7.

I'm looking for a size ____	**Ich suche etwas in Größe ____**
	Ee[ch] SOO-[ch]eh at-vahs inn
	gr[oe]sseh ____
small.	**S.**
	ess.
medium.	**M.**
	emm.
large.	**L.**
	ell.
extra-large.	**XL.**
	ICKS ell.
I'm looking for ____	**Ich suche ____**
	Ee[ch] SOO-[ch]eh ____
a silk blouse.	**eine Seidenbluse.**
	eye-neh SYE-denn-bloo-seh.
cotton pants.	**eine Baumwollhose.**
	BOWM-voll-hoh-seh.
a hat.	**einen Hut.**
	eye-nen HOOT.
sunglasses.	**eine Sonnenbrille.**
	eye-neh SONN-en-brrill-eh.
underwear.	**Unterwäsche.**
	OONN-tehr-v[ae]sh-eh.
cashmere.	**nach etwas aus Kaschmir.**
	nah[ch] at-vahs ous KHASH-mere.
socks.	**nach Socken.**
	nah[ch] SOKKEN.
sweaters.	**nach Pullovern.**
	nah[ch] pull-OH-vehrn.

Ohrringe

Halskette

Armbanduhr

Kleid

Hemd

Krawatte

Jackett

Gürtel

Hose

Schuhe

a coat.	**eine Jacke.** *eye-ne YAKK-eh.*
a swimsuit.	**einen Badeanzug.** *eye-nen BAH-deh-un-tsoog.*
May I try it on?	**Kann ich das anprobieren?** *Khann ee[ch] dahs UN-proh-bee-ren?*
Do you have fitting rooms?	**Haben Sie Umkleidekabinen?** *Hah-ben zee OOMM-klye-deh-kah-bee-nen?*
This is _____	**Das ist _____** *Dahs isst _____*
too tight.	**zu eng.** *tsoo ENNG.*
too loose.	**zu weit.** *tsoo VYTE.*
too long.	**zu lang.** *tsoo LAHNGG.*
too short.	**zu kurz.** *tsoo KOORRTS.*

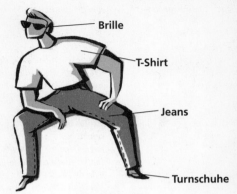

Brille

T-Shirt

Jeans

Turnschuhe

This fits great!	**Das passt gut!**
	Dahs pahsst GOOT!
Thanks, I'll take it.	**Danke, das nehme ich.**
	Dunk-eh, dahs NEH-meh ee[ch].
Do you have that in ___	**Haben Sie das ___**
	Hah-ben zee dahs ___
a smaller / larger size?	**kleiner / größer?**
	KLYE-nehr / GR[OE]-ssehr?
a different color?	**in einer anderen Farbe?**
	inn eye-nehr un-deh-ren FARR-beh?
How much is it?	**Wie viel kostet das?**
	Vee feel COSS-tet dahs?

ARTISAN MARKET SHOPPING

Is there a craft / artisan market?	**Gibt es hier einen Handwerksmarkt / Künstlermarkt?**
	Gheebt as hear eye-nen HAHNND-vehrrks-marrkt / K[UE]NNST-lehr-marrkt?

That's beautiful. May I look at it?	**Das ist wunderschön. Darf ich mir das näher ansehen?**
	Dahs isst voohn-dehr-SH[OE]HN. Dharrf ee[ch] mere dahs N[AE]-hehr un-seh-hen?
When is the farmers' market open?	**Wann hat der Bauernmarkt geöffnet?**
	Vahnn hut dehr BOW-errn-marrkt gheh-[OE]FF-net?
Is that open every day of the week?	**Ist das die ganze Woche über geöffnet?**
	Isst dahs dee GHANN-tseh voh-[ch]eh [ue]h-behr ghe-[oe]ff-net?
How much does that cost?	**Wie viel kostet das?**
	Vee feel COSS-tet dahs?
That's too expensive.	**Das ist zu teuer.**
	Dahs isst tsoo TOY-ehr.
How much for two?	**Wie viel für zwei Stück?**
	Vee feel f[ue]hr TSVAIH sht[ue]ck?
Do I get a discount if I buy two or more?	**Bekomme ich einen Nachlass, wenn ich zwei oder mehr kaufe?**
	Beh-com-meh ee[ch] eye-nen NA[CH]-lahss, venn ee[ch] tsvaih oder mehhr cow-feh?
Do I get a discount if I pay in cash?	**Bekomme ich einen Nachlass bei Barzahlung?**
	Beh-com-meh ee[ch] eye-nen na[ch]-lahss bye BAAR-tsah-loong?
No thanks, maybe I'll come back.	**Nein, danke. Vielleicht komme ich später nochmal vorbei.**
	Nine, dunk-eh, feel-lye[ch]t kom-meh ee[ch] SHP[AE]-tehr noh[ch]-mahl fohr-bye.

Listen Up: Market Lingo

Wenden Sie sich bei Fragen zu den Artikeln an das Personal.	Please ask for help before handling goods.
Venn-denn zee see[ch] by FRAH-ghenn tsoo dehn arr-TEE-kelln un dahs perr-soh-NAHL.	
Hier ist Ihr Wechselgeld.	Here is your change.
Hear isst eehr VECK-sell-gelld.	
Zwei für vierzig, der Herr.	Two for forty, sir.
Tsvaih f[ue]hr FEER-tsigg, dehr herr.	

Would you take €____?	**Sagen wir ____ Euro?**
	Sah-ghen veer ____ OY-roh?
For a full list of numbers, see p7.	
That's a deal!	**Abgemacht!**
	UP-gheh-mah[ch]t!
Do you have a less expensive one?	**Haben Sie eine günstigere Ausführung?**
	Hah-ben zee eye-neh GH[UE]NS-tee-gheh-reh ous-f[ue]h-roong?
Is there tax?	**Fällt Steuer an?**
	F[ae]llt SHTOYER un?
May I have the VAT forms? (Europe only)	**Könnte ich bitte die Formulare für die Mehrwertsteuer haben?**
	K[oe]nn-teh ee[ch] bit-eh dee fohr-moo-LAAH-reh f[ue]hr dee MEHHR-vehrt-shtoyer hah-ben?

BOOKSTORE / NEWSSTAND SHOPPING

Is there a ____ nearby?	**Gibt es in der Nähe ____ ?**
	Gheebt as inn dehr n[ae]h-heh ____?
a bookstore	**eine Buchhandlung**
	eye-neh BOO[CH]-hahnd loong
a newsstand	**einen Zeitungsstand**
	eye-nen TSITE-oongs-shtahnd
Do you have ____ in English?	**Haben Sie ____ in englischer Sprache?**
	Hah-ben zee ____ in eng-lisher SHPRAH-[ch]eh?
books	**Bücher**
	B[ue]h-[ch]ehr
newspapers	**Zeitungen**
	Tsite-oong-en
magazines	**Zeitschriften**
	Tsite-shriff-ten
books about local history	**Bücher zur örtlichen Geschichte**
	B[ue]h-[ch]ehr tsoor [oe]rrt-li[ch]-en gheh-SHI[CH]-teh
picture books	**Bilderbücher**
	BILL-dehr-b[ue]h-[ch]ehr

SHOPPING FOR ELECTRONICS

With some exceptions, shopping for electronic goods in Germany, Switzerland or Austria is generally not recommended. Many DVDs, CDs, and other products contain different signal coding from that used in the United States or Canada, to help deter piracy. In addition, electronic goods are generally more expensive than in the United States or Canada. They can be even more epensive if the exchange rate is high.

Can I play this in the United States?	**Lässt sich das in den USA abspielen?**
	L[ae]sst zee[ch] dahs inn dehn ohh ess AH up-shpee-len?
Will this game work on my game console in the United States?	**Funktioniert dieses Spiel auf meiner Spielekonsole in den USA?**
	Foonnk-tsee-yoh-NEERT dee-sehs shpeel ouf minor SHPEE-leh-con-soh-leh inn dehn ohh ess AH?
Do you have this in a U.S. market format?	**Haben Sie das in einem US-kompatiblen Format?**
	Hah-ben zee dahs in eye-nem ohh ESS-com-pah-tee-blenn forr-MAHT?
Can you convert this to a U.S. market format?	**Können Sie das in ein US-kompatibles Format umwandeln?**
	K[oe]n-nen zee dahs inn aihn ohh ESS-com-pah-tee-bles forr-maht OOMM-vahnn-delln?
Will this work with a 110 VAC adapter?	**Funktioniert das mit einem 110-Volt-Adapter?**
	Foonnk-tsee-yoh-NEERT dahs mit eye-nem hoon-dehrt-tsehn-VOLLT ah-dahpp-tehr?
Do you have an adapter plug for 110 to 220?	**Haben Sie einen Adapterstecker von 110 auf 220 Volt?**
	Hah-ben zee eye-nen ah-DAHPP-tehr-shteck-ehr fonn hoon-dehrt-TSEHN ouf tsvaih-honn-dehrt-TSVANN-tsigg vollt?
Do you sell electronics adapters here?	**Gibt es hier Elektronikadapter?**
	Gheebt as hear ehlec-TROH-nick-ah-dahpp-tehr?

Is it safe to use my laptop with this adapter?	**Kann ich mein Notebook mit diesem Adapter betreiben?** *Khann ee[ch] mine NOTE-book mitt dee-sem ah-dahpp-tehr beh-TRYE-ben?*
If it doesn't work, may I return it?	**Kann ich den Artikel zurückgeben, wenn er nicht funktioniert?** *Khann ee[ch] dehn arr-tee-kell tsoo-R[UE]CK-gheh-ben, venn air ni[ch]t foonnk-tsee-yoh-NEERT?*
May I try it here in the store?	**Kann ich den Artikel hier im Laden ausprobieren?** *Khann ee[ch] dehn arr-tee-kell hear im lah-denn OUS-proh-bee-ren?*

AT THE BARBER / HAIRDRESSER

Do you have a style guide?	**Haben Sie einen Frisurenkatalog?** *Hah-ben zee eye-nen frree-SOO-ren-kah-tah-lohg?*
A trim, please.	**Schneiden, bitte.** *SHNYE-denn, bit-eh.*
I'd like it bleached.	**Ich hätte mein Haar gern blondiert.** *Ee[ch] hat-teh mine haahr ghern blonn-DEERT.*
Would you make the color ____	**Könnten Sie die Farbe bitte ____** *K[oe]nn-ten zee dee fahrr-beh bit-eh ____*
darker?	**dunkler machen?** *DOONNK-lehr mah[ch]-en?*
lighter?	**heller machen?** *HELL-ehr mah[ch]-en?*

Would you just touch it up a little?

Könnten Sie es bitte nur ein wenig nachschneiden?

K[oe]nn-ten zee as bit-eh noohr aihn veh-nigg NAH[CH]-shnye-denn?

I'd like it curled.

Ich hätte mein Haar gern gelockt.

Ee[ch] hat-teh mine haahr ghern gheh-LOCKT.

Do I need an appointment?

Benötige ich einen Termin?

Beh-n[oe]-tiggeh ee[ch] eye-nen tehr-MEEN?

Wash, dry, and set.

Waschen, Trocknen und Legen.

VAHSH-en, TROKK-nen oonnd LEH-ghenn.

Do you do permanents?

Kann ich bei Ihnen eine Dauerwelle bekommen?

Khann ee[ch] by eeh-nen eye-neh DOWER-vell-eh beh-com-men?

May I make an appointment?

Ich hätte gern einen Termin.

Ee[ch] hat-eh ghern eye-nen tehr-MEEN.

Please use low heat.

Bitte nicht zu heiß.

Bit-eh ni[ch]t tsoo HYE-ss.

Please don't blow dry it.

Bitte nicht trockenföhnen.

Bit-eh ni[ch]t TROKK-en-f[oe]h-nen.

Please dry it curly / straight.

Föhnen Sie die Haare bitte lockig / glatt.

F[oe]h-nen zee dee haah-reh bit-eh LOCK-igg / GLAHTT.

Would you fix my braids?

Könnten Sie sich bitte um meinen Zopf kümmern?

K[oe]nn-ten zee see[ch] bit-eh oomm my-nen TSOPF k[ue]m-mehrn?

Would you fix my highlights?	**Könnten Sie sich bitte um meinen Strähnen kümmern?**
	K[oe]nn-ten zee see[ch] bit-eh oomm my-neh SHTR[AE]H-nen k[ue]m-mehrn?
Do you wax?	**Bieten Sie Enthaarungen an?**
	Beaten zee ent-HAAH-roongen un?
Please wax my ____	**Bitte enthaaren Sie meine ____**
	Bit-eh ent-haah-ren zee my-neh
legs.	**Beine.**
	BY-neh.
bikini line.	**Bikinilinie.**
	bee-KEE-nee-lee-nee-eh.
eyebrows.	**Augenbrauen.**
	OW-ghenn-brown.
under my nose.	**Oberlippe.**
	OH-behr-lipp-eh.
Please trim my beard.	**Trimmen Sie bitte meinen Bart.**
	Trimmen zee bit-eh my-nen BAHRRT.
A shave, please.	**Rasieren, bitte.**
	Rah-SEE-ren, bit-eh.
Use a fresh blade please.	**Verwenden Sie bitte eine neue Klinge.**
	Fair-venn-denn zee bit-eh eye-neh noy-eh KLING-eh.
Sure, cut it all off.	**Klar, schneiden Sie ruhig alles ab.**
	Klahr, shnye-denn zee ROO-higg ull-es up.

CHAPTER NINE
SPORTS & FITNESS

GETTING FIT

Is there a gym nearby?

Gibt es ein Fitnessstudio in der Nähe?
Gheebt as aihn FIT-ness-shtoo-dee-oh inn dehr n[ae]h-heh?

Do you have free weights?

Haben Sie Hanteln und Gewichte?
Hah-ben zee HAHN-teln oond gheh-WI[CH]-teh?

I'd like to go for a swim.

Ich möchte gern schwimmen gehen.
Ee[ch] m[oe][ch]-teh ghern SHVIMM-en gheh-hen.

Do I have to be a member?

Muss ich Mitglied sein?
Mooss ee[ch] MITT-gleed syne?

May I come here for one day?

Kann ich Ihr Angebot an einem einzelnen Tag nutzen?
Khann ee[ch] eehr un-gheh-boht un eye-nem AIHN-tsell-nen tahgg noott-senn?

149

How much does a membership cost?	**Wie viel kostet die Mitgliedschaft?** *Vee feel coss-tet dee MITT-gleed-shufft?*
I need to get a locker please.	**Ich hätte gern einen Spind.** *Ee[ch] hat-eh ghern eye-nen SHPINNT.*
Do you have a lock?	**Haben Sie ein Schloss?** *Hah-ben zee aihn SHLOSS?*
Do you have a treadmill?	**Haben Sie ein Laufband?** *Hah-ben zee aihn LOUF-bund?*
Do you have a stationary bike?	**Haben Sie ein Trainingsrad?** *Hah-ben zee aihn TRAI-nings-rahd?*
Do you have squash / American handball courts?	**Haben Sie einen Squashplatz / Platz für American Handball?** *Hah-ben zee eye-nen SQUASH-plahts / plahts f[ue]hr american HAND-ball?*
Are they indoors?	**In der Halle?** *Inn dehr HULL-eh?*
I'd like to play tennis.	**Ich würde gern Tennis spielen.** *Ee[ch] v[ue]rr-deh ghern TEN-nis shpee-len.*
Would you like to play?	**Möchten Sie gern spielen?** *M[oe][ch]-ten zee ghern SHPEE-len?*
I'd like to rent a racquet.	**Ich würde gern einen Schläger mieten.** *Ee[ch] v[ue]rr-deh ghern eye-nen SHL[AE]h-gher meeten.*
I need to buy some _____	**Ich benötige _____** *Ee[ch] beh-n[oe]-tiggeh _____*
new balls.	**neue Bälle.** *noy-eh B[AE]LL-eh.*
safety glasses.	**eine Schutzbrille.** *eye-neh SHOOTTS-brill-eh.*

May I rent a court for tomorrow?	**Kann ich für morgen einen Platz mieten?**
	Khann ee[ch] f[ue]r morr-ghenn eye-nen PLAHTS meeten?
May I have clean towels?	**Könnte ich bitte saubere Handtücher bekommen?**
	K[oe]nn-teh ee[ch] bit-eh sow-beh-reh HAHND-t[ue]h-[ch]ehr beh-com-men?
Where are the showers / locker-rooms?	**Wo finde ich die Duschen / Umkleiden?**
	Voh fin-deh ee[ch] dee DOO-shenn / OOMM-klye-denn?
Do you have a workout room for women only?	**Haben Sie einen Trainingsraum für Frauen?**
	Hah-ben zee eye-nen trainings-roum f[ue]hr FROW-en?
Do you have aerobics classes?	**Bieten Sie Aerobic-Kurse an?**
	Bee-ten zee aeROBic-koorr-seh un?
Do you have a women's pool?	**Haben Sie einen Pool für Frauen?**
	Hah-ben zee eye-nen pool f[ue]hr FROW-en?
Let's go for a jog.	**Gehen wir eine Runde joggen.**
	Gheh-hen veer eye-neh roonn-deh JOG-en.
That was a great workout.	**Das war ein großartiges Training.**
	Dahs vahr aihn GROHS-arr-tee-ghess training.

CATCHING A GAME

Where is the stadium?

Wo finde ich das Stadion?
Voh fin-deh ee[ch] dahs SHTAH-dee-on?

Who is your favorite player?

Wer ist Ihr Lieblingsspieler?
Vehr isst eehr LEEB-links-shpeel-er?

Who is the best goalie?

Wer ist der beste Torwart?
Vehr isst dehr bess-teh TOHR-wahrrt?

Where can I watch a soccer game?

Wo kann ich ein Fußballspiel sehen?
Voh khann ee[ch] aihn FOOSS-bahl-speel seh-en?

Where can I see a volleyball game?

Wo kann ich ein Volleyballspiel sehen
Voh khann ee[ch] aihn VOL-ley-bahl-speel seh-en?

Are there any women's teams?

Gibt es Frauenteams?
Gheebt as FROW-en-teams?

Do you have any amateur / professional teams?

Gibt es hier Amateurteams / Profiteams?
Gheebt as hear ama-TEUR-teams / PROH-fee-teams?

Is there a game I could play in?	**Gibt es ein Spiel, bei dem ich mitspielen kann?**
	Gheebt as aihn shpeel, by dehm ee[ch] MITT-shpee-len khann?
Which is the best team?	**Welches Team ist das beste?**
	Vell-[ch]ess team isst dahs BESS-teh?
Will the game be on television?	**Wird das Spiel im Fernsehen übertragen?**
	Virrd dahs shpeel im FEHRN-sehh-hen [ue]h-behr-trah-ghenn?
Where can I buy tickets?	**Wo kann ich Karten kaufen?**
	Voh khann ee[ch] KAHRR-ten cow-fen?
The best seats, please.	**Die besten Plätze, bitte.**
	Dee bess-ten PL[AE]TT-seh, bit-eh.
The cheapest seats, please.	**Die billigsten Plätze, bitte.**
	Dee bill-igg-sten PL[AE]TT-seh, bit-eh.
How close are these seats?	**Wie nah sind diese Plätze?**
	Vee NAH sinnd dee-seh pl[ae]tt-seh?
May I have box seats?	**Könnte ich bitte Logenplätze haben?**
	K[oe]nn-teh ee[ch] bit-eh LOH-shen-pl[ae]tt-seh hah-ben?
Wow! What a game!	**Wow! Was für ein Spiel!**
	Wow! VAHS f[ue]hr aihn shpeel!
Go Go Go!	**Los, los, los!**
	LOHS, LOHS, LOHS!
Oh No!	**Oh nein!**
	Oh NINE!
Give it to them!	**Gebt ihnen Saures!**
	Ghehbt eeh-nen SOW-ress!

Go for it!	**Auf geht's!**
	OUF ghehts!
Score!	**Tor!**
	TOHHR!
What's the score?	**Wie lautet der Spielstand?**
	Vee loutet dehr SHPEEL-shtahnd?
Who's winning?	**Wer gewinnt?**
	Vehr gheh-VINNT?

HIKING

Where can I find a guide to hiking trails?	**Wo finde ich einen Führer für Wandertouren?**
	Voh fin-deh ee[ch] eye-nen f[ue]h-rehr f[ue]hr VAHNN-dehr-touren?
Do we need to hire a guide?	**Benötigen wir einen Führer?**
	Beh-n[oe]-tiggen veer eye-nen F[UE]H-rehr?
Where can I rent equipment?	**Wo kann ich Ausrüstung mieten?**
	Voh khann ee[ch] OUS-r[ue]ss-toong meeten?
Do they have rock climbing there?	**Gibt es hier eine Möglichkeit zum Felsenklettern?**
	Gheebt as hear eye-neh m[oe]g-lee[ch]-kite tsoom FELL-senn-klet-tern?

We need more ropes and carabiners.

Wir benötigen mehr Seile und Karabiner.
Veer beh-n[oe]-tiggen mehhr SYE-leh oonnd kah-rah-BEE-nehr.

Where can we go mountain climbing?

Wo können wir hier bergsteigen?
Voh k[oe]n-nen veer hear BEHRRG-shtye-ghenn?

Are the routes _____

Sind die Routen _____
Sinnd dee roo-ten _____

well marked?

gut gekennzeichnet?
goot gheh-KENN-tsye[ch]-net?

in good condition?

in gutem Zustand?
inn goo-tem TSOO-shtahnd?

What is the altitude there?

Wie hoch ist es dort?
Vee HOH[CH] isst as dohrrt?

How long will it take?

Wie lange dauert die Tour?
Vee lahng-eh DOWERT dee tour?

Is it very difficult?

Ist die Tour sehr schwierig?
Isst dee tour sehr SHVEE-rigg?

I'd like a challenging climb but I don't want to take oxygen.

Ich möchte eine herausfordernde Tour unternehmen, aber keine Sauerstoffflaschen mitnehmen.
Ee[ch] m[oe][ch]-teh eye-neh heh-ROUS-forr-derrn-deh tour oonntehr-neh-men, ah-behr kye-neh SOUER-shtoff-flahshenn mitt-neh-men.

I want to hire someone to carry my excess gear.

Ich möchte einen Träger für meine Zusatzausrüstung engagieren.
Ee[ch] m[oe][ch]-teh eye-nen tr[ae]-ghehr f[ue]hr my-ne TSOO-sutts-ous-r[ue]ss-toong ong-ghah-SHEE-ren.

We don't have time for a long route.	**Wir haben nicht genügend Zeit für eine lange Tour.**
	Veer hah-ben ni[ch]t gheh-n[ue]h-ghennd TSITE f[ue]hr eye-ne lahng-eh tour.
I don't think it's safe to proceed.	**Ich denke, wir sollten aus Sicherheitsgründen nicht weitergehen.**
	Ee[ch] dehng-keh, veer soll-ten ous SI[CH]-ehr-hytes-gr[ue]nn-den nee[ch]t VYE-tehr-gheh-hen.
Do we have a backup plan?	**Haben wir einen Notfallplan?**
	Hah-ben veer eye-nen NOHT-fahll-plahn?
If we're not back by tomorrow, send a search party.	**Sollten wir bis morgen nicht zurück sein, schicken Sie einen Suchtrupp.**
	Soll-ten veer biss morr-ghenn nee[ch]t tsoo-R[UE]CK syne, shick-en zee eye-nehn SOO[CH]-troopp.
Are the campsites marked?	**Sind die Zeltplätze gekennzeich-net?**
	Sinnd dee tsellt-pl[ae]tt-seh gheh-KENN-tsye[ch]-net?
Can we camp off the trail?	**Können wir abseits der Strecke campieren?**
	K[oe]nn-en veer UP-sites dehr shtrek-keh cumpeeren?
Is it okay to build fires here?	**Ist hier Feuermachen erlaubt?**
	Isst hear foyer-mah-[ch]en air-LOUBT?
Do we need permits?	**Benötigen wir eine Genehmigung?**
	Beh-n[oe]-tiggen veer eye-ne gheh-NEH-mee-goong?

For more camping terms, see p70.

BOATING OR FISHING

When do we sail?	**Wann legen wir ab?**
	Vahnn leh-ghenn veer UP?
Where are the life preservers?	**Wo befinden sich die Schwimmwesten?**
	Voh beh-fin-den si[ch] dee SHVIMM-vess-ten?
Can I purchase bait?	**Kann ich Köder kaufen?**
	Khann ee[ch] K[OE]H-dehr cow-fen?
Can I rent a pole?	**Kann ich eine Angel leihen?**
	Khann ee[ch] eye-neh UNG-ell lye-hen?
How long is the voyage?	**Wie lang dauert die Reise?**
	Vee lahng DOW-ert dee rye-seh?
Are we going up river or down?	**Fahren wir flussauf- oder flussabwärts?**
	Fah-ren veer flooss-OUF oh-dehr flooss-UP-v[ae]rrts?
How far are we going?	**Wie weit fahren wir?**
	Vee vite FAH-ren veer?
How fast are we going?	**Wie schnell fahren wir?**
	Vee SHNELL fah-ren veer?
How deep is the water here?	**Wie tief ist das Wasser hier?**
	Vee teef isst dah VAHS-ser hear?

I got one!	**Ich hab einen!**
	Ee[ch] HUB eye-nen!
I can't swim.	**Ich kann nicht schwimmen.**
	Ee[ch] khann nee[ch]t SHVIMM-men.
Can we go ashore?	**Können wir an Land gehen?**
	K[oe]nn-en veer un LAHNND gheh-hen?

For more boating terms, see p54.

DIVING

I'd like to go snorkeling.	**Ich würde gern schnorcheln gehen.**
	Ee[ch] v[ue]rr-deh ghern SHNORR-[ch]elln gheh-hen.
I'd like to go scuba diving.	**Ich würde gern mit Atemgerät tauchen gehen.**
	Ee[ch] v[ue]rr-deh ghern mitt AH-tehm-gheh-r[ae]ht TOU-[ch]enn gheh-hen.
I have a NAUI / PADI certification.	**Ich habe ein NAUI / PADI-Zertifikat.**
	Ee[ch] hah-beh aihn NAUI / PADI-tserr-tee-fee-KAHT.
I need to rent gear.	**Ich muss Ausrüstung mieten.**
	Ee[ch] mooss OUS-r[ue]ss-toong meeten.
We'd like to see some shipwrecks if we can.	**Wir würden gern ein paar Wracks sehen.**
	Veer v[ue]rr-den ghern aihn paahr VRRAHCKS seh-hen.
Are there any good reef dives?	**Gibt es hier schöne Riffe zum Tauchen?**
	Gheebt as hear sh[oe]h-neh riff-eh tsoomm TOU-[ch]en?

I'd like to see a lot of sea-life.	**Ich möchte gern viel von der Unterwasserwelt sehen.** *Ee[ch] m[oe][ch]-teh ghern feel fonn dehr oonter-VAHS-sehr-vellt seh-hen.*
Are the currents strong?	**Ist die Strömung stark?** *Isst dee shtr[oe]h-moonng SHTARRK?*
How clear is the water?	**Wie klar ist das Wasser?** *Vee klaar isst dahs VAHS-sehr?*
I want / don't want to go with a group.	**Ich möchte gern / nicht mit einer Gruppe tauchen.** *Ee[ch] m[oe][ch]-teh ghern / nee[ch]t mitt eye-ner GROOPP-eh tou-[ch]en.*
Can we charter our own boat?	**Können wir ein eigenes Boot chartern?** *K[oe]nn-en veer aihn EYE-ghenn-es boht chartehrn?*

SURFING

I'd like to go surfing.	**Ich würde gern surfen gehen.** *Ee[ch] v[ue]rr-deh ghern SUR-fen gheh-hen.*
Are there any good beaches?	**Gibt es hier schöne Strände?** *Gheebt as hear sh[oe]h-neh SHTR[AE]N-deh?*
Can I rent a board?	**Kann ich ein Surfbrett leihen?** *Khann ee[ch] aihn SURF-brrett lye-hen?*
How are the currents?	**Wie ist die Strömung?** *Vee isst dee SHTR[OE]H-moonng?*

How high are the waves?	**Wie hoch sind die Wellen?** *Vee hoh[ch] sinnd dee VELL-ehn?*
Is it usually crowded?	**Sind viele Menschen dort?** *Sinnd FEE-leh menn-shenn dohrrt?*
Are there facilities on that beach?	**Gibt es Einrichtungen an diesem Strand?** *Gheebt as AIHN-ri[ch]-toong-en un dee-sem shtrahnd?*
Is there wind surfing there also?	**Ist dort auch Windsurfing möglich?** *Isst dohrrt ouh[ch] WIND-surfing m[oe]h-gli[ch]?*

GOLFING

I'd like to reserve a tee-time, please.	**Ich möchte eine Tee-Time reservieren.** *Ee[ch] m[oe][ch]-teh eye-neh TEE-time reh-sehr-vee-renn.*
Do we need to be members to play?	**Müssen wir Mitglied sein, um spielen zu dürfen?** *M[ue]ss-ehn veer MITT-gleed syne, oomm shpee-len tsoo d[ue]rr-fen?*
How many holes is your course?	**Wie viele Löcher hat Ihr Platz?** *Vee fee-leh l[oe][ch]-ehr hut eehr PLAHTS?*

What is par for the course?	**Wie hoch ist das Par auf diesem Platz?**
	Vee hoh[ch] isst dahs PAAR ouf dee-sem plahts?
I need to rent clubs.	**Ich möchte Schläger mieten.**
	Ee[ch] m[oe][ch]-teh SHL[AE]H-ghehr meeten.
I need to purchase a sleeve of balls.	**Ich möchte Golfbälle kaufen.**
	Ee[ch] m[oe][ch]-teh GOLLF-b[ae]ll-eh cow-fen.
I need a glove.	**Ich benötige einen Handschuh.**
	Ee[ch] beh-n[oe]h-tiggeh eye-nen HAHND-shoo.
I need a new hat.	**Ich brauche einen neuen Hut.**
	Ee[ch] brow-[ch]eh eye-nen noy-en HOOT.
Do you require soft spikes?	**Muss ich weiche Spikes tragen?**
	Mooss ee[ch] VYE-[ch]eh spikes trah-ghenn?
Do you have carts?	**Haben Sie Golfwägen?**
	Hah-ben zee GOLLF-v[ae]h-ghenn?
I'd like to hire a caddy.	**Ich würde gern einen Caddy mieten.**
	Ee[ch] v[ue]rr-deh ghern eye-nen CADDY meeten.
Do you have a driving range?	**Haben Sie eine Driving Range?**
	Hah-ben zee eye-neh DRIving Range?
How much are the greens fees?	**Wie hoch ist die Green Fee?**
	Vee hoh[ch] isst dee GREEN fee?
Can I book a lesson with the pro?	**Kann ich eine Unterrichtseinheit mit dem Profi buchen?**
	Khann ee[ch] eye-neh oon-tehr-ri[ch]ts-aihn-hyte mitt dehm PRO-fee boo-[ch]enn?

I need to have a club repaired.	**Ich benötige eine Schlägerreparatur.**
	Ee[ch] beh-n[oe]h-tiggeh eye-neh SHL[AE]H-ghehr-reh-pah-rah-tour.
Is the course dry?	**Ist der Platz trocken?**
	Isst dehr plahts TROKK-en?
Are there any wildlife hazards?	**Besteht eine Gefahr durch wilde-bende Tiere?**
	Beh-shteht eye-neh gheh-fahr doohr[ch] villd-leh-benn-deh TEE-reh?
How many meters is the course?	**Wie groß ist der Platz in Metern?**
	Vee grohs isst dehr plahts inn MEH-terrn?
Is it very hilly?	**Ist der Platz sehr hügelig?**
	Isst dehr plahts sehr H[UE]H-gheh-lligg?

CHAPTER TEN

NIGHTLIFE

For coverage of movies and cultural events, see p132, Chapter Seven, "Culture."

CLUB HOPPING

Where can I find ____	**Wo finde ich ____**
	Voh fin-deh ee[ch] ____
a good nightclub?	**einen guten Nachtclub?**
	eye-nen gooten NAH[CH]T-cloopp?
a club with a live band?	**einen Club mit Liveband?**
	eye-nen cloopp mitt LIVE-band?
a reggae club?	**einen Reggaeclub?**
	eye-nen REGGAE-cloopp?
a hip hop club?	**einen Hiphop-Club?**
	eye-nen HIP-hop-cloopp?
a techno club?	**einen Technoclub?**
	eye-nen TEKK-noh-cloopp?
a jazz club?	**einen Jazzclub?**
	eye-nen JAZZ-cloopp?
a country-western club?	**einen Country-und-Western-Club?**
	eye-nen country oonnd WESS-tern cloopp?
a gay / lesbian club?	**einen Schwulen- / Lesbenclub?**
	eye-nen SHVOO-len / LESS-ben-cloopp?
a club where I can dance?	**einen Tanzclub?**
	eye-nen TUNNTS-cloopp?

a club with Salsa music?	**einen Club mit Salsa-Musik?**
	eye-nen CLOOPP mitt SAL-sa moo-SEEK?
the most popular club in town?	**den beliebtesten Club der Stadt?**
	dehn beh-LEEB-tess-ten cloopp dehr shtahtt?
a singles bar?	**eine Singlebar?**
	eye-ne SINGLE-bahr?
a piano bar?	**eine Pianobar?**
	eye-ne pee-AH-noh-bahr?
the most upscale club?	**den exklusivsten Club?**
	dehn ekks-cloo-SEEVS-ten cloopp?
What's the hottest bar these days?	**Welcher Club ist zurzeit besonders angesagt?**
	Vell-[ch]ehr cloopp isst tsoor-tsite beh-SONN-dehrs un-gheh-sahggt?
What's the cover charge?	**Wie viel kostet der Eintritt?**
	Vee feel coss-tet dehr AIHN-tritt?
Do they have a dress code?	**Ist eine bestimmte Kleidung vorge-schrieben?**
	Isst eye-ne beh-shtimm-teh KLYE-doong fohr-gheh-shree-ben?
Is it expensive?	**Ist es dort teuer?**
	Isst as dohrrt TOY-ehr?
What's the best time to go?	**Wann geht man dort am besten hin?**
	Vahnn gheht mahnn dohrrt um bess-ten HINN?
What kind of music do they play there?	**Welche Art von Musik wird dort gespielt?**
	Vell-[ch]eh arrt fonn moo-SEEK virrd dohrrt gheh-shpeelt?

Is it smoking?	**Darf geraucht werden?**
	Dahrrf gheh-RAU[CH]T vehr-denn?
Is it nonsmoking?	**Ist das Rauchen dort verboten?**
	Isst dahs rauh-[ch]en dohrrt fehr-BOH-ten?
I'm looking for ____	**Ich suche ____**
	Ee[ch] SOO-[ch]eh ____
a good cigar shop.	**ein gutes Zigarrengeschäft.**
	aihn goo-tess tsee-GHARR-en-gheh-sh[ae]fft.
a pack of cigarettes.	**eine Packung Zigaretten.**
	eye-neh pahkk-oong tsee-ghah-RET-ten.
I'd like ____	**Ich hätte gern ____**
	Ee[ch] hat-eh ghern ____
a drink please.	**etwas zu trinken.**
	at-vahs tsoo TRING-ken.
a bottle of beer please.	**ein Bier aus der Flasche.**
	aihn beer ous dehr FLUSH-eh.

Do You Mind If I Smoke?

Haben Sie eine Zigarette?	Do you have a cigarette?
Hah-ben zee eye-neh tsee-ghah-RETT-eh?	
Haben Sie Feuer?	Do you have a light?
Hah-ben zee FOY-ehr?	
Darf ich Ihnen Feuer geben?	May I offer you a light?
Dharrf ee[ch] eeh-nen FOY-ehr gheh-ben?	
Rauchen verboten.	Smoking not permitted.
Rauh-[ch]en fair-BOH-ten.	

A beer on tap please.	**ein Bier vom Fass.**
	aihn beer fomm FAHSS.
a shot of ____ please.	**einen ____.**
	eye-nen ____.

For a full list of drinks, see p80.

Make it a double please!	**Einen Doppelten, bitte!**
	Eye-nen DOPP-ell-ten, bit-eh!
With ice, please.	**Mit Eis, bitte.**
	Mitt ICE, bit-eh.
And one for the lady / the gentleman!	**Und einen für die Dame / den Herrn!**
	Oonnd eye-nen f[ue]hr dee DAH-meh / dehn HERRN.
How much for a bottle / glass of beer?	**Wie viel kostet eine Flasche / ein Glas Bier?**
	Vee feel coss-tet eye-neh FLUSH-eh/aihn GLAHS beer?
I'd like to buy a drink for that woman / man over there.	**ch würde der Dame / dem Herrn da drüben gern einen Drink spendieren.**
	Ee[ch] v[ue]rr-deh dehr DAH-meh / dem HEHRRN dah dr[ue]h-ben ghern eye-nen DRINK shpenn-dee-ren.
A pack of cigarettes, please.	**Eine Packung Zigaretten, bitte.**
	Eye-neh pahkk-oong tsee-ghah-RET-ten, bit-eh.
Do you have a lighter or matches?	**Hast du Feuer?**
	Hahsst doo FOY-ehr?
Do you smoke?	**Rauchst du?**
	RAU[CH]ST doo?
Would you like a cigarette?	**Darf ich dir eine Zigarette anbieten?**
	Dharrf ee[ch] deer eye-ne tsee-ghah-RETT-eh un-bee-ten?

May I run a tab?	**Kann ich die Getränke bezahlen, wenn ich gehe?** *Khann ee[ch] dee ghe-trank-eh beh-tsah-len, venn ee[ch] GHEH-heh?*
What's the cover?	**Was kostet der Eintritt?** *Vahs coss-tet dehr AIHN-tritt?*

ACROSS A CROWDED ROOM

Excuse me, may I buy you a drink?	**Verzeihung. Darf ich dich auf einen Drink einladen?** *Fehr-TSYE-oong. Dharrf ee[ch] di[ch] ouf eye-nen DRINK aihn-lah-den?*
You look amazing.	**Du siehst umwerfend aus.** *Doo seehst OOMM-vehrr-fennd ous.*
You look like the most interesting person in the room.	**Du bist mit Abstand die interessanteste Person im Raum.** *Doo bisst mitt up-shtahnnd dee in-teh-ress-UN-tess-teh pehr-sohn imm rowm.*

Would you like to dance?	**Möchtest du gern tanzen?**
	M[oe][ch]-test doo ghern TUNN-tsenn?
Do you like to dance fast or slow?	**Tanzt du lieber schnell oder langsam?**
	Tunntst doo lee-behr SHNELL oh-der LUNG-sahm?
Give me your hand.	**Gib mir deine Hand.**
	Gheeb mere dye-neh HAHND.
What would you like to drink?	**Was möchtest du trinken?**
	Vahs m[oe][ch]-test doo TRING-kenn?
You're a great dancer.	**Du tanzt großartig.**
	Doo tunntst GROHS-urr-tigg.
I don't know that dance!	**Diesen Tanz kenne ich nicht!**
	Dee-sen tunnts KEN-neh ee[ch] nee[ch]t!
Do you like this song?	**Magst du dieses Lied?**
	MAHGGST doo dee-ses leed?
You have nice eyes!	**Du hast wunderschöne Augen!**
	Doo hahsst VOON-dehr-sh[oe]h-neh ow-ghenn!

For a full list of features, see p106.

May I have your phone number?	**Gibst du mir deine Telefonnummer?**
	Gheebst doo mere dye-neh tehleh-PHON-noommer?

GETTING CLOSER

You're very attractive.	**Du siehst unglaublich gut aus.** *Doo seehst oon-gloub-li[ch] GOOT ous.*
I like being with you.	**Ich bin gern mit dir zusammen.** *Ee[ch] bin ghern mitt deer tsoo-SAHMM-en.*
I like you.	**Ich mag dich.** *Ee[ch] MAHGG di[ch].*
I want to hold you.	**Ich möchte dich in den Arm nehmen.** *Ee[ch] m[oe][ch]-teh di[ch] inn dehn AHRRM neh-men.*
Kiss me.	**Küss mich.** *K[UE]SS mee[ch].*
May I give you _____	**Darf ich dich _____** *Dharff ee[ch] di[ch] _____*
a hug?	**umarmen?** *oomm-AHRR-men?*
a kiss?	**küssen?** *K[UE]SS-en?*
Would you like _____	**Möchtest du gern _____** *M[oe][ch]-test doo ghern _____*
a back rub?	**eine Rückenmassage?** *eye-neh R[UE]K-ken-mah-ssah-sheh?*

| a massage? | **eine Massage?** |
| | *eye-neh ma-SSAH-sheh?* |

GETTING INTIMATE

Would you like to come inside?	**Möchtest du mit reinkommen?**
	M[oe][ch]-test doo mitt RYNE-kom-men?
May I come inside?	**Darf ich noch mit reinkommen?**
	Dharrf ee[ch] no[ch] mitt RYNE-kom-men?
Let me help you out of that.	**Lass mich dir damit helfen.**
	Lahss mee[ch] deer dah-mitt HELL-fen.
Would you help me out of this?	**Könntest du mir damit bitte behilflich sein?**
	K[oe]nn-test doo mere dah-mitt bit-eh beh-HILLF-li[ch] syne?
You smell so good.	**Du riechst so gut.**
	Doo REE[CH]ST soh goot.
You're beautiful / handsome.	**Du bist wunderschön / sehr gut-aussehend.**
	Doo bisst voohn-dehr-SH[OE]HN / sehr GOOT-ous-seh-hend.
May I?	**Darf ich?**
	DHARRF ee[ch]?
OK?	**OK?**
	Okay?
Like this?	**So?**
	Soh?
How?	**Wie?**
	Vee?

HOLD ON A SECOND

Please don't do that.
Das möchte ich nicht.
Dahs M[OE][CH]-teh ee[ch] ni[ch]t.

Stop, please.
Hör bitte auf.
H[oe]hr bit-eh OUF.

Do you want me to stop?
Soll ich aufhören?
Sohll ee[ch] OUF-h[oe]h-ren?

Let's just be friends.
Lass uns einfach Freunde sein.
Lahss oonns aihn-fah[ch] FROYN-deh syne.

Do you have a condom?
Hast du ein Kondom?
Hahsst doo aihn con-DOHM?

Are you on birth control?
Nimmst du die Pille?
Nimmst doo dee PILL-eh?

I have a condom.
Ich habe ein Kondom.
Ee[ch] hah-beh aihn con-DOHM.

Do you have anything you should tell me first?
Sollte ich vorher noch etwas wissen?
Soll-teh ee[ch] fohr-hehr noh[ch] at-vahs VISS-en?

BACK TO IT

That's it.
Genau so.
Gheh-NOW soh.

That's not it.
Nicht so.
Ni[ch]t SOH.

Here.
Hier.
Hear.

There.
Da.
Dahh.

For a full list of features, see p106.
For a full list of body parts, see p179.

More.	**Weiter.**
	VYE-tehr.
Harder.	**Härter.**
	H[AE]RR-tehr.
Faster.	**Schneller.**
	SHNELL-ehr.
Deeper.	**Tiefer.**
	TEE-fehr.
Slower.	**Langsamer.**
	LUNG-sah-mehr.
Easier.	**Sanfter.**
	SAHNNF-tehr.

COOLDOWN

You're great.	**Du bist fantastisch.**
	Doo bisst fahn-TAHSS-tish.
That was great.	**Das war fantastisch.**
	Dahs vahr fahn-TAHSS-tish.
Would you like _____	**Möchtest du gern _____**
	M[oe][ch]-test doo ghern _____
a drink?	**etwas zu trinken?**
	at-vahs tsoo TRING-ken?
a snack?	**einen Imbiss?**
	eye-nen IMM-biss?
a shower?	**duschen?**
	DOO-shen?
May I stay here?	**Kann ich hierbleiben?**
	Khann ee[ch] HEAR-blye-ben?
Would you like to stay here?	**Möchtest du bleiben?**
	M[oe][ch]-test doo BLYE-ben?
I'm sorry. I have to go now.	**Es tut mir leid. Ich muss jetzt gehen.**
	As toot mere LYDE. Ee[ch] mooss yetst gheh-hen.
Where are you going?	**Wohin gehst du?**
	Voh-hinn GHEHST doo?

I have to work early.	**Ich muss früh arbeiten.** *Ee[ch] mooss fr[ue]h ARR-byten.*
I'm flying home in the morning.	**Ich fliege morgen früh nach Hause.** *Ee[ch] flee-gheh morr-ghenn fr[ue]h nah[ch] HOW-seh.*
I have an early flight.	**Mein Flug geht frühmorgens.** *Mine floog gheht fr[ue]h-MORR-ghenns.*
I think this was a mistake.	**Ich glaube, das war ein Fehler.** *Ee[ch] GLOU-beh, dahs vahr aihn FEH-lehr.*
Will you make me breakfast too?	**Bekomme ich auch ein Frühstück?** *Beh-com-meh ee[ch] OU[CH] aihn FR[UE]H-sht[ue]ck?*
Stay. I'll make you breakfast.	**Geh nicht. Ich mach dir Frühstück.** *Gheh ni[ch]t. Ee[ch] mah[ch] deer FR[UE]H-sht[ue]ck.*

IN THE CASINO

How much is this table?	**Wie hoch ist der Einsatz an diesem Tisch?** *Vee hoh[ch] isst der AIHN-sahtts un dee-sem tish?*
Deal me in.	**Ich bin dabei.** *Ee[ch] bin dah-BYE.*
Put it on red!	**Setzen Sie das auf Rot!** *Set-senn zee dahs ouf ROHHT!*
Put it on black!	**Setzen Sie das auf Schwarz!** *Set-senn zee dahs ouf SHVAHRRZ!*
Let it ride!	**Los geht's!** *Lohs GHEHTS!*
21!	**21!** *aihn-oonnd-TSVAHNN-tsigg!*

NIGHTLIFE

Snake-eyes!	**Schlangenaugen!**
	SHLAHNG-en-ow-ghenn!
Seven.	**Sieben.**
	Zee-ben.

For a full list of numbers, see p7.

Damn, eleven.	**Elf, verdammt.**
	ELLF, fehr-DAHMMT.
I'll pass.	**Ich passe.**
	Ee[ch] PAHSS-eh.
Hit me!	**Karte!**
	KAHRR-teh!
Split.	**Split.**
	Split.
Are the drinks complimentary?	**Sind die Getränke gratis?**
	Sinnd dee ghe-trank-eh GRAH-tees?
May I bill it to my room?	**Kann ich die Kosten über mein Zimmer abrechnen?**
	Khann ee[ch] dee coss-ten [ue]h-behr mine TSIMMER up-re[ch]-nen?
I'd like to cash out.	**Ich möchte meinen Gewinn aus-zahlen lassen.**
	Ee[ch] m[oe][ch]-teh my-nen gheh-VINN ous-tsah-len lahss-en.
I'll hold.	**Ich schiebe.**
	Ee[ch] SHEEH-beh.
I'll see your bet.	**Ich gehe mit.**
	Ee[ch] gheh-heh MITT.
I call.	**Ich will sehen.**
	Ee[ch] vill SEH-hen.
Full house!	**Full House!**
	Full HOUSE!
Royal flush.	**Royal Flush.**
	Royal FLUSH.
Straight.	**Straße.**
	SHTRAH-sseh.

CHAPTER ELEVEN

This chapter covers the terms you'll need to maintain your health and safety—including the most useful phrases for the pharmacy, the doctor's office, and the police station.

AT THE PHARMACY

Please fill this prescription.	**Ich möchte das Rezept hier ein-lösen.** *Ee[ch] m[oe][ch]-teh dahs reh-tseppt hear AIHN-l[oe]h-sen.*
Do you have something for _____	**Haben Sie etwas gegen _____** *Hah-ben zee at-vahs ghe-ghenn _____*
a cold?	**eine Erkältung?** *eye-ne air-KELL-toong?*
a cough?	**Husten?** *WHO-stenn?*
I need something _____	**Ich brauche etwas _____** *Ee[ch] brow-[ch]eh at-vahs _____*
to help me sleep.	**zum Einschlafen.** *tsoomm AIHN-shlah-fen.*
to help me relax.	**zum Entspannen.** *tsoomm ent-SHPAHNN-en.*
I want to buy _____	**Ich hätte gern _____** *Ee[ch] hat-eh ghern _____*
condoms.	**Kondome.** *con-DOH-meh.*
an antihistamine.	**ein Antihistamin.** *aihn un-tee-his-tah-MEEN.*
antibiotic cream.	**eine antibiotische Salbe.** *eye-ne un-tee-bee-OH-tish-eh SULL-beh.*

175

aspirin.	**Aspirin.**
	ahss-pee-REEN.
non-aspirin pain reliever.	**ein aspirinfreies Schmerzmittel.**
	aihn ahss-pee-REEN-frye-ess SHMEHRTTS-mittel.
medicine with codeine.	**ein Medikament mit Kodein.**
	aihn meh-dee-kah-meant mitt koh-deh-EEN.
insect repellant.	**ein Insektenschutzmittel.**
	aihn in-SECK-ten-shoohts-mittel.
I need something for _____	**Ich brauche etwas gegen _____**
	Ee[ch] brow-[ch]eh at-vahs gheh-ghenn _____
corns.	**Hühneraugen.**
	H[UE]H-nehr-ow-ghenn.
congestion.	**Verstopfung.**
	fehr-SHTOPP-foong.
warts.	**Warzen.**
	VAHRR-tsenn.
constipation.	**Darmträgheit.**
	DHARRM-tr[ae]hgg-hyte.
diarrhea.	**Durchfall.**
	DOORR[CH]-fahll.
indigestion.	**Verdauungsstörungen.**
	fehr-DOW-oongs-sht[oe]h-roong-en.
nausea.	**Übelkeit.**
	[UE]H-bell-kite.
motion sickness.	**Reisekrankheit.**
	RYE-seh-krahnk-hyte.
seasickness.	**Seekrankheit.**
	SEHH-krahnk-hyte.
acne.	**Akne.**
	AHKK-neh.

AT THE DOCTOR'S OFFICE

I would like to see _____

Ich brauche einen Termin bei einem _____
Ee[ch] brow-[ch]eh eye-nen tehr-MEEN bye eye-nem _____

a doctor.
Arzt.
artst.

a chiropractor.
Chiropraktiker.
[ch]ee-roh-PRAHKK-tee-kehr.

a gynecologist.
Frauenarzt.
FROW-en-artst.

an eye / ears / nose / throat specialist.
Augenspezialisten / Ohrenspezialisten / Nasenspezialisten / Halsspezialisten.
OW-ghenn-shpeh-tsee-yah-liss-ten / OH-ren-shpeh-tsee-yah-liss-ten / NAH-senn-shpeh-tsee-yah-liss-ten / HAHLLS-shpeh-tsee-yah-liss-ten.

a dentist.
Zahnarzt.
TSAAHN-artst.

an optometrist.
Optiker.
OPP-tee-kehr.

Do I need an appointment?
Benötige ich einen Termin?
Beh-n[oe]-tiggeh ee[ch] eye-nen tehr-MEEN?

I have an emergency.
Das ist ein Notfall.
Dahs isst aihn NOHT-fahll.

I need an emergency prescription refill.
Ich benötige dringend eine erneute Rezepteinlösung.
Ee[ch] beh-n[oe]h-tigge dring-end eye-neh air-noy-teh reh-TSEPPT-aihn-l[oe]h-soong.

Please call a doctor.	**Rufen Sie bitte einen Arzt.**
	Roofen zee bit-eh eye-nen ARTST.
I need an ambulance.	**Ich brauche einen Krankenwagen.**
	Ee[ch] brow-[ch]eh eye-nen KRAHNK-en-vah-ghenn.

SYMPTOMS

For a full list of body parts, see p179.

My ____ hurts.	**Mein ____ schmerzt. (sing.) / Meine ____ schmerzen. (pl.)**
	Mine ____ shmehrtst. / My-neh ____ shmehr-tsenn.
My ____ is stiff.	**Mein ____ ist steif. (sing.) / Meine ____ sind steif. (pl.)**
	Mine ____ isst shtyfe. / My-neh ____ sinnd shtyfe.
I think I'm having a heart attack.	**Ich glaube, ich habe einen Herzinfarkt.**
	Ee[ch] glauh-beh, ee[ch] hah-beh eye-nen HERRTS-in-farrkt.
I can't move.	**Ich kann mich nicht bewegen.**
	Ee[ch] khann mee[ch] nee[ch]t beh-VEH-ghenn.
I fell.	**Ich bin gestürzt.**
	Ee[ch] bin ghe-SHT[UE]RRTST.
I fainted.	**Ich habe das Bewusstsein verloren.**
	Ee[ch] hah-beh dahs beh-VOOSST-syne fehr-loh-ren.
I have a cut on my ____.	**Ich habe eine Schnittwunde in meiner / meinem ____.**
	Ee[ch] hah-beh eye-neh SHNITT-voonn-deh in minor/my-nem ____.
I have a headache.	**Ich habe Kopfschmerzen.**
	Ee[ch] hah-beh COPF-shmair-tsenn.
My vision is blurry.	**Ich sehe verschwommen.**
	Ee[ch] seh-heh fehr-SHVOMM-en.

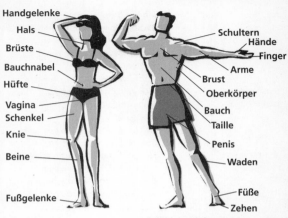

Handgelenke
Hals
Brüste
Bauchnabel
Hüfte
Vagina
Schenkel
Knie
Beine
Fußgelenke

Schultern
Hände
Finger
Arme
Brust
Oberkörper
Bauch
Taille
Penis
Waden
Füße
Zehen

I feel dizzy.	**Ich fühle mich benommen.** *Ee[ch] f[ue]h-leh mee[ch] beh-NOMM-en.*
I think I'm pregnant.	**Ich glaube, ich bin schwanger.** *Ee[ch] glau-beh, ee[ch] bin SHVAHNNG-ehr.*
I don't think I'm pregnant.	**Ich glaube nicht, dass ich schwanger bin.** *Ee[ch] glau-beh NI[CH]T, dahss ee[ch] shvahnng-ehr bin.*
I'm having trouble walking.	**Ich habe Probleme beim Gehen.** *Ee[ch] hah-beh proh-bleh-meh byme GEH-hen.*
I can't get up.	**Ich kann nicht aufstehen.** *Ee[ch] khann ni[ch]t OUF-shteh-hen.*
I was mugged.	**Ich wurde überfallen.** *Ee[ch] voorr-deh [ue]h-behr-FAHLL-en.*

I was raped.	**Ich wurde vergewaltigt.** *Ee[ch] voorr-deh fehr-gheh-VAHLL-tiggt.*
A dog attacked me.	**Ich wurde von einem Hund ange-griffen.** *Ee[ch] voorr-deh fonn eye-nem HOONND un-gheh-griff-en.*
A snake bit me.	**Ich wurde von einer Schlange gebissen.** *Ee[ch] voorr-deh fonn eye-nehr SHLUNG-eh gheh-biss-en.*
I can't move my ____ without pain.	**Ich kann mein/meinen/meine ____ nicht schmerzfrei bewegen.** *Ee[ch] khann mine/my-nen/my-neh ____ ni[ch]t shmehrts-frye beh-veh-ghenn.*

MEDICATIONS

I need morning-after pills.	**Ich brauche Pillen für den Morgen danach.** *Ee[ch] brau-[ch]eh PILL-en f[ue]hr dehn morr-ghenn dah-NAH[CH].*
I need birth control pills.	**Ich brauche Antibabypillen.** *Ee[ch] brau-[ch]eh un-tee-BEH-bee-pill-en.*
I lost my eyeglasses and need new ones.	**Ich habe meine Brille verloren und benötige eine neue.** *Ee[ch] hah-beh my-neh BRILL-eh fehr-loh-ren oonnd beh-n[oe]h-tigge eye-neh NOY-eh.*
I need new contact lenses.	**Ich benötige neue Kontaktlinsen.** *Ee[ch] beh-n[oe]h-tigge noye konn-TAHKKT-lin-sen.*

I need erectile dysfunction pills.	**Ich benötige Pillen gegen Erektionsstörungen.** *Ee[ch] beh-n[oe]h-tigge pill-en gheh-ghenn eh-rekk-tsee-YOHNS-sht[oe]h-roong-en.*
Please fill this prescription.	**Ich möchte das hier abholen.** *Ee[ch] m[oe][ch]-teh dahs hear UP-hoh-len.*
I need a prescription for ____.	**Ich benötige ein Rezept für ____.** *Ee[ch] beh-N[OE]-tiggeh aihn reh-TSEPT f[ue]hr ____.*
I am allergic to ____	**Ich bin allergisch gegen ____** *Ee[ch] bin ah-LERR-ghish gheh-ghenn ____*
penicillin.	**Penizillin.** *penn-ee-tsee-LEAN.*
antibiotics.	**Antibiotika.** *un-tee-bee-YOH-tee-kah.*
sulfa drugs.	**schwefelhaltige Medikamente.** *SHVEHH-fell-hahll-tiggeh meh-dee-kah-menn-teh.*
steroids.	**Steroide.** *shteh-roh-EE-deh.*
I have asthma.	**Ich habe Asthma.** *Ee[ch] hah-beh USST-mah.*

DENTAL PROBLEMS

I have a toothache.	**Ich habe Zahnschmerzen.** *Ee[ch] hah-beh TSAAHN-shmehrts-en.*
I chipped a tooth.	**Ich habe einen abgebrochenen Zahn.** *Ee[ch] hah-beh eye-nen up-gheh-broh[ch]en-en TSAAHN.*
My bridge came loose.	**Meine Brücke hat sich gelöst.** *My-neh BR[UE]KKEH hut see[ch] gheh-l[oe]hst.*

I lost a crown.	**Ich habe eine Krone verloren.** *Ee[ch] hah-beh eye-ne KROH-ne fehr-loh-ren.*
I lost a denture plate.	**Ich habe eine Zahnprotese verloren.** *Ee[ch] hah-beh eye-ne TSAAHN-proh-teh-se fehr-loh-ren.*

AT THE POLICE STATION

I'm sorry, did I do something wrong?	**Verzeihung, habe ich etwas falsch gemacht?** *Fehr-TSYE-oong, hah-beh ee[ch] at-vahs FAHLLSH gheh-mah[ch]t?*
I am _____	**Ich bin _____** *ee[ch] bin _____*
an American.	**Amerikaner (m.) / Amerikanerin (f.).** *ah-meh-ree-KAH-nehr / ah-meh-ree-KAH-nehr-in.*
British.	**Brite (m.) / Britin (f.).** *BREE-teh / BREE±tin.*
a Canadian.	**Kanadier (m.) / Kanadierin (f.).** *kah-NAH-dee-er / kah-NAH-dee-er-in.*
Irish.	**Ire (m.) / Irin (f.).** *EE-re / EE-rin.*
an Australian.	**Australier (m.) / Australierin (f.).** *ous-TRAH-lee-er / ous-TRAH-lee-er-in.*
a New Zealander.	**Neuseeländer (m.) / Neuseeländerin (f.).** *noy-SEHH-lander / noy-SEHH-lander-in.*
The car is a rental.	**Das Auto ist ein Mietwagen.** *Dahs ou-toh isst aihn MEET-vah-ghenn.*

Listen Up: Police Lingo

Führerschein, Fahrzeug- und Versicherungspapiere, bitte.	Your license, registration and insurance, please.
F[ue]h-rehr-shine, faahrtsoygg oonnd fehr-SI[CH]-eh-roongs-pah-peer-eh, bit-eh.	
Die Strafe beträgt 10 €. Sie können direkt bezahlen.	The fine is €10. You can pay me directly.
Dee shtrah-feh beh-tr[ae]hggt tsehn OY-roh. Zee k[oe]nn-en dee-RECKT beh-tsah-len.	
Ihren Ausweis, bitte?	Your passport please?
Eehren OUS-vise, bit-eh?	
Wohin sind Sie unterwegs?	Where are you going?
Voh-hinn sinnd zee oonn-ter-VEHGGS?	
Warum haben Sie es denn so eilig?	Why are you in such a hurry?
Vah-roomm hah-ben zee as denn soh EYE-ligg?	

Do I pay the fine to you?	**Zahle ich die Strafe direkt an Sie?**
	Tsah-leh ee[ch] dee shtrah-feh dee-reckt un Zee?
Do I have to go to court?	**Komme ich vor Gericht?**
	Com-meh ee[ch] fohr ghe-RI[CH]T?
When?	**Wann?**
	Vahnn?

I'm sorry, my German isn't very good.	**Verzeihung, mein Deutsch ist nicht besonders gut.** *Fehr-TSYE-oong, mine doytsch isst ni[ch]t beh-sonn-dehrs GOOT.*
I need an interpreter.	**Ich benötige einen Dolmetscher.** *Ee[ch] beh-n[oe]h-tiggeh eye-nen DOLL-match-ehr.*
I'm sorry, I don't understand the ticket.	**Verzeihung, ich verstehe den Strafzettel nicht.** *Fehr-TSYE-oong, ee[ch] fair-shteh-heh dehn SHTRAHF-tsettel ni[ch]t.*
May I call my embassy?	**Darf ich meine Botschaft anrufen?** *Dharrf ee[ch] my-neh BOHT-shahfft unroofen?*
I was robbed.	**Ich wurde ausgeraubt.** *Ee[ch] voorr-deh OUS-gheh-raubt.*
I was mugged.	**Ich wurde überfallen.** *Ee[ch] voorr-deh [ue]h-behr-FAHLL-en.*
I was raped	**Ich wurde vergewaltigt.** *Ee[ch] voorr-deh fehr-gheh-VAHLL-tiggt.*
Do I need to make a report?	**Muss ich eine Aussage machen?** *Mooss ee[ch] eye-neh OUS-sah-gheh mah-[ch]en?*
Somebody broke into my room.	**In mein Zimmer wurde eingebrochen.** *Inn mine tsimmer voorr-deh AIHN-gheh-broh-[ch]en.*
Someone stole my purse / wallet.	**Meine Handtasche / Geldbörse wurde gestohlen.** *My-neh HAHND-tah-sheh / GELLD-b[oe]r-seh voorr-deh gheh-shtoh-len.*

ENGLISH—GERMAN

DICTIONARY KEY

n	noun	m	masculine
v	verb	f	feminine
adj	adjective	gn	gender neutral
prep	preposition	s	singular
adv	adverb	pl	plural
pron	pronoun		

All verbs are listed in infinitive (to + verb) form, cross-referenced to the appropriate conjugations page. Adjectives are listed first in masculine singular form, followed by the feminine ending.

For food terms, see the Menu Reader (p83) and Grocery section (p89) in Chapter 4, Dining.

A

able, to be able to (can) *v*
können p26

above *adj* über p69

accept, to accept *v* p20
akzeptieren

Do you accept credit cards?
*Akzeptieren Sie
Kreditkarten?* p31

accident *n* der Unfall *m* p49

I've had an accident. *Ich
hatte einen Unfall.*

account *n* das Konto *gn* p123

**I'd like to transfer to / from
my checking / savings
account.** *Ich möchte etwas
auf mein / von meinem
Girokonto / Sparkonto
überweisen.*

acne *n* die Akne *f* p176

across *prep* über p6

across the street *auf der
anderen Straßenseite*

actual *adj* tatsächlich,
eigentlich, wirklich p15

adapter plug *n* der
Adapterstecker *m*

address *n* die Adresse *f* p112

What's the address?
Wie lautet die Adresse?

admission fee *n* die
Eintrittsgebühr *f* p136

in advance *im Voraus*

African-American *adj*
afroamerikanisch p107

afternoon *n* der Nachmittag
m p12

in the afternoon *am
Nachmittag*

age *n* das Alter *gn* p104

What's your age? *Wie alt
sind Sie? (formal) / Wie alt
bist du? (informal)*

agency *n* die Agentur / das
Büro *f*/*gn* p42

car rental agency *die
Autovermietung f*

agnostic *adj* agnostisch

air conditioning *n* die
Klimaanlage *f* p60

Would you lower / raise the air conditioning? *Könnten Sie die Klimaanlage bitte auf eine höhere / niedrigere Temperatur einstellen?*

airport *n der Flughafen m*

I need a ride to the airport. *Ich muss zum Flughafen.*

How far is it from the airport? *Wie weit ist das vom Flughafen entfernt?*

airsickness bag *n die Spucktüte f p41*

aisle (in store) *n der Gang m*

Which aisle is it in? *In welchem Gang finde ich das?*

alarm clock *n der Wecker m p67*

alcohol *n der Alkohol m p80*

Do you serve alcohol? *Haben Sie alkoholische Getränke?*

I'd like nonalcoholic beer. *Ich hätte gerne ein alkoholfreies Bier.*

all *n Alles p10*

all *adj ganz; alle p10*

all of the time *die ganze Zeit*

That's all, thank you. *Danke, das ist alles.*

allergic *adj allergisch p67*

I'm allergic to ____. *Ich bin allergisch gegen ____.* See p79 and 181 for common allergens.

also *auch adv p15*

altitude *n die Höhe f p155*

aluminum *n das Aluminium gn*

ambulance *n der Krankenwagen m*

American *n der Amerikaner m, die Amerikanerin f p109*

amount *n die Menge (things) / der Betrag (money) f/m p56*

angry *adj wütend*

animal *n das Tier gn*

another *adj noch ein / eine / einen p40, 64*

answer *n die Antwort f*

answer, to answer (phone call, question) *v p20 beantworten (question) / entgegennehmen (phone call)*

Answer me, please. *Antworten Sie mir bitte.*

antibiotic *n das Antibiotikum gn*

I need an antibiotic. *Ich brauche ein Antibiotikum.*

antihistamine *n das Antihistamin gn p175*

anxious *adj besorgt p109*

any *adj beliebig*

anything *n alles / irgend etwas*

anywhere *adv überall / irgendwo*

April *n der April m p13*

appointment *n der Termin m p136*

Do I need an appointment? *Benötige ich einen Termin?*

are *v See* **be, to be** p23

arrive, to arrive *v ankommen*

arrival(s) *n die Ankunft f*

art *n die Kunst f*

exhibit of art *die Kunstausstellung*

art *adj Kunst-*

art museum *das Kunstmuseum*

artist *n der Künstler m, die Künstlerin f*

Asian *adj asiatisch* p72

ask for (request) *v bitten um* p24

ask a question *v fragen* p24

aspirin *n das Aspirin gn* p176

assist *v helfen* p24

assistance *n die Hilfe f*

asthma *n das Asthma gn* p181

I have asthma. *Ich habe Asthma.*

atheist *adj atheistisch* p115

ATM *n der Geldautomat m*

I'm looking for an ATM. *Ich suche einen Geldautomaten.*

attend *v teilnehmen (meeting) / behandeln (doctor)* p22/24

audio *adj Audio-* p57

August *n der August m* p13

aunt *n die Tante f* p104

Australian *n der Australier m, die Australierin*

Austrian *n der Österreicher m, die Österreicherin* p108

autumn *n der Herbst m* p14

available *adj verfügbar* p135

B

baby *n das Baby gn* p105

baby *adj Baby- / für Babys* p89

Do you sell baby food? *Verkaufen Sie Babynahrung?*

babysitter *n der Babysitter m*

Do you have babysitters who speak English? *Haben Sie englischsprachige Babysitter?*

back *n der Rücken m* p179

My back hurts. *Mein Rücken schmerzt.*

back rub *n die Rückenmassage f* p169

backed up (toilet) *adj verstopft*

The toilet is backed up. *Die Toilette ist verstopft.*

bad *schlecht adj* p15

bag *n die Tasche f, die Tüte f*

airsickness bag *die Spucktüte* p41

My bag was stolen. *Meine Tasche wurde gestohlen.*

I lost my bag. *Ich habe meine Tasche verloren.*

bag *v einpacken* p20

baggage *n das Gepäck gn* p33

baggage *adj Gepäck-* p33

baggage claim *Gepäckausgabe*

bait *n* der Köder *m*

balance (on bank account) *n* der Kontostand *m* p123

balance *v balancieren* p20 (something shaky) / begleichen (invoice) p24

balcony *n* der Balkon *m* p59

bald *adj kahl* p15

ball (sport) *n* der Ball *m*

ballroom dancing *n* der Gesellschaftstanz *m* p133

band (musical ensemble) *n* die Band *f* p163

band-aid *n* das Pflaster *gn*

bank *n* die Bank *f* p120

Can you help me find a bank? *Könnten Sie mir bitte helfen, eine Bank zu finden?*

bar *n* die Bar *f*

barber *n* der (Herren-) Frisör *m* p146

bass (instrument) *n* der Bass *m*

bath (spa) *n* das Bad *gn*

bathroom (restroom) *n* die Toilette / das WC *f/gn* p60

Where is the nearest public bathroom? *Wo finde ich das nächste öffentliche WC?*

bathtub *n* die Badewanne *f* p60

bathe, to bathe oneself *v baden / ein Bad nehmen* p20, 24

battery (for flashlight) *n* die Batterie *f*

battery (for car) *n* die Batterie *f*

bee *n* die Biene *f*

I was stung by a bee. *Ich wurde von einer Biene gestochen.*

be, to be *v sein* p23

beach *n* der Strand *m* p118

beach *v stranden* p20

beard *n* der Bart *m*

beautiful *adj schön* p105

bed *n* das Bett *gn* p59

beer *n* das Bier *gn* p80

beer on tap *das Bier vom Fass*

begin *v beginnen / anfangen* p24

behave *v sich benehmen* p24

well behaved *brav* p15

behind *adv hinter* p5

Belgian *n* der Belgier *m*, die Belgierin *f* p108

below *adv unter* p69

belt *n* der Gürtel *m* p140

conveyor belt *das Transportband*

berth *n* die Koje *f*

best *am besten*

bet, to bet *v wetten* p20

better *besser*

big *adj groß* p11

bilingual *adj zweisprachig*

bill (currency) *n* der (Geld-)Schein *m*

bill *v berechnen* p20

billion *n* die Milliarde *f* p15

biography *n* die Biografie *f*

bird *n* der Vogel *m*

birth control n *die Verhütung f* p171, 180

birth control adj *Antibaby-* p171, 180

I'm out of birth control pills. *Ich habe keine Antibabypillen mehr.*

I need more birth control pills. *Ich brauche mehr Antibabypillen.*

bit (small amount) n *ein bisschen g* n

black adj *schwarz* p106

blanket n *die (Bett-)Decke f* p40

bleach n *das Bleichmittel g* n

blend v *mischen* p15

blind adj *blind*

block v *blockieren* p20

blond(e) adj *blond* p106

blouse n *die Bluse f* p139

blue adj *blau* p107

blurry adj *verschwommen* p178

board n *die Tafel f*

on board *an Bord*

board v *einsteigen / an Bord gehen* p24

boarding pass n *die Bordkarte f* p38

boat n *das Boot g* n

bomb n *die Bombe f* p15

book n *das Buch g* n p144

bookstore n *die Buchhandlung f* p144

bordello n *der Puff m* p15

boss n *der Chef m, die Chefin f*

bottle n *die Flasche f* p165

May I heat this (baby) bottle someplace? *Kann ich dieses (Baby-)Fläschchen irgendwo aufwärmen?*

box (seat) n *die Loge f* p153

box office n *der Kartenverkauf m*

boy n *der Junge m*

boyfriend n *der Freund m* p103

braid n *der Zopf m* p147

braille, American n *die englische Blindenschrift f*

brake n *die Bremse f* p46

emergency brake *die Notbremse*

brake v *bremsen* p20

brandy n *der Brandy m* p81

brave adj *tapfer* p15

bread n *das Brot n* p89

break v *(zer-)brechen* p24

breakfast n *das Frühstück g* n

What time is breakfast? *Um wie viel Uhr gibt es Frühstück?*

bridge (across a river, dental) n *die Brücke f* p181

briefcase n *der Aktenkoffer m* p41

bright adj *hell*

broadband n *Breitband-*

bronze adj *bronzefarben*

brother n *der Bruder m* p103

brown adj *braun* p107

brunette n *die Brünette f* p106

Buddhist n der Buddhist m, die Buddhistin f p115

budget n das Budget gn

buffet n das Buffet gn

bug n der Käfer m, das Insekt gn

burn v brennen p24

Can I burn a CD here? Kann ich hier eine CD brennen? p127

bus n der Bus m p50

Where is the bus stop? Wo ist die nächste Bushaltestelle?

Which bus goes to ____? Welcher Bus fährt nach ____? p53

business n das Unternehmen gn p37

business adj Geschäfts- p65

business center das Geschäftszentrum

busy adj gut besucht (restaurant), besetzt (phone)

butter n die Butter f p78

buy, to buy v kaufen p20

C

café n das Café gn p31

Internet café das Internetcafé

call, to call v rufen (shout) anrufen (phone) p24

camp, to camp v zelten p20

camper n das Wohnmobil (van) / der Wohnwagen (trailer) gn/m

camping adj Camping-

Do we need a camping permit? Benötigen wir eine Campingerlaubnis?

campsite n der Campingplatz m

can n die Dose f

can (able to) v können p26

Canada n Kanada

Canadian adj kanadisch

cancel, to cancel v stornieren p20

My flight was canceled. Mein Flug wurde storniert.

canvas n die Leinwand f (for painting), das Segeltuch gn p42 (material)

cappuccino n der Cappuccino m

car n das Auto gn

car rental agency die Autovermietung

I need a rental car. Ich benötige einen Mietwagen.

card n die Karte f p110

Do you accept credit cards? Akzeptieren Sie Kreditkarten?

May I have your business card? Könnte ich bitte Ihre Visitenkarte haben?

car seat (child's safety seat) n der Kindersitz m

Do you rent car seats for children? Vermieten Sie Kindersitze?

ENGLISH—GERMAN

carsickness n die
Autokrankheit f

cash n das Bargeld gn p121

cash only Nur gegen
Barzahlung p122

cash, to cash v einlösen
(check) p20

to cash out (gambling)
auszahlen lassen p174

cashmere n der Kaschmir m

casino n das Kasino gn p58

cat n die Katze f

cathedral n der Dom m p15

Catholic adj katholisch p115

cavity (tooth cavity) n das
Loch gn

I think I have a cavity. Ich
glaube, ich habe ein Loch
im Zahn.

CD n die CD f p127

CD player n der CD-Player
m p43

celebrate, to celebrate v
feiern p20

cell phone n das
Mobiltelefon / das Handy
gn p122

centimeter n der Zentimeter m

chamber music n die
Kammermusik f

change (money) n das
Wechselgeld gn

I'd like change, please.
Geben Sie mir bitte
Wechselgeld.

This isn't the correct
change. Das Wechselgeld
stimmt leider nicht.

change (to change money,
clothes) v wechseln p20

changing room n die
Umkleidekabine f

charge, to charge (money) v
abbuchen p20

charge, to charge (a battery)
v aufladen p24

charmed adj entzückt

charred (meat) adj verkohlt
p77

charter, to charter v chartern
p22

cheap adj billig p44

check n der Scheck m p83

Do you accept travelers'
checks? Akzeptieren Sie
Reiseschecks?

check, to check v überprüfen
/ sich vergewissern p20

checked (pattern) adj kariert

check-in n der Check-In m
p30

What time is check-in?
Um wie viel Uhr wird
eingecheckt?

check-out n der Check-Out gn

check-out time Uhrzeit für
das Auschecken

What time is check-out?
Um wie viel Uhr wird
ausgecheckt?

check out, to check out v
auschecken p20

cheese n der Käse m p89

chicken n das Hähnchen gn
p86

child n das Kind gn

children n Kinder gn p38

  Are children allowed? Sind Kinder erlaubt?

  Do you have children's programs? Haben Sie ein Programm für Kinder?

  Do you have a children's menu? Haben Sie ein Kindermenü?

chiropractor n der Chiropraktiker m p177

church n die Kirche f p114

cigar n die Zigarre f p138

cigarette n die Zigarette f

  a pack of cigarettes eine Schachtel Zigaretten

cinema n das Kino gn

city n die Stadt f p61

claim n die Reklamation f

  I'd like to file a claim. Ich möchte etwas reklamieren.

clarinet n die Klarinette f

class n die Klasse f p34

  business class die Businessklasse

  economy class die Economyklasse

  first class die Erste Klasse

classical (music) adj klassisch

clean adj sauber

clean, to clean v reinigen p20

  Please clean the room today. Reinigen Sie bitte heute das Zimmer.

clear v räumen p20

clear adj klar p159

climbing n das Klettern gn p155

climb, to climb v klettern (mountain) I steigen (stairs) p20, 24

  to climb a mountain bergsteigen

  to climb stairs Treppen steigen

close, to close v schließen p24

close (near) nah p5

closed adj geschlossen p49

cloudy adj bewölkt p113

clover n der Klee m

go clubbing, to go clubbing v einen Nachtclub besuchen p20

coat n die Jacke f p140

coffee n der Kaffee m p84

  iced coffee der Eiskaffee

cognac n der Kognak m p81

coin n die Münze f

cold n die Erkältung f p99

  I have a cold. Ich habe eine Erkältung.

cold adj kalt p113

  I'm cold. Mir ist kalt.

  It's cold out. Es ist kalt draußen.

coliseum n die Sporthalle f

collect adj unfrei

  I'd like to place a collect call. Ich möchte ein R-Gespräch führen.

collect, to collect v sammeln p20

college *n die Hochschule f*

color *n die Farbe f* **p141**

color *v färben* **p20**

computer *n der Computer m*

concert *n das Konzert gn* p118

condition *n der Zustand m*

in good / bad condition *in gutem / schlechtem Zustand*

condom *n das Kondom gn* p171

Do you have a condom? *Hast du ein Kondom?*

not without a condom *nicht ohne Kondom*

condor *n der Kondor m*

confirm, to confirm *v bestätigen* **p20**

I'd like to confirm my reservation. *Ich möchte meine Reservierung bestätigen.*

confused *adj verwirrt*

congested *adj überfüllt*

connection speed *n die Verbindungs-geschwindigkeit f* p128

consequently *folglich adv* p15

consistent *konsequent adj* p15

constipated *adj verstopft*

I'm constipated. *Ich habe Verstopfung.*

contact lens *n die Kontaktlinse f*

I lost my contact lens. *Ich habe meine Kontaktlinse verloren.*

continue, to continue *v fortsetzen* **p20**

convertible *n das Cabrio gn*

cook, to cook *v kochen* **p20**

I'd like a room where I can cook. *Ich hätte gerne ein Zimmer mit Kochgelegenheit.*

cookie *n der Keks m* p89

copper *adj Kupfer-*

corner *n die Ecke f*

on the corner *an der Ecke*

correct *v korrigieren* **p23**

correct *adj richtig* p51

Am I on the correct train? *Bin ich im richtigen Zug?*

cost, to cost *v kosten* **p20**

How much does it cost? *Wie viel kostet das?*

Costa Rican *adj costa-ricanisch*

costume *n das Kostüm gn*

cotton *n die Baumwolle f* p139

cough *n der Husten m* p175

cough *v husten* **p20**

counter (in bar) *n die Theke f* p30

country-and-western *n die Country-Musik f* p116

court (legal) *n das Gericht gn* p183

court (sport) *n der Platz m*

courteous *adj zuvorkommend* p70

cousin *n der Cousin m, die Cousine f*

cover charge (in bar) *n der Eintrittspreis m* p164

cow *n die Kuh f*

crack (in glass object) *n der Sprung m*

craftsperson *n der Handwerker m, die Handwerkerin f* p110

cream *n die Sahne f* p84

credit card *n die Kreditkarte f* p121

Do you accept credit cards? *Akzeptieren Sie Kreditkarten?*

crib *n das Kinderbett gn* p61

crown (dental) *n die Krone f*

curb *n der Bordstein m*

curl *n die Locke f*

curly *adj gelockt* p106

currency exchange *n die Geldwechselstube f* p31, 121

Where is the nearest currency exchange? *Wo finde ich die nächste Geldwechselstube?*

current *aktuell adj* p15

current (water) *n die Strömung f*

customs *n der Zoll m* p33

cut (wound) *n der Schnitt m* p178

I have a bad cut. *Ich habe eine tiefe Schnittwunde.*

cut, to cut *v schneiden* p24

cybercafé *n das Internetcafé gn*

Where can I find a cybercafé? *Wo finde ich ein Internetcafé?*

Czech *n der Tscheche m, die Tschechin f* p109

D

damaged *adj beschädigt* p41

Damn! *expletive Verdammt!*

dance *v tanzen* p20

danger *n die Gefahr f* p49

Danish *n der Däne m, die Dänin f* p108

dark *n die Dunkelheit f*

dark *adj dunkel*

daughter *n die Tochter f* p105

day *n der Tag m* p149

the day before yesterday *vorgestern* p13

these last few days *die letzten paar Tage*

dawn *n die Morgendämmerung f* p12

at dawn *bei Tagesanbruch*

dazzle *v blenden* p15

deaf *adj taub*

deal (bargain) *n das Schnäppchen gn*

What a great deal! *Was für ein großartiges Schnäppchen!*

deal (cards) *v geben* p24

Deal me in. *Ich bin dabei.*

December *n der Dezember m* p14

declined *adj abgelehnt*

Was my credit card declined? *Wurde meine Kreditkarte nicht akzeptiert?*

declare *v verzollen (customs)* **p20**

I have nothing to declare. *Ich habe nichts zu verzollen.*

deep *adj tief* **p157**

delay *n die Verspätung f* **p36**

How long is the delay? *Wie viel beträgt die Verspätung?*

delighted *adj erfreut*

democracy *n die Demokratie f*

dent *v verbeulen* **p20**

He / She dented the car. *Er / Sie hat das Auto verbeult.*

dentist *n der Zahnarzt m* **p177**

denture *n das Gebiss gn*

denture plate *die Zahnprothese*

departure *n die Abreise f*

designer *n der Designer m, die Designerin f* **p110**

dessert *n die Nachspeise f* **p80**

dessert menu *die Dessertkarte*

destination *n das Ziel gn*

diabetic *adj Diabetiker-* **p77**

dial (a phone) *v wählen* **p20**

dial direct *durchwählen*

diaper *n die Windel f*

Where can I change a diaper? *Wo kann ich hier Windeln wechseln?*

diarrhea *n der Durchfall m* **p176**

dictionary *n das Wörterbuch gn*

different (other) *adj anders* **p141**

difficult *adj schwierig* **p155**

dinner *n das Abendessen gn* **p119**

directory assistance (phone) *n die Telefonauskunft f*

disability *n die Behinderung f*

disappear *v verschwinden* **p24**

disco *n die Disko f* **p116**

disconnected *adj unterbrochen* **p126**

Operator, I was disconnected. *Vermittlung, mein Gespräch wurde unterbrochen.*

discount *n der Preisnachlass m*

Do I qualify for a discount? *Bekomme ich einen Preisnachlass?*

dish *n das Gericht gn* **p77**

dive *v tauchen* **p20**

scuba dive *tauchen (mit Atemgerät)* **p158**

divorced *adj geschieden*

dizzy *adj benommen* **p179**

do, to do *v tun* **p24**

doctor n der Arzt m, die Ärztin f p110, 177

doctor's office n die Arztpraxis f

dog n der Hund m p36

service dog der Blindenhund p62

dollar n der Dollar m

dome n die Kuppel f p15

door n die Tür f p69

double adj Doppel- p8

double bed das Doppelbett p59

double vision doppelt sehen

down adj abwärts p5

download v herunterladen p24

downtown n das Stadtzentrum gn p137

dozen n das Dutzend gn p11

drain n der Abfluss m

drama n das Drama gn

drawing (work of art) n die Zeichnung f

dress (garment) n das Kleid gn

dress (general attire) n die Kleidung f p164

What's the dress code? Welche Kleidung ist vorgeschrieben?

dress v anziehen p24, 29

Should I dress up for that affair? Muss ich mich dafür herausputzen?

dressing (salad) n das Dressing gn

dried adj getrocknet / Trocken- p96

drink n das Getränk gn p165

I'd like a drink. Ich hätte gerne etwas zu trinken.

drink, to drink v trinken p24

drip v tropfen p20

drive v fahren p24

driver n der Fahrer m p49

driving range n die Driving Range f

drum n die Trommel f

dry adj trocken

This towel isn't dry. Dieses Handtuch ist nicht trocken.

dry, to dry v trocknen p20

I need to dry my clothes. Ich muss meine Kleidung trocknen.

dry cleaner n die chemische Reinigung f

dry cleaning n das chemische Reinigen f

duck n die Ente f

Dutch n der Niederländer m, die Niederländerin f p108

duty-free adj zollfrei p31

duty-free shop n der Duty-free-Shop m p31

DVD n die DVD f p44

Do the rooms have DVD players? Gibt es auf den Zimmern einen DVD-Player?

Where can I rent DVDs or videos? Wo kann ich DVDs oder Videos ausleihen?

E

early *adj früh* p12
　It's early. *Es ist früh.*
eat *v essen* p24
　to eat out *auswärts essen*
economy *n die Wirtschaft f*
editor *n der Redakteur m,
　die Redakteurin f* p110
educator *n der Erzieher m,
　die Erzieherin f* p110
eight *n acht* p7
eighteen *n Achtzehn* p7
eighth *n achter* p9
eighty *n achtzig* p7
election *n die Wahl f* p114
electrical hookup *n der
　Elektroanschluss m* p71
elevator *n der Aufzug m* p61
eleven *n elf* p7
e-mail *n die E-Mail f* p112
　**May I have your e-mail
　address?** *Kann ich Ihre
　(formal) / deine (informal)
　E-Mail-Adresse haben?*
　e-mail message *die E-Mail-
　Nachricht*
e-mail, to send e-mail *v eine
　E-Mail senden* p20
embassy *n die Botschaft f*
emergency *n der Notfall m*
emergency brake *n die
　Notbremse f*
emergency exit *n der
　Notausgang m* p34
employee *n der Mitarbeiter
　m, die Mitarbeiterin f* p110
employer *n der Arbeitgeber
　m*

engine *n der Motor m* p46
engineer *n der Ingenieur m,
　die Ingenieurin f* p110
England *n England*
English *n, adj englisch,
　der Engländer m, die
　Engländerin f* p64, 108
　Do you speak English?
　Sprechen Sie Englisch? p2
enjoy, to enjoy *v genießen*
　p24
enter, to enter *v betreten*
　p24
　Do not enter. *Kein Eingang.*
enthusiastic *adj begeistert*
　p109
entrance *n der Eingang m*
　p33
envelope *n das Kuvert gn*
　p130
environment *n die Umwelt f*
escalator *n die Rolltreppe f*
espresso *n der Espresso m*
exchange rate *n der
　Wechselkurs m* p121
　**What is the exchange rate
　for US / Canadian dollars?**
　*Welcher Wechselkurs gilt
　für US-Dollar / kanadische
　Dollar?*
excuse (pardon) *v
　entschuldigen* p20
　Excuse me. *Entschuldigung.*
exhausted *adj erschöpft*
exhibit *n die Ausstellung f*
exit *n der Ausgang m* p33
　not an exit *kein Ausgang*

exit v verlassen p24

expensive adj teuer p164

explain v erklären p20

express adj Express- p34, 53

express check-in der Express-Check-In

extra (additional) adj zusätzlich p66

extra-large adj besonders groß

eye n das Auge gn p177

eyebrow n die Augenbraue f

eyeglasses n die Brille f

eyelash n die Wimper f

F

fabric n der Stoff m

face n das Gesicht gn p107

faint v ohnmächtig werden p24

fall (season) n der Herbst m

fall v fallen p24

family n die Familie f p103

fan n der Ventilator (blower) / der Fan (sport) m

far weit p5

How far is it to _____? Wie weit ist es nach / zur / zum _____?

fare n der Fahrpreis m

fast adj schnell p49, 128

fat adj beleibt p11, 107

father n der Vater m p103

faucet n der Wasserhahn m

fault n der Fehler m p49

I'm at fault. Es war mein Fehler.

It was his fault. Es war sein Fehler.

fax n das Fax gn p111

February n der Februar m p13

fee n die Gebühr f

female adj weiblich

fiancé(e) n der Verlobte m, die Verlobte f p104

fifteen adj fünfzehn p7

fifth adj fünfter p9

fifty adj fünfzig m p7

find v finden p24

fine (for traffic violation) n die Strafe f p183

fine gut p1

I'm fine. Mir geht es gut.

fire! n Feuer! gn

first adj erste / erster / erstes p9

fishing pole n die Angelrute f

fitness center n das Fitness-Center gn p59

fit (clothes) v passen p20, 141

Does this look like it fits? Passt mir das?

fitting room n die Umkleidekabine f

five adj fünf p7

flight n der Flug m p32

Where do domestic flights arrive / depart? Wo finde ich den Ankunftsbereich / Abflugbereich für Inlandsflüge?

Where do international flights arrive / depart?

ENGLISH–GERMAN

Wo finde ich den Ankunftsbereich / Abflugbereich für Auslandsflüge?
What time does this flight leave? *Welche Abflugzeit hat dieser Flug?*
flight attendant *der Flugbegleiter (m) / die Flugbegleiterin (f)*
floor n *die Etage f* p61
  ground floor *das Erdgeschoß*
  second floor *das erste Stockwerk*
Note that in German, the second floor is called the first, the third is the second, etc.
flower n *die Blume f*
flush (gambling) n *der Flush m*
flush, to flush v *spülen* p20
  This toilet won't flush. *Die Toilettenspülung funktioniert nicht.*
flute n *die Flöte f*
food n *das Essen* gn p80
foot (body part, measurement) n *(der) Fuß*
forehead n *die Stirn f*
formula n *die Formel f*
  Do you sell infants' formula? *Haben Sie Säuglingsanfangsnahrung?*
forty adj *vierzig* p7
forward adj *vorwärts* p6
four adj *vier* p7
fourteen adj *vierzehn* p7

fourth adj *vierter* p9
  one-fourth *ein Viertel*
fragile adj *zerbrechlich* p129
freckle n *die Sommersprosse f*
French n *der Franzose m, die Französin f* p108
fresh adj *frisch* p90
Friday n *der Freitag m* p13
friend n *der Freund m, die Freundin f* p103
front adj *Vorder-* p34
  front desk *die Rezeption* p65
  front door *die Vordertür*
fruit n *die Frucht f* p89
fruit juice n *der Fruchtsaft m*
full, to be full (after a meal) adj *satt* p82
Full house! n *Full House!*
fuse n *die Sicherung f*

G
garlic n *der Knoblauch m* p95
gas n *das Gas (for cooking) n, das Benzin (for cars) gn* p46
  gas gauge *die Tankanzeige*
  out of gas *kein Benzin mehr*
gate (at airport) n *das Gate gn* p30
German n *der/die Deutsche m/f* p108
gift n *das Geschenk gn*
gin n *der Gin m* p81
girl n *das Mädchen gn*
girlfriend n *die Freundin f* p103
give, to give v *geben* p24

glass n das Glas gn p76

> **Do you have it by the glass?** Schenken Sie das als offenes Getränk aus?
> **I'd like a glass please.** Ich hätte gerne ein Glas.

glasses (eye) n die Brille f

> **I need new glasses.** Ich brauche eine neue Brille.

glove n der Handschuh m p161

go, to go v gehen p24

goal (sport) n das Tor gn

goalie n der Torwart m p152

gold adj Gold-

golf n das Golf(-spiel) gn p42

golf, to go golfing v Golf spielen p20

good adj gut p99

goodbye n der Abschied m p100

grade (school) n die Note f

gram n das Gramm gn

grandfather n der Großvater m

grandmother n die Großmutter f

grandparents n die Großeltern pl only

grape n die Traube f

gray adj grau

great adj großartig

Greek n der Grieche m, die Griechin f p108

Greek Orthodox adj griechisch-orthodox p115

green adj grün p107

groceries n die Lebensmittel gn

group n die Gruppe f p37

grow, to grow (get larger) v wachsen p24

> **Where did you grow up?** Wo sind Sie (formal) / bist du (informal) aufgewachsen?

guard n der Wachmann m p30

> **security guard** der Sicherheitsbeamte

guest n der Gast m

guide (of tours) n der Fremdenführer / die Fremdenführerin m/f p135

guide (publication) n der Reiseführer m

guide, to guide v führen p20

guided tour n die Fremdenführung f

guitar n die Gitarre f p117

gym n das Fitnessstudio gn p149

gynecologist n der Frauenarzt m

H

hair n das Haar gn, die Haare pl

haircut n der Haarschnitt m

> **I need a haircut.** Ich muss mir die Haare schneiden lassen.
> **How much is a haircut?** Wie viel kostet ein Haarschnitt?

hairdresser n der Frisör m, die Frisörin f

hair dryer n der Haartrockner m p67

half n die Hälfte f
   one-half halb- p8
hallway n der Gang m
hand n die Hand f p168
handicapped-accessible adj
   behindertengerecht
handle, to handle v
   handhaben p20
handsome adj gut aussehend
   p105
hangout (hot spot) n der
   Treff m
hang out (to relax) v
   entspannen / abhängen
   (slang) p20, 24
hang up (to end a phone
   call) v auflegen p20
hanger n der Kleiderbügel m
happy adj fröhlich p109
hard adj schwierig (difficult),
   hart (firm) p42
hat n der Hut m
have v haben p24
hazel adj nussbraun p107
headache n die
   Kopfschmerzen pl p99
headlight n der Scheinwerfer m
headphones n der Kopfhörer
   m
hear v hören p20
hearing-impaired adj
   hörgeschädigt
heart n das Herz gn p178
heart attack n der
   Herzinfarkt m p178
hello n Hallo p1
Help! n Hilfe!

help, to help v helfen p24
hen n die Henne f
her adj ihr p3
herb n das Kraut gn
here n hier p5
high adj hoch p160
highlights (hair) n die
   Strähnchen pl p148
highway n die Autobahn f
hike, to hike v wandern p20
him pron ihm / ihn p3
hip-hop n Hiphop p163
his adj sein / seine
historical adj historisch
history n die Geschichte f
   p119
hobby n das Hobby gn
hold, to hold v halten p24
   to hold hands Händchen
   halten
   Would you hold this for
   me? Könnten Sie (formal)
   / Kannst du (informal) das
   bitte für mich halten?
hold, to hold (to pause) v
   innehalten p24
   Hold on a minute! Einen
   Moment bitte!
   I'll hold. Ich warte.
hold, to hold (gambling) v
   schieben p22
holiday n der Feiertag m
home n das Zuhause gn, das
   Haus gn
homemaker n die Hausfrau f
horn n die Hupe f
horse n das Pferd gn

hostel n die Jugendherberge f p58

hot adj heiß p82

hot chocolate n die heiße Schokolade f p82

hotel n das Hotel gn p58

Do you have a list of local hotels? Haben Sie eine Liste der örtlichen Hotels?

hour n die Stunde f p127

hours (at museum) n die Öffnungszeiten pl

how adv wie p3, 11

humid adj feucht p113

hundred n Hundert

hurry v sich beeilen p29

I'm in a hurry. Ich bin in Eile.
Hurry, please! Beeilung, bitte!

hurt, to hurt v verletzen p20

Ouch! That hurts! Autsch! Das tut weh!

husband n der Ehemann m p103

I

I pron ich p3

ice n das Eis gn p79

identification n die Papiere pl p38

indigestion n die Verdauungsstörung f

inexpensive adj günstig p32

infant n das Kleinkind gn

Are infants allowed? Sind Kleinkinder erlaubt?

information n die Information f

information booth n der Informationsstand m

insect repellent n das Insektenschutzmittel gn p176

inside drinnen p76

insult v beleidigen p20

insurance n die Versicherung f p183

intercourse (sexual) n der (Geschlechts-)Verkehr m

interest rate n der Zinssatz m p121

intermission n die Pause f

Internet n das Internet gn p31

High-speed Internet Hochgeschwindigkeits-Internet

Do you have Internet access? Haben Sie einen Internetanschluss?

Where can I find an Internet café? Wo finde ich ein Internetcafé?

interpreter n der Dolmetscher / die Dolmetscherin m/f p184

I need an interpreter. Ich benötige einen Dolmetscher.

introduce, to introduce v vorstellen p20

I'd like to introduce you to _____. Ich möchte Sie (formal) / dich (informal) mit _____ bekannt machen.

ENGLISH–GERMAN

Ireland n Irland
Irish n der Ire m, die Irin f p108
is v See be (to be) p23
Italian n der Italiener m, die Italienerin f 108

J

jacket n die Jacke f p39
January n der Januar m p13
Japanese adj japanisch p72
jazz n der Jazz m p116
Jewish adj jüdisch p115
jog, to run v joggen p20
juice n der Saft m p89
June n der Juni m p13
July n der Juli m p13

K

keep, to keep v behalten p24
kid n das Kind gn
   Are kids allowed? Sind Kinder erlaubt?
   Do you have kids' programs? Haben Sie ein Programm für Kinder?
   Do you have a kids' menu? Haben Sie ein Kindermenü?
kilo n das Kilo p10
kilometer n der Kilometer m
kind (type) n die Art f
   What kind is it? Um welche Art handelt es sich?
kiss n der Kuss m p169
kitchen n die Küche f p65
know, to know (something) v (etwas) wissen p33

know, to know (someone) v (jemanden) kennen p26
kosher adj koscher p77

L

lactose-intolerant adj mit Laktoseunverträglichkeit p78
land, to land v landen p20
landscape n die Landschaft f
language n die Sprache f
laptop n das Notebook gn p146
large adj groß p11
last, to last v dauern p20
last adv letzter p9
late adj spät p12
   Please don't be late. Bitte pünktlich sein.
later adv später
   See you later. Bis später.
laundry n die Wäscherei f p66
lavender adj Lavendel-
law n das Gesetz gn
lawyer n der Anwalt / die Anwältin m/f p110
least n das Mindeste gn
least adj mindestens
leather n das Leder gn p42
leave, to leave (depart) v abreisen p20
left adj links p5
   on the left auf der linken Seite
leg n das Bein gn
lemonade n die Limonade f
less adj weniger p143

lesson n die Unterrichtseinheit f p161

license n die Lizenz f p183

driver's license der Führerschein

life preserver n die Schwimmweste f

light n (lamp) das Licht gn p46

light (for cigarette) n das Feuer gn p165

May I offer you a light? Darf ich Ihnen (formal) / dir (informal) Feuer geben?

lighter (cigarette) n das Feuerzeug m p166

like, desire v gern haben p24

I would like ____. Ich hätte gerne ____.

like, to like v gefallen p34

I like this place. Mir gefällt es hier.

limo n die Limousine f p50

liquor n das alkoholische Getränk gn p37

liter n der Liter m p10

little adj klein (size), gering (amount)

live, to live v leben p20

Where do you live? Wo wohnen Sie? (formal) / Wo wohnst du? (informal)

living n der Lebensunterhalt m p110

What do you do for a living? Was machen Sie (formal) / machst du (informal) beruflich?

local adj örtlich p53

lock n das Schloss gn p150

lock, to lock v abschließen p24

I can't lock the door. Die Tür lässt sich nicht abschließen.

I'm locked out. Ich bin ausgesperrt.

locker n der Spind m p150

storage locker der Aufbewahrungsschrank

locker room die Umkleide p151

long adv lang p11

For how long? Für wie lange?

long adj lang

look, to look v (to observe) umsehen p24

I'm just looking. Ich sehe mich nur um.

Look here! Schau her!

look, to look v (to appear) aussehen p24

How does this look? Wie sieht das aus?

look for, to look for (to search) v suchen p20

I'm looking for a porter. Ich suche einen Träger für mein Gepäck.

loose adj locker p140

lose, to lose v verlieren p24

I lost my passport. Ich habe meinen Pass verloren.

I lost my wallet. Ich habe meine Geldbörse verloren.

I'm lost. *Ich habe mich verirrt.*
lost *See* **lose** *verlieren* p38
loud *adj laut* p69
loudly *adv laut*
lounge *n das Foyer gn*
lounge, to lounge *v faulenzen* p20
love *n die Liebe f*
love, to love *v lieben* p20
  to love (family) *lieben*
  to love (a friend) *mögen*
  to love (a lover) *lieben*
  to make love *miteinander schlafen*
low *adj niedrig* p77
lunch *n das Mittagessen gn* p74
luggage *n das Gepäck gn* p31
  Where do I report lost luggage? *Wo kann ich verloren gegangenes Gepäck melden?*
  Where is the lost luggage claim? *Wo finde ich die Ausgabe für verloren gegangenes Gepäck?*

M
machine *n die Maschine f* p66
made of *adj aus*
magazine *n die Zeitschrift f*
maid (hotel) *n das Zimmermädchen gn*
maiden *adj Mädchen-*

That's my maiden name. *Das ist mein Mädchenname.*
mail *n die Post f*
  air mail *die Luftpost*
  registered mail *das Einschreiben*
mail *v versenden* p20
make, to make *v machen* p20
makeup *n das Make-up gn*
make up, to make up (apologize) *v wiedergutmachen* p20
make up, to make up (apply cosmetics) *v schminken* p20
male *n der Mann m* p38
male *adj männlich*
mall *n das Einkaufszentrum gn*
man *n der Mann m*
manager *n der Manager / die Managerin m/f*
manual (instruction booklet) *n das Handbuch gn* p45
many *adj viele* p10
map *n die Karte f* p43
March (month) *n der März m* p13
market *n der Markt m* p141
  flea market *Flohmarkt* p138
  open-air market *der Freiluftmarkt*
married *adj verheiratet* p104
marry, to marry *v heiraten* p20
massage, to massage *v massieren* p20, 170

match (sport) n das Spiel gn

match n das Streichholz gn

book of matches das Streichholzbriefchen

match, to match v passen p20

Does this match my outfit? Passt das zu meinem Outfit?

May (month) n der Mai m p13

may v aux dürfen p24

May I? Darf ich?

meal n die Mahlzeit f p35

meat n das Fleisch gn p79

meatball n die Frikadelle f

medication n das Medikament gn

medium (size) adj mittel

medium rare (meat) adj halb gar p76

medium well (meat) adj medium p77

member n das Mitglied gn

menu n die Speisekarte f p74

May I see a menu? Könnte ich bitte die Speisekarte bekommen?

children's menu Kindermenü

diabetic menu Diabetikermenü

kosher menu koscheres Menü

metal detector n der Metalldetektor m

meter n der Meter m p10

middle adj Mittel-

midnight n Mitternacht f

military n das Militär gn

milk n die Milch f p82

milk shake der Milchshake

milliliter n der Milliliter m

millimeter n der Millimeter m

minute n die Minute f p4

in a minute sofort

miss, to miss (a flight) v verpassen p20

missing adj fehlend

mistake n der Fehler m p70

moderately priced adj der mittleren Preiskategorie p58

mole (facial feature) n das Muttermal gn

Monday n der Montag m p12

money n das Geld gn p120

money transfer die Überweisung

month n der Monat m p4

morning n der Morgen m p12

in the morning morgens

mosque n die Moschee f

mother n die Mutter f p103

mother, to mother v bemuttern p20

motorcycle n das Motorrad gn

mountain n der Berg m

mountain climbing das Bergsteigen p155

mouse n die Maus f

mouth n der Mund m

move, to move v bewegen p20

movie n der Film m p132

much n viel p10

mug, to mug (someone) v überfallen p24

mugged adj überfallen

museum n das Museum gn p118

music n die Musik f p116

live music die Livemusik

musician n der Musiker m, die Musikerin f p110

muslim adj muslimisch p115

mustache n der Schnurrbart m

mystery (novel) n der Mystery-Roman m

N

name n der Name m p102

My name is ___. Ich heiße ___. p1

What's your name? Wie heißen Sie? (formal) / Wie heißt du? (informal)

napkin n die Serviette f

narrow adj schmal p11

nationality n die Nationalität f

nausea n die Übelkeit f p176

near adj nähe p5

nearby adj in der Nähe p73

neat (tidy) adj ordentlich

need, to need v benötigen p20

neighbor n der Nachbar m, die Nachbarin f p103

nephew n der Neffe m p104

network n das Netzwerk gn

new adj neu p150

newspaper n die Zeitung f

newsstand n der Zeitungsstand m p31

New Zealand n Neuseeland

New Zealander adj der Neuseeländer m, die Neuseeländerin f

next prep neben

next to neben

the next station der nächste Halt

nice adj nett

niece n die Nichte f p104

night n die Nacht f p12

at night nachts

per night pro Übernachtung p62

nightclub n der Nachtclub m

nine adj neun p7

nineteen adj neunzehn p7

ninety adj neunzig p7

ninth adj neunter p9

no adv nein p1

noisy adj laut p68

none n keiner, keine, kein p10

nonsmoking adj Nichtraucher-

nonsmoking area der Nichtraucherbereich

nonsmoking room das Nichtraucherzimmer

noon n der Mittag m p12

Norwegian n der Norweger m, die Norwegerin f p109

nose n die Nase f p177

novel n der Roman m

November n der November m p14

now *adv jetzt* p4

number *n die Nummer f*
p112

Which room number?
Welche Zimmernummer?

**May I have your phone
number?** *Kann ich bitte
Ihre Telefonnummer
haben?*

nurse *n der Krankenpfleger
m*, *die Krankenpflegerin
f* p110

nurse *v stillen* p20

**Do you have a place where
I can nurse?** *Haben Sie
einen Raum zum Stillen?*

nursery *n die Kinderkrippe f*

Do you have a nursery?
*Haben Sie eine
Kinderkrippe?*

nut *n die Nuss f*

O

o'clock *adv Uhr* p4

two o'clock *zwei Uhr*

October *n der Oktober m* p14

offer, to offer *v anbieten* p24

officer *n der Polizist m*, *die
Polizistin f* p38

oil *n das Öl gn* p46, 77

okay *adv OK, in Ordnung*

old *adj alt*

olive *n die Olive f*

one *adj ein / eine* p7

one way (traffic sign) *adj
Einbahnstraße*

open (business) *adj geöffnet*
p142

Are you open? *Haben Sie
geöffnet?*

opera *n die Oper f* p116

operator (phone) *n die
Vermittlung f*

optometrist *n der Optiker m*,
die Optikerin f

orange (color) *adj orange*

orange juice *n der
Orangensaft m* p39

order, to order (demand) *v
befehlen* p24

order, to order (request) *v
bestellen* p20

organic *adj Bio-*

Ouch! *interj Au!*

outside *n draußen* p76

overcooked *adj zerkocht*

overheat, to overheat *v
überhitzen* p20, 35

The car overheated. *Das
Auto hat sich überhitzt.*

overflowing *adv überlaufend*

oxygen tank *n die
Sauerstoffflasche f*

P

package *n das Paket gn* p97

pacifier *n der Schnuller m*

page, to page (someone) *v
anpiepen* p20

paint, to paint *v streichen*
p24

painting *n das Gemälde gn*

pale *adj blass* p106

paper *n das Papier gn* p89

parade *n der Umzug m*

parent *n der Elternteil m*

ENGLISH—GERMAN

park n der Park m p119

park, to park v parken p20

no parking das Parkverbot

parking fee die Parkgebühr

parking garage das Parkhaus

partner n der Partner m, die Partnerin f

party n die Partei f p114

party n die Party f

political party die Partei

pass, to pass v passen p20

I'll pass. Ich passe.

passenger n der Passagier m

passport n der Ausweis m

I've lost my passport. Ich habe meinen Ausweis verloren.

pay, to pay v bezahlen p20

peanut n die Erdnuss f

pedestrian adj Fußgänger-

pediatrician n der Kinderarzt m, die Kinderärztin f

Can you recommend a pediatrician? Können Sie mir einen Kinderarzt empfehlen?

permit n die Genehmigung f

Do we need a permit? Benötigen wir eine Genehmigung?

permit, to permit v erlauben p20

phone n das Telefon gn p168

May I have your phone number? Kann ich bitte Ihre Telefonnummer haben?

Where can I find a public phone? Wo finde ich eine Telefonzelle?

phone operator die Vermittlung

Do you sell prepaid phones? Verkaufen Sie Prepaid-Telefone?

phone adj Telefon-

Do you have a phone directory? Haben Sie ein Telefonbuch?

phone call n der Telefonanruf m

I need to make a collect phone call. Ich möchte ein R-Gespräch führen.

an international phone call ein Auslandsgespräch

photocopy, to photocopy v (foto-)kopieren p20

piano n das Klavier gn p117

pillow n das Kissen gn p40

down pillow das Daunenkissen

pink adj rosa

pizza n die Pizza f p72

place, to place v platzieren p20

plastic n der Kunststoff m p42

play n das Theaterstück gn

play, to play (a game) v spielen p20

play, to play (an instrument) v spielen p20

playground n der Spielplatz m

Do you have a playground?
Haben Sie einen Spielplatz?

please (polite entreaty) *adv bitte*

please, to be pleasing to *v gefallen* p28

pleasure *n die Freude f* p1

It's a pleasure. *Freut mich.*

plug *n der Stecker m* p145

plug, to plug *v einstecken* p20

point, to point *v zeigen, weisen* p20, 24

Would you point me in the direction of ____? *Wie komme ich zu / zum / zur ____?*

poison *n das Gift gn* p15

police *n die Polizei f* p30

police station *n die Polizeiwache f* p30

Polish *n der Pole m, die Polin f* p109

pool *n der (Swimming-)Pool m* p58

pool (the game) *n das Poolbillard gn*

pop music *n die Popmusik f*

popular *adj beliebt* p164

port (beverage) *n der Portwein m*

port (for ship) *n der Hafen m*

porter *n der Portier m* p30

portion *n die Portion f*

portrait *n das Porträt gn*

Portuguese *n der Portugiese m, die Portugiesin f* p108

postcard *n die Postkarte f*

post office *n das Postamt gn*

Where is the post office? *Wo befindet sich das Postamt?*

poultry *n das Geflügel gn*

pound *n das Pfund gn* p97

prefer, to prefer *v bevorzugen* p20

pregnant *adj schwanger*

prepared *adj vorbereitet*

prescription *n das Rezept gn* p38

price *n der Preis m*

print, to print *v drucken* p20

private berth / cabin *n eine eigene Kabine f* p54

problem *n das Problem gn* p2

process, to process *v verarbeiten* p20

product *n das Produkt gn*

professional *adj professionell*

program *n das Programm gn*

May I have a program? *Geben Sie mir bitte ein Programm.*

Protestant *n der Protestant m die Protestantin f*

publisher *n der Verleger m die Verlegerin f*

puff *n der Hauch / Zug m* p15

pull, to pull *v ziehen* p24

purple *adj violett*

purse *n die Handtasche f*

push, to push *v drücken* p20

put, to put v setzen, stellen, legen p20

Q

quarter adj Viertel- p8
  one-quarter Viertel-
quiet adj ruhig p76

R

rabbit n der Hase m p86
radio n das Radio gn p43
  satellite radio das Satellitenradio
rain, to rain v regnen p20
  Is it supposed to rain? Soll es regnen?
rainy adj regnerisch p113
  It's rainy. Es ist regnerisch.
ramp (wheelchair) n die Rampe (Rollstuhl) f p57
rare (meat) adj blutig p76
rate (for car rental, hotel) n der Preis m p44
  What's the rate per day? Wie hoch ist der Preis pro Tag?
  What's the rate per week? Wie hoch ist der Preis pro Woche?
rate plan (cell phone) n die Tariftabelle f
rather adv lieber
read, to read v lesen p24
really adv wirklich
receipt n die Quittung f p121
receive, to receive v erhalten p23

recommend, to recommend v empfehlen p24
red adj rot p173
redhead n der Rothaarige m, die Rothaarige f p106
reef n das Riff gn p158
refill to refill (of beverage) v nachschenken
refill (of prescription) n die erneute Einlösung f p177
reggae adj Reggae- p116
relative (family) n der / die Verwandte m/f
remove, to remove v entfernen p20
rent, to rent v mieten p20
  I'd like to rent a car. Ich möchte ein Auto mieten.
repeat, to repeat v wiederholen p20
  Would you please repeat that? Könnten Sie das bitte wiederholen? p2
reservation n die Reservierung f
  I'd like to make a reservation for ____. Ich möchte eine Reservierung für ____. p62
  See p7 for numbers.
restaurant n das Restaurant gn
  Where can I find a good restaurant? Wo finde ich ein gutes Restaurant? p72
restroom n die Toilette f p30
  Do you have a public restroom? Gibt es hier eine öffentliche Toilette?

return, to return (to a place) v zurückkehren p20

return, to return (something to a store) v zurückgeben p24

ride, to ride v fahren (vehicle) / reiten (horse) p23

right adj rechts p48

_____ **is on the right.**
_____ befindet sich auf der rechten Seite.

Turn right at the corner.
Biegen Sie an der Ecke nach rechts ab.

rights n die Rechte gn, pl

civil rights die Bürgerrechte

river n der Fluss m p157

road n die Straße f p48

road closed sign n das Straßensperrschild gn p49

rob, to rob v ausrauben p20

I've been robbed. Ich wurde ausgeraubt.

rock and roll n Rock'n'Roll m

rock climbing n das Felsenklettern gn

rocks (ice) n die Würfel f, pl p80

I'd like it on the rocks. Ich hätte das gerne auf Eis.

romance (novel) n der Liebesroman m

romantic adj romantisch

room (hotel) n das Zimmer gn

room for one / two Einzelzimmer / Doppelzimmer

room service der Zimmerservice

rose n die Rose f

royal flush n der Royal Flush m

rum n der Rum m p81

run, to run v rennen p24

Russian n der Russe m, die Russin f p109

S

sad adj traurig p109

safe (for storing valuables) n der Tresor m p67

Do the rooms have safes? Verfügen die Zimmer über einen Tresor?

safe (secure) adj sicher

Is this area safe? Ist dieses Gebiet sicher?

sail n das Segel gn

sail, to sail v ablegen (start) / segeln (on a sailboat) p20

When do we sail? Wann legen wir ab? p54

salad n der Salat m p97

salesperson n der Verkäufer m, die Verkäuferin f p110

salt n das Salz gn p95

Is that low-salt? Enthält das wenig Salz?

satellite n der Satellit m p43

satellite radio das Satellitenradio

satellite tracking das Navigationssystem

Saturday n der Sonntag m p13

sauce *n die Soße f*

say, to say *v sagen* **p20**

scan, to scan *v (document) scannen* **p20**

schedule *n der Fahrplan m*

school *n die Schule f*

scooter *n der Roller m* **p43**

score *n der Spielstand f* **p154**

Scottish *adj schottisch*

scratched *adj zerkratzt* **p45**

scratched surface *die zerkratzte Oberfläche*

scuba dive, to scuba dive *v tauchen (mit Atemgerät)* **p20**

sculpture *n die Skulptur f*

seafood *n die Meeresfrüchte f, pl* **p73**

search *n die Suche f*

hand search *das Abtasten*

search, to search *v suchen* **p20**

seasick *adj seekrank* **p54**

I am seasick. *Ich bin seekrank.*

seasickness pill *n die Tablette gegen Seekrankheit f*

seat *n der Platz m* **p34, 134**

child seat *der Kindersitz*

second *adj zweiter* **p9**

security *n die Sicherheit f* **p30**

security checkpoint *die Sicherheitsschleuse*

security guard *der Sicherheitsbeamte*

sedan *n die Limousine f* **p43**

see, to see *v sehen* **p24**

May I see it? *Dürfte ich das mal sehen?*

self-serve *adj Selbstbedienungs-*

sell, to sell *v verkaufen* **p20**

seltzer *n das Selters gn* **p80**

send, to send *v versenden* **p20**

separated (marital status) *adj getrennt lebend* **p104**

September *n der September m* **p14**

serve, to serve *v servieren* **p20**

service *n der Service m* **p36**

services (religious) *n der Gottesdienst m* **p115**

service charge *n die Servicegebühr f* **p64**

seven *adj sieben* **p7**

seventy *adj siebzig* **p7**

seventeen *adj siebzehn* **p7**

seventh *adj siebter* **p9**

sew, to sew *v nähen* **p20**

sex (gender) *n das Geschlecht gn*

sex, to have (intercourse) *v Sex haben* **p24**

shallow *adj seicht*

sheet (bed linen) *n das Bettlaken gn*

shellfish *n das Schalentier gn* **p79**

ship *n das Schiff gn* **p54**

ship, to ship *v versenden* **p20**

**How much to ship this to
____?** *Wie viel kostet der
Versand hiervon nach
____?*

shipwreck *n das Schiffswrack
gn*

shirt *n das Hemd gn*

shoe *n der Schuh m* p137

shop *n das Geschäft gn* p138

shop *v einkaufen* p20

**I'm shopping for
mens' clothes.** *Ich bin
auf der Suche nach
Herrenbekleidung.*

**I'm shopping for
womens' clothes.** *Ich
bin auf der Suche nach
Damenbekleidung.*

**I'm shopping for
childrens' clothes.** *Ich
bin auf der Suche nach
Kinderbekleidung.*

short *adj kurz* p10

shorts *n die kurze Hose f* p75

shot (liquor) *n der Kurze m*

shout *v rufen* p24

show (performance) *n die
Vorstellung f*

What time is the show?
*Wann beginnt die
Vorstellung?*

show, to show *v zeigen* p20

Would you show me?
*Könnten Sie mir das bitte
zeigen?*

shower *n die Dusche f* p60

Does it have a shower? *Gibt
es eine Dusche?*

shower, to shower *v duschen*
p20, 29

shrimp *n die Garnele f* p91

shuttle bus *n der Pendelbus
m*

sick *adj krank* p41

I feel sick. *Mir ist schlecht.*

side *n die Beilage f* p78

**on the side (e.g., salad
dressing)** *dazu*

sidewalk *n der Gehweg m*

sightseeing *n das Sightseeing
gn*

sightseeing bus *n der
Sightseeing-Bus m*

sign, to sign *v unterschreiben*
p24

Where do I sign? *Wo muss
ich unterschreiben?*

silk *n die Seide f* p139

silver *n das Silber-*

sing, to sing *v singen* p24

single (unmarried) *adj ledig*
p104

Are you single? *Sind Sie
ledig?*

single (one) *adj Einzel-*

single bed *das Einzelbett*

sink *n das Waschbecken gn*

sister *n die Schwester f* p103

sit, to sit *v sitzen*

six *adj sechs* p7

sixteen *adj sechzehn* p7

sixty *adj sechzig* p7

size (clothing, shoes) *n die
Kleidergröße f* p139

ENGLISH–GERMAN

skin n die Haut f
sleeping berth n das Schlafabteil gn
slow adj langsam p168
slow, to slow v verlangsamen p20
  Slow down! Fahren Sie bitte langsamer. p51
slow(ly) adv langsam
  Speak more slowly. Sprechen Sie bitte etwas langsamer. p101
small adj klein p11
smell, to smell v riechen
smoke, to smoke v rauchen p20
smoking n das Rauchen gn p31
  smoking area Raucherbereich
  No Smoking Rauchen verboten p33
snack n der Imbiss m p172
Snake eyes! n Schlangenaugen! p173
snorkel n der Schnorchel m
sock n die Socke f
soda n die Limonade f p39
  diet soda die Diätlimonade
soft adj weich
software n die Software f
sold out adj ausverkauft
some adj etwas (uncountable) / einige (countable)
someone n jemand p31
something n etwas m p41
son n der Sohn m p105

song n das Lied gn p168
soon adv bald p15
sorry adj leid
  I'm sorry. Tut mir leid.
spa n das Heilbad m p59
Spain n Spanien
Spanish n der Spanier m, die Spanierin f p108
spare tire n der Reservereifen m
speak, to speak v sprechen p24
  Do you speak English? Sprechen Sie Englisch?
  Would you speak louder, please? Könnten Sie bitte etwas lauter sprechen?
  Would you speak slower, please? Könnten Sie bitte etwas langsamer sprechen?
special (featured meal) n die Spezialität f
specify, to specify v angeben p24
speed limit n die Geschwindigkeitsbegrenzung f p48
  What's the speed limit? Welche Geschwindigkeitsbegrenzung gilt hier?
speedometer n der Tacho m
spell, to spell v buchstabieren p20
  How do you spell that? Wie schreibt sich das?
spice n das Gewürz gn

spill, to spill *v verschütten* **p20**

split (gambling) *n der Split m*

sports *n der Sport m* **p118**

spring (season) *n der Frühling m* **p14**

stadium *n das Stadion gn* **p152**

staff (employees) *n die Mitarbeiter pl* **p70**

stamp (postage) *n die Briefmarke f*

stair *n die Stufe f*

> **Where are the stairs?** *Wo finde ich das Treppenhaus?*
> **Are there many stairs?** *Gibt es viele Stufen?*

stand, to stand *v stehen* **p24**

start, to start (commence) *v beginnen*

start, to start (a car) *v anlassen* **p24**

state *n der Staat (gov.) / der Status (status) m*

station *n der Bahnhof m* **p51**

> **Where is the nearest____?** *Wo ist die nächste _____?*
> **gas station** *Tankstelle*
> **bus station** *Bushaltestelle*
> **subway station** *U-Bahn-Haltestelle*
> **Where is the nearest train station?** *Wo ist der nächste Bahnhof?*

stay, to stay *v Aufenthalt, bleiben* **p24**

> **We'll be staying for ____ nights.** *Wir bleiben ____ Nächte. See numbers, p7.*

steakhouse *n das Steakhaus gn* **p72**

steal, to steal *v stehlen* **p24**

stolen *adj gestohlen* **p41**

stop *n die Haltestelle f* **p52**

> **Is this my stop?** *Ist das hier meine Haltestelle?*
> **I missed my stop.** *Ich habe meine Haltestelle verpasst.*

stop, to stop *v anhalten* **p24**

> **Please stop.** *Halten Sie bitte an.*
> **STOP (traffic sign)** *STOP*
> **Stop, thief!** *Haltet den Dieb!*

store *n das Lager gn* **p137**

straight *adj gerade (street) / glatt (hair)* **p106**

> **straight ahead** *geradeaus* **p5**
> **straight (drink)** *pur*
> **Go straight.** *Gehen Sie geradeaus* **p48**

straight (gambling) *n der Straight m* **p174**

street *n die Straße f* **p6**

> **across the street** *gegenüber*
> **down the street** *am Ende der Straße*
> **Which street?** *Welche Straße?*
> **How many more streets?** *Wie viele Straßen noch?*

stressed *adj gestresst*

striped *adj gestreift*

stroller *n der Kinderwagen m*

> **Do you rent baby strollers?** *Vermieten Sie Kinderwagen?*

ENGLISH—GERMAN

substitution n der Ersatz m

subway n die U-Bahn f p55

subway line die U-Bahn-Linie

subway station die U-Bahn-Haltestelle

Which subway do I take for _____? Mit welcher U-Bahn komme ich zu / zur / zum _____?

subtitle n die Untertitel m, pl

suitcase n der Koffer m p41

suite n die Suite f p58

summer n der Sommer m p14

sun n die Sonne f

sunburn n der Sonnenbrand m

I have a bad sunburn. Ich habe einen starken Sonnenbrand.

Sunday n der Sonntag m p12

sunglasses n die Sonnenbrille f

sunny adj sonnig p113

It's sunny out. Draußen scheint die Sonne.

sunroof n das Sonnendach gn

sunscreen n die Sonnencreme f

Do you have sunscreen SPF _____? Haben Sie Sonnencreme mit Lichtschutzfaktor _____? See numbers p7.

supermarket n der Supermarkt m

surf v surfen p20

surfboard n das Surfbrett gn

suspiciously adv verdächtig p41

swallow, to swallow v schlucken p20

sweater n der Pullover m p39

Swedish n der Schwede m, die Schwedin f p109

swim, to swim v schwimmen p24

Can one swim here? Kann man hier schwimmen?

swimsuit n der Badeanzug m

swim trunks n die Badehose f

Swiss n der Schweizer m, die Schweizerin f p108

symphony n die Symphonie f

T

table n der Tisch m p21

table for two der Tisch für zwei

tailor n der Schneider m die Schneiderin f p66

Can you recommend a good tailor? Können Sie mir einen guten Schneider empfehlen?

take, to take v nehmen, bringen p24

Take me to the station. Bringen Sie mich bitte zum Bahnhof.

How much to take me to _____? Wieviel kostet die Fahrt zu / zur / zum _____?

takeout menu n das Essen zum Mitnehmen gn

talk, to talk v *sprechen* p24

tall adj *groß* p107

tanned adj *gebräunt*

taste (flavor) n *der Geschmack* m

taste n **(discernment)** *der Geschmack* m

taste, to taste v *schmecken* p20

tax n *die Steuer* f p143

value-added tax (VAT) *Mehrwertsteuer (MwSt.)*

taxi n *das Taxi* gn p50

Taxi! *Taxi!*
Would you call me a taxi? *Könnten Sie mir bitte ein Taxi rufen?*

tea n *der Tee* m p82

team n *das Team* gn p152

Techno n *der Techno* m p116, 163

television n *der Fernseher* m

temple n *der Tempel* m p114

ten adj *zehn* p7

tennis n *das Tennis* gn p59

tennis court *der Tennisplatz*

tent n *das Zelt* gn

tenth adj *zehnter* p9

terminal n **(airport)** *das Terminal* gn p33

thank you *danke* p1

that (near) adj *diese / dieser / dieses*

that (far away) adj *jene / jener / jenes*

theater n *das Theater* gn p133

them (m/f) *sie* p3

there (demonstrative) adv *da* **(nearby)**, *dort* **(far)**

Is / Are there _____ over there? *Tatsächlich _____ dort drüben?*

these adj *diese* p6

thick adj *dick*

thin adj *dünn* p107

third adj *dritter* p9

thirteen adj *dreizehn* p7

thirty adj *dreißig* p7

this adj *diese / dieser / dieses* p6

those *jene / jener / jenes* adj

thousand *Eintausend* p7

three *drei* p7

Thursday n *der Donnerstag* m p12

thus (therefore) *also* adv p15

ticket n *das Ticket* gn p30

ticket counter *der Kartenschalter*
one-way ticket *das einfache Ticket* p32
round-trip ticket *das Hin- und Rückreiseticket* p32

tight adj *eng* p140

time n *die Zeit* f p156

Is it on time? *Ist er (train, bus) pünktlich? / Ist es (plane, ship) pünktlich?*
At what time? *Um wie viel Uhr?*
What time is it? *Wie spät ist es?*

timetable n **(train)** *der Fahrplan* m p51

tip (gratuity) *das Trinkgeld* gn p83

tire n *der Reifen* m p45

I have a flat tire. *Ich habe einen platten Reifen.*

tired *adj müde* p109

today *n heute*

today's special *n das Menü gn* p15

toilet *n die Toilette f* p68

The toilet is overflowing. *Die Toilette läuft über.*

The toilet is backed up. *Die Toilette ist verstopft.*

toilet paper *n das Toilettenpapier gn*

You're out of toilet paper. *Sie haben kein Toilettenpapier mehr.*

toiletries *n die Hygieneartikel m, pl* p89

toll *n die Gebühr f* p49

tomorrow *n morgen* p4

ton *n die Tonne f*

too (excessively) *adv zu*

too (also) *adv auch* p173

tooth *n der Zahn m* p181

I lost my tooth. *Ich habe einen Zahn verloren.*

toothache *n die Zahnschmerzen m, pl*

I have a toothache. *Ich habe Zahnschmerzen.*

total *n die Gesamtsumme f*

What is the total? *Wie hoch ist die Gesamtsumme?*

tour *n der Ausflug m*

Are guided tours available? *Werden Fremdenführungen angeboten?*

Are audio tours available? *Werden Audioführungen angeboten?*

towel *n das Handtuch gn*

May we have more towels? *Könnten wir bitte mehr Handtücher bekommen?*

toy *n das Spielzeug gn*

toy store *n das Spielwarengeschäft gn*

Do you have any toys for the children? *Haben Sie Kinderspielzeug?*

traffic *n der Verkehr m* p45

How's traffic? *Wie ist der Verkehr?*

traffic rules *die Verkehrsregeln*

trail *n der Weg m* p156

Are there trails? *Gibt es dort Wege?*

train *n der Zug m* p51

express train *der Expresszug*

local train *der Nahverkehrszug*

Does the train go to ____? *Fährt der Zug nach / zum ____?*

May I have a train schedule? *Könnte ich bitte einen Zugfahrplan bekommen?*

Where is the train station? *Wo finde ich den Bahnhof?*

train, to train *v trainieren* p20

transfer, to transfer *v* überweisen **p24**

I need to transfer funds. *Ich möchte eine Überweisung tätigen.*

transmission *n* das Getriebe *gn*

automatic transmission *das Automatikgetriebe*

standard transmission *das Schaltgetriebe*

travel, to travel *v* reisen **p20**

travelers' check *n* der Reisescheck *m*

Do you cash travelers' checks? *Kann ich mir hier Reisechecks auszahlen lassen?*

trillion *n* die Billion *f* p15

trim, to trim (hair) *v* schneiden **p24**

trip *n* die Reise *f* p99

triple *adj* dreifach **p8**

trumpet *n* die Trompete *f*

trunk *n* der Koffer *m* (luggage) p42, der Kofferraum *m* (car)

try, to try (attempt) *v* versuchen **p20**, ausprobieren **p20**

try, to try on (clothing) *v* anprobieren **p20**

try, to try (food) *v* probieren

Tuesday *n* der Dienstag *m* p12

Turkish *n* der Türke *m*, die Türkin *f* p109

turn, to turn *v* abbiegen (car) / sich wenden (person) **p24**

to turn left / right *links / rechts abbiegen*

to turn off / on *ausschalten / einschalten* **p20**

twelve *adj* zwölf p7

twenty *adj* zwanzig p7

twine *n* die Paketschnur *f* p129

two *adj* zwei p7

U

umbrella *n* der Regenschirm *m*

uncle *n* der Onkel *m* p104

undercooked *adj* noch nicht durch

understand, to understand *v* verstehen **p24**

I don't understand. *Ich verstehe nicht.*

Do you understand? *Verstanden?*

underwear *n* die Unterwäsche *f*

university *n* die Universität *f*

up *adv* aufwärts p5

update, to update *v* aktualisieren **p20**

upgrade *n* die höhere Kategorie *f* p44

upload, to upload *v* hochladen **p24**

upscale *adj* gehoben

us *pron* uns p3

USB port *n* der USB-Anschluss *m*

use, to use *v* verwenden **p20**

V

vacation *n der* Urlaub *m* p37
  on vacation *im Urlaub*
  to go on vacation *in Urlaub gehen*

vacancy *n das* freie Zimmer (hotel) *gn*

van *n der* Kleinbus *m, der* Van *m*

VCR *n der* Videorekorder *m*
  Do the rooms have VCRs? *Gibt es auf den Zimmern einen Videorekorder?*

vegetable *n das* Gemüse *gn*

vegetarian *n der* Vegetarier *m, die* Vegetarierin *f* p35

vending machine *n der* Automat *m*

version *n die* Version *f*

very *sehr* p70

video *n das* Video *gn*
  Where can I rent videos or DVDs? *Wo kann ich Videos oder DVDs ausleihen?*

view *n die* Aussicht *f* p60
  beach view *die Aussicht auf den Strand*
  city view *die Aussicht auf die Stadt*

vineyard *n das* Weingut *gn*

vinyl *n das* Vinyl *gn* p42

violin *n die* Geige *f*

visa *n das* Visum *gn*
  Do I need a visa? *Benötige ich ein Visum?*

vision *n die* Sicht *f* p178

visit, to visit *v besuchen* p20

visually-impaired *adj sehbehindert*

vodka *n der* Wodka *m* p81

voucher *n der* Gutschein *m* p37

W

wait, to wait *v warten* p20
  Please wait. *Warten Sie bitte.*
  How long is the wait? *Wie lange muss ich warten? (sing.) / Wie lange müssen wir warten? (pl.)*

waiter *n der* Kellner *m, die* Kellnerin *f*

waiting area *n der* Wartebereich *m* p30

wake-up call *n der* Weckruf *m* p67

wallet *n die* Geldbörse *f* p38
  I lost my wallet. *Ich habe meine Geldbörse verloren.*
  Someone stole my wallet. *Meine Geldbörse wurde gestohlen.*

walk, to walk *v gehen* p24

walker (ambulatory device) *n die* Gehhilfe *f* p36

walkway *n der* Fußgängerweg *m*
  moving walkway *der Fahrsteig*

want, to want *v wollen* p25

war *n der* Krieg *m* p114

warm *adj warm* p113

watch, to watch *v zusehen* p24

water n das Wasser gn p39
  Is the water potable? *Ist das Wasser trinkbar?*
  Is there running water? *Gibt es fließend Wasser?* p71
wave, to wave v winken p20
waxing n das Enthaaren (mit Wachs) gn
wear, to wear v tragen p24
weather forecast n der Wetterbericht m
Wednesday n der Mittwoch m
week n die Woche f p4, 13
  this week *diese Woche*
  last week *letzte Woche*
  next week *nächste Woche*
weigh v wiegen p24
  I weigh ____. *Ich wiege ____.*
  It weighs ____. *Das wiegt ____. See p7 for numbers.*
weights n die Gewichte gn, pl p149
welcome adv willkommen
  You're welcome. *Gern geschehen.*
well adv gut
  well done (meat) *gut durch* p77
  well done (task) *gut gemacht*
  I don't feel well. *Ich fühle mich nicht gut.*
western adj westlich, abendländisch
whale n der Wal m
what adv welche / welcher / welches p3
  What sort of ____? *Welche Art von ____?*
  What time is ____? *Wann gibt es ____?* p11
  See p100 for questions.
wheelchair n der Rollstuhl m p36
  wheelchair access *der Zugang per Rollstuhl* p62
  wheelchair ramp *die Rampe für Rollstuhlfahrer*
  power wheelchair *der elektrisch betriebene Rollstuhl*
wheeled (luggage) adj mit Rollen
when adv wann p3
  See p100 for questions.
where adv wo p3
  Where is ____? *Wo ist ____?*
  See p100 for questions.
which adv welche / welcher / welches p3
  Which one? *Welche / Welcher / Welches?*
  See p100 for questions.
white adj weiß
who adv wer p3
whose adj wessen / dessen
wide adj breit p11
widow, widower n die Witwe f, der Witwer m p104

wife *n die Ehefrau f* p103
wi-fi *n das Wi-Fi gn*
window *n das Fenster gn, der Schalter m* p34, 130

> **drop-off window**
> *Abgabeschalter*
> **pickup window**
> *Abholschalter*

windshield *n die Frontscheibe f*
windshield wiper *n der Scheibenwischer m*
windy *adj windig* p113
wine *n der Wein m* p39, 76
winter *n der Winter m* p14
wiper *n der Wischer m*
with *prep mit* p79
withdraw *v abheben* p24
   I need to withdraw money.
   Ich möchte Geld abheben.
without *prep ohne* p79
woman *n die Frau f*
work, to work *v arbeiten (person), funktionieren (device)* p20

> _____ **doesn't work.** _____
> *funktioniert nicht.*

workout *n das Training m*
worse *schlimmer*
worst *am schlimmsten*
write, to write *v schreiben* p24

> **Would you write that down for me?** *Könnten Sie mir das bitte aufschreiben?*

writer *n der Autor m* p110

X
x-ray machine *n das Röntgengerät gn*

Y
yellow *adj gelb*
yes *adv ja*
yesterday *n gestern* p4

> **the day before yesterday**
> *vorgestern* p13

yield sign *n das Schild „Vorfahrt gewähren" gn*
you *pron Sie / du / ihr* p3

> **you (singular, informal)** *du*
> **you (singular, formal)** *Sie*
> **you (plural informal)** *ihr*
> **you (plural formal)** *Sie*

your, yours *adj Ihr / Ihre (formal); dein / deine (informal)*
young *adj jung* p105

Z
zoo *n der Zoo m* p118

A

abbiegen (car) to turn v **p24**

abbiegen to turn v **p24**

Biegen Sie links / rechts ab. Turn left / right.

abbuchen to charge (money) v **p20**

das Abendessen gn dinner n

der Abfluss m drain n

abgelehnt declined adj

Ihre Kreditkarte wurde abgelehnt. Your credit card was declined.

abheben to withdraw v **p24**

die Abhebung f withdrawal n

ablegen to sail v **p20**

Wann legen wir ab? When do we sail?

die Abreise f departure n **p33**

abreisen to leave (depart) v **p20**

abschließen to lock v **p22**

abwärts down adv **p5**

acht eight adj **p7**

achter eighth adj **p9**

drei Achtel three eighths

achtzehn eighteen adj **p7**

achtzig eighty adj **p7**

der Adapterstecker m adapter plug n

der Adler m eagle n

die Adresse f address n **p112**

Wie lautet die Adresse? What's the address?

Afro- afro adj

afroamerikanisch African American adj **p107**

die Agentur / das Büro f/gn agency n **p42**

der Agnostiker m, **die Agnostikerin** f agnostic n **p115**

die Akne f acne n **p176**

der Aktenkoffer m briefcase n **p41**

aktualisieren to update v **p20**

aktuell current adj **p15**

akzeptieren to accept v **p20**

Wir akzeptieren Kreditkarten. Credit cards accepted.

der Alkohol m alcohol n **p80**

die Allergie f allergy n

allergisch allergic adj **p5, 79**

Ich bin allergisch gegen _____. I'm allergic to _____.

alles / irgend etwas anything n

also thus, therefore adv **p15**

alt old adj

das Alter gn age n

Wie alt sind Sie? (formal) / Wie alt bist du? (informal) What's your age?

das Aluminium gn aluminum n

am besten best. See gut

am schlimmsten worst. See schlecht

am wenigsten *least. See wenig*

der Amerikaner *m*, die Amerikanerin *f American n* p109

amerikanisch *American adj*

an Bord *on board*

anbieten *to offer v* **p24**

anders *different (other) adj* p141

angeben *to specify v* **p24**

die Angelegenheit *f matter, affair*

Kümmern Sie sich um Ihre eigenen Angelegenheiten. *Mind your own business.*

die Angelrute *f fishing pole n*

anhalten *to stop v* **p24**

Halten Sie bitte an. *Please stop.*

ankommen *to arrive v* **p24**

die Ankunft *f arrival n*

anlassen *to start (a car) v*

anpiepen *to page (someone) v* **p20**

anrufen *to call (to phone) v* **p20**

Antibaby- *birth control adj*

Ich habe keine Antibabypillen mehr. *I'm out of birth control pills.*

das Antibiotikum *gn antibiotic n*

das Antihistamin *gn antihistamine n* p175

die Antwort *f answer n*

Ich benötige eine Antwort. *I need an answer.*

antworten (auf eine Frage) *to answer (respond to a question) v* **p20**

Antworten Sie mir bitte. *Answer me, please.*

der Anwalt / die Anwältin *m/f lawyer n* p110

anziehen *to dress v* **p24 p29**

der April *m April n* p13

arbeiten (person) *to work v* **p20**

der Arbeitgeber *m employer n*

die Art *f kind (sort, type) n*

Um welche Art handelt es sich? *What kind is it?*

der Arzt *m* / die Ärztin *f doctor n* p110, 177

die Arztpraxis *f doctor's office n*

asiatisch *Asian adj* p72

das Aspirin *gn aspirin n* p176

das Asthma *gn asthma n* p181

Ich habe Asthma. *I have asthma.*

atheistisch *atheist adj*

auch *too (also) adv* p173

Audio- *audio adj* p57

das Audio *gn audio n* p136

der Aufenthalt *m wait n* p74

aufladen *to charge (a battery) v* **p24**

auflegen *hang up (to end a phone call) v* **p24**

aufwärts *up adv* p5

der Aufzug *m elevator n* p61

das Auge *gn eye n* p173

die Augenbraue *f eyebrow n*

der August *m August n* p13

aus *made of adj*

auschecken *to check out (of hotel) v* **p20**

der Ausflug *m tour n*

ausrauben, stehlen *to rob v, to steal v* **p20, 24**

die Ausrüstung *f equipment n* p37

ausschalten *to turn off (lights) v* **p20**

aussehen *to look (appear) v* **p24**

die Aussicht *f view n* p60

die Aussicht auf den Strand *beach view* p60

die Aussicht auf die Stadt *city view*

die Ausstellung *f exhibit n*

Australien *Australia n*

australisch *Australian adj*

ausverkauft *sold out adj*

auswärts essen *to eat out v*

der Ausweis *m passport n*

auszahlen lassen *to cash out (gambling)* **p24**, p174

auszahlen *to cash v* **p30**

das Auto *gn car n*

die Autovermietung *car rental agency*

die Autobahn *f highway n*

die Autokrankheit *f carsickness n*

der Autor / die Autorin *m/f writer n* p110

die Autovermietung *f car rental agency*

Autsch! *Ouch! interj*

B

das Baby *gn baby n* p105

Baby-, für Babys *for babies adj*

Kinderwagen *baby stroller*

Babynahrung *baby food*

der Babysitter *m babysitter n*

das Bad *gn bath, spa n* p15

der Badeanzug *m swimsuit n*

baden *to bathe v* **p20, 29**

die Badewanne *f bathtub n* p60

das Badezimmer *gn bathroom n, bath n* p30

der Bahnhof *m station n* p51

Wo finde ich die nächste Tankstelle? *Where is the nearest gas station?*

balancieren (something shaky) / begleichen (invoice) *to balance v* p20, 24

bald *soon adv* p15

der Balkon *m balcony n* p59

der Ball *m ball (sport) n*

die Band *f band n*

Bank- *bank adj*

das Bankkonto *bank account*

die Bankkarte *bank card*

die Bank *f bank n* p120

die Bar *f bar n* p31

die **Pianobar** *piano bar*
die **Single-Bar** *singles bar*
p164

das **Bargeld** *gn cash n* p121

Nur gegen Barzahlung.
Cash only. p122

der **Bass** *m bass (instrument)*
n

die **Batterie** *f battery (for*
flashlight) n

die **Batterie** *f battery (for*
car) n

die **Baumwolle** *f cotton n*
p139

bearbeiten *to process (a*
transaction) v p20

sich **beeilen** *to hurry v* **p20,**
35

begeistert *enthusiastic adj*
p109

beginnen *to begin v, to start*
(commence) v **p24**

behalten *to keep v* **p24**

die **Behinderung** *f disability*
n

die **Behinderung** *f handicap*
n

das **Bein** *gn leg n*

beleibt *fat adj* p11, 107

beleidigen *to insult v* **p20**

der **Belgier** *m,* die **Belgierin** *f*
Belgian n p108

beliebig *any adj*

beliebt *popular adj* p164

bemuttern *to mother v* **p20**

sich **benehmen** *to behave*
v **p24**

benommen *dizzy adj* p62,
179

das **Benzin** *gn gas n*

berechnen *to bill v* **p20**

der **Berg** *m mountain n*

das **Bergsteigen** *mountain*
climbing

das **Bergsteigen** *gn*
mountain climbing n

beschädigt *damaged adj* p41

besetzt *busy adj (phone*
line), occupied adj p138

besorgt *anxious adj* p109

Ich brauche ein
Antibiotikum. *I need an*
antibiotic.

besser *better. See gut*

bestätigen *to confirm v* **p20**

die **Bestätigung** *f*
confirmation n

bestellen *(restaurant) to*
order v **p20**

besuchen *to visit v* **p20**

betreten *to enter v* **p24**

Kein Eingang. *Do not enter.*
Zutritt verboten. *Entry*
forbidden.

das **Bett** *gn bed n*

das **Bettlaken** *gn sheet (bed*
linen) n

die **Beule** *f dent n*

bevorzugen *to prefer v* **p20**

bevorzugt *preferably adj*

bewegen *to move v* **p20**

bewölkt *cloudy adj* p113

bezahlen *to pay v* **p20**

die **Biene** *f bee n*

das Bier *gn beer n* p80

das Bier vom Fass *beer on tap, draft beer* p177

billig *cheap adj* p44

billig *cheap* p44
billiger *cheaper* p44
am billigsten *cheapest*

die Billion *f trillion n* p15

Bio- *organic adj*

Bis später. *See you later.*

bitte *please (polite entreaty) adv* p1

blass *pale adj* p106

blau *blue adj* p107

bleiben *to stay v* p24

das Bleichmittel *gn bleach n*

blenden *to dazzle, to blind v* p15

blind *blind adj*

der Block *m block n*

blockieren *to block v* p20

der Blonde *m,* **die Blondine** *f blond(e) n* p106

die Blume *f flower n*

die Bluse *f blouse n* p139

blutig *rare (meat) adj* p76

das Boot / Schiff *gn boat n / ship n* p54

die Bordkarte *f boarding pass n* p38

der Bordstein *m curb n*

die Botschaft *f embassy n*

der Brandy *m brandy n* p81

brauchen *to need v* p20

braun *brown adj* p107

brav *well behaved adj* p15

breit *wide adj* p11

Breitband- *broadband n*

die Bremse *f brake n* p46

bremsen *to brake v* p20

das Bremslicht *brake light*

die Motorkontrollleuchte *check engine light* p46
der Scheinwerfer *headlight*
die Ölkontrollleuchte *oil light* p46

brennen *to burn v* p24

die Briefmarke *f stamp (postage) n*

die Brille *f eyeglasses n*

bronzefarben *bronze (color) adj*

das Brot *gn bread n* p89

die Brücke *f bridge (across a river) n / bridge (dental structure) n* p181

der Bruder *m brother n* p103

der Brünette *m,* **die Brünette** *f brunette n* p106

buchstabieren *to spell v* p20

Wie schreibt sich das? *How do you spell that?*

der Buddhist *m,* **die Buddhistin** *f Buddhist n* p115

das Budget *gn budget n*

das Buffet *gn buffet n*

der Bus *m bus n* p50

die Bushaltestelle *bus stop*
der Pendelbus *shuttle bus*
der Sightseeing-Bus *sightseeing bus*

die Butter *f butter n* p78

C

das Cabrio *gn convertible n*

das Café *(coffee house) n*

der Campingplatz *m campsite n*

der Cappuccino *m cappuccino n*

die CD *f CD n* p127

Charter- *charter adj*

  der Charterflug *charter flight*

chartern *to charter (transportation) v* **p20**

der Check-In *check-in n* **p30**

  der Curbside-Check-In *curbside check-in*

  der elektronische Check-In *electronic check-in* p34

  der Express-Check-In *express check-in* p34

der Chef *m,* **die Chefin** *f boss n*

die chemische Reinigung *f dry cleaner n*

der Chiropraktiker *m chiropractor n* p177

der Computer *m computer n*

die Country-Musik *f country-and-western adj*

der Cousin *m,* **die Cousine** *f cousin n*

die Creme *f cream n* p84

cremefarben *off-white adj*

D

da *there (nearby) adv (demonstrative)* p171

das Dach *gn roof n*

  das Sonnendach *sunroof*

die Damentoilette *women's restroom*

der Däne *m,* **die Dänin** *f Danish n* p108

danke *thank you*

Darf ich Ihnen ____ vorstellen? *I'd like to introduce you to ____.*

das *this n* p6

dauern *to last v* p20

die Dauerwelle *f permanent (hair)*

die (Bett-)Decke *f blanket n* p40

dein *your, yours adj sing (informal)*

die Demokratie *f democracy n*

der Designer *m,* **die Designerin** *f designer n* p110

der Deutsche *m,* **die Deutsche** *f German n* p108

der Dezember *m December n*

Diabetiker- *diabetic adj* p77

dick *thick adj*

der Dienstag *m Tuesday n* p12

diese *these adj pl* p6

diese *those (near) adj pl*

diese *those adj pl*

dieser / diese / dieses *that (near) adj*

dieser / diese / dieses *this adj* p6

die Disko *f disco* n p116

der Dollar *m dollar* n

der Dolmetscher / die Dolmetscherin *m/f interpreter* n p184

der Dom *m cathedral* n **p15**

der Donnerstag *m Thursday* n p12

Doppel- *double adj* p8

dort drüben *over there adv*

dort *there (far) adv (demonstrative)* p5

der Download *m download* n

das Drama *gn drama* n

draußen *outside* n p76

drei *three adj* p7

dreifach *triple adj* p8

dreißig *thirty adj* p7

dreizehn *thirteen adj* p7

das Dressing *gn dressing (salad)* n

drinnen *inside adj* p76

dritter *third adj* p9

die Driving Range *f driving range* n

drucken *to print v* **p20**

drücken *to push v* **p20**

du *you pron sing (informal)*

dunkel *dark adj*

die Dunkelheit *f darkness* n

dünn *thin (fine, skinny, slender) adj*

der Durchfall *m diarrhea* n p176

durchwählen *to dial direct*

die Dusche *f shower* n p60

duschen *to shower v* **p20, 29**

das Dutzend *gn dozen* n p11

die DVD *f DVD* n p44

E

die Ecke *f corner* n

an der Ecke *on the corner*

die Ehefrau *f wife* n p103

der Ehemann *m husband* n p103

eigentlich / wirklich *actual adv* **p15**

ein / eine *one adj* p7

eine E-Mail senden *to send e-mail v* **p20**

einen Nachtclub besuchen *to go clubbing v* **p20**

einfach *single adj / simple adj*

ohne Eis *straight up (drink)*

das einfache Ticket *one-way ticket* p38

der Eingang *m entrance* n p39

einkaufen *to shop v* **p20**

das Einkaufszentrum *gn mall* n

einpacken *to bag v* **p20**

einstecken *to plug v* **p20**

einsteigen / an Bord gehen *to board v* **p24**

das Eis *gn ice* n p79

die Eismaschine *ice machine*

der Elefant *m elephant* n

der Elektroanschluss *m electrical hookup* n **p71**

elf *eleven adj* p7

die E-Mail *f e-mail* n p112

Kann ich Ihre (formal) / deine (informal) E-Mail-Adresse haben? *May I have your e-mail address?* p112

die E-Mail-Nachricht *e-mail message* p112

empfehlen *to recommend* v p24

eng *tight adj* p140

England *England n*

der Engländer *m,* **die Engländerin** *f English n* p108

englisch *English adj* p64

die englische Blindenschrift *f braille (American) n*

die Ente *f duck n*

entfernen *to remove* v p20

das Enthaaren (mit Wachs) *gn waxing n*

entschuldigen *to excuse (pardon)* v p20

Verzeihung. *Excuse me.*

entspannen / abhängen (slang) *to hang out (relax)* v p20, 24

entzückt *charmed adj*

er *he pron* p3

erbitten *to request, demand* v p24

die Erdnuss *f peanut n*

erfreut *delighted adj*

erhalten *to receive* v p24

die Erkältung *f cold (illness) n*

erklären *to explain* v p20

erlauben *to permit* v p20

die erneute Einlösung *f refill (of prescription) n* p177

der Ersatz *m substitution n*

erschöpft *exhausted adj*

erster *first adj* p9

der Erzieher *m,* **die Erzieherin** *f educator n* p110

der Esel *m donkey n*

das Essen *gn food n* p80

essen *to eat* v p24

das Essen zum Mitnehmen *takeout menu*

die Etage *f floor n* p61

das erste Stockwerk *ground floor, first floor* p61

etwas *bit (small amount) n*

etwas (uncountable) / einige (countable) *some adj*

etwas *gn something n* p41

Express- *express adj* p34, 53

der Express-Check-In *express check-in* p34

F

fahren *to drive* v p24

fahren *to ride* vp24

der Fahrer *m driver n* p49

der Fahrplan *m schedule n, timetable (train) n* p51

der Fahrpreis *m fare n*

fallen *to fall* v p24

die Familie *f family n* p103

die Farbe *f color n* p141

färben *to color* v p20

faulenzen *to lounge* v p20

das Fax *gn fax n* p111

der Februar *m February n* p13

fehlend *missing adj* p41

der Fehler *m fault n* p49

Es war mein Fehler. *I'm at fault.* p49

Es war sein Fehler. *It was his fault.*

der Fehler *m mistake n* p70

feiern *to celebrate v* **p20**

der Feiertag *m holiday n*

der Fels *m rock n* p80

auf Eis *on the rocks*

das Fenster *gn window n* p34

der Fernseher *m television n*

das Kabelfernsehen *cable television* p60

das Satellitenfernsehen *satellite television* p60

das Festival *gn festival n*

feucht *humid adj* p113

das Feuer *gn fire n*

das Feuer *gn light (for cigarette) n* p165

Darf ich Ihnen (formal) / dir (informal) Feuer geben? *May I offer you a light?*

das Feuerzeug *gn lighter (cigarette) n* p166

der Film *m movie n* p132

finden *to find v* **p24**

das Fitness-Center *gn fitness center n* p59

das Fitnessstudio *gn gym n* p149

die Flasche *f bottle n* p165

das Fleisch *gn meat n* p79

die Flöte *f flute n*

der Flug *m flight n* p32

der Flugbegleiter / die Flugbegleiterin *m / f flight attendant*

der Flughafen *m airport n*

der Fluss *m river n* p157

folglich *consequently adv* p15

das Format *gn format n* p145

die Formel *f formula n*

der Fortschritt *m advance n*

fortsetzen *to continue v* **p20**

(foto-)kopieren *to photocopy v* **p20**

das Foyer *gn lounge n*

fragen *to ask v* **p20**

der Franzose *m,* **die Französin** *f French n* p108

französisch *French adj* p108

die Frau *f woman n*

der Frauenarzt / die Frauenärztin *m/f gynecologist n*

das freie Zimmer (hotel) *gn vacancy n*

der Freitag *m Friday n* p13

der Fremdenführer / die Fremdenführerin *m/f guide (of tours) n*

die Fremdenführung *f guided tour n*

die Freude *f pleasure n* p1

Freut mich. *It's a pleasure.*

der Freund *m / die Freundin* *f friend n* p103

der Freund *m boyfriend n* p103

die Freundin f girlfriend n
p103

die Frikadelle f meatball n

frisch fresh adj p90

der Frisör m, die Frisörin f
hairdresser n

fröhlich happy adj p109

die Frontscheibe f windshield
n

die Frucht f fruit n p89

der Fruchtsaft m fruit juice n

früh early adj p12

der Frühling m spring
(season) n p14

das Frühstück gn breakfast n

führen to guide v p20

Full House! Full house! n

fünf five adj p7

fünfter m fifth adj

fünfzehn m fifteen adj

fünfzig fifty adj p7

(der) Fuß m foot (body
part) n

Fußgänger- pedestrian adj

die Fußgängerzone
pedestrian shopping
district

der Fußgängerweg m
walkway n

der Fahrsteig moving
walkway

G

der Gang m aisle (in store)
n / hallway n p89

ganz all adj p10

die ganze Zeit all the time
Das ist alles. That's all.

die Garnele f shrimp n p91

das Gas (for cooking) / das
Benzin (for cars) gn gas
n p46

die Tankanzeige gas gauge
kein Benzin mehr out of
gas

der Gast m guest n

geben to deal (cards) v p24
Ich bin dabei. Deal me in.
p173

geben to give v p24

das Gebiss gn dentures,
denture plate n p182

gebräunt tanned adj

die Gebühr f fee n

die Gebühr f toll n p49

der Gedanke m thought n

die Gefahr f danger n p49

gefallen to please v to be
pleasing to v p24

das Geflügel gn poultry n

gehen to go v p24

die Gehhilfe f walker
(ambulatory device) n p36

gehoben upscale adj p175

Geht es Ihnen (formal) / dir
(informal) gut? Are you
okay?

der Gehweg m sidewalk n

die Geige f violin n

gelb yellow adj

der (Geld-)Schein m bill
(currency) n

das Geld gn money n p120

die Überweisung *money transfer* p120

der Geldautomat *m* ATM *n*

die Geldbörse *f* wallet *n*

die Geldwechselstube *f* currency exchange *n* p31, 121

gelockt *curly adj* p106

das Gemälde *gn* painting *n*

das Gemüse *gn* vegetable *n*

die Genehmigung *f* permit *n*

genießen *to enjoy v* **p24**

geöffnet *open (business) adj*

Gepäck- *baggage adj* p33

die Gepäckausgabe *baggage claim* p33

das Gepäck *gn* baggage, luggage *n* p33

das verloren gegangene Gepäck *lost baggage*

gerade *straight adj*

das Gericht *gn* court (legal) *n* p183

das Gericht für Verkehrsdelikte *traffic court*

das Gericht *gn* dish *n* p77

die Gesamtsumme *f* total *n*

Wie hoch ist die Gesamtsumme? *What is the total?*

Ich arbeite bei ____. *I work for ____.*

das Geschäft *gn* shop *n*, store *n*

das Zelt *gn* tent *n*

Geschäfts- *business adj* p65

das Geschäftszentrum *business center* p65

das Geschenk *gn* gift *n*

die Geschichte *f* history *n* p119

geschieden *divorced adj*

das Geschlecht *gn* sex (gender) *n*

der (Geschlechts-) Verkehr *m* intercourse (sexual) *n*

geschlossen *closed adj* p49

der Geschmack *m* taste (discernment) *n*

der Geschmack *m* taste, flavor *n*

der Schokoladengeschmack *chocolate flavor*

der Gesellschaftstanz *m* ballroom dancing *n* p133

das Gesicht *gn* face *n* p107

gestern *yesterday adv* p4

gestohlen *stolen adj* p41

gestreift *striped adj*

gestresst *stressed adj*

das Getränk *gn* drink *n* p165

das Gratisgetränk *complimentary drink*

getrennt lebend *separated (marital status) adj* p104

das Getriebe *gn* transmission *n*

das Automatikgetriebe *automatic transmission* p44

das Schaltgetriebe *standard transmission* p44

getrocknet / Trocken- *dried adj* p96

die Gewichte *gn, pl* weights n p149

das Gewürz *gn* spice n

Gibt es hier ____? Is / Are there ____?

Gibt es hier eine öffentliche Toilette? Do you have a public restroom?

das Gift *gn* poison n **p15**

der Gin *m* gin n p81

die Gitarre *f* guitar n p117

das Glas *gn* glass (drinking) n

Schenken Sie das als offenes Getränk aus? Do you have it by the glass?

Ich hätte gerne ein Glas. I'd like a glass please.

das Gold *gn* gold n

golden gold (color) adj

golden golden adj

Golf spielen to go golfing v p24

das Golf (-spiel) *gn* golf n p42

der Golfplatz golf course

der Gottesdienst *m* service (religious) n p115

das Gramm *gn* gram n

grau gray adj

der Grieche *m*, die Griechin *f* Greek n p108

griechisch Greek adj p73

griechisch-orthodox Greek Orthodox adj p115

groß big adj, large adj p12

groß big, large p11

größer bigger, larger p69, 141

am größten biggest, largest

Großartig! Great! interj

die Großmutter *f* grandmother n

der Großvater *m* grandfather n

grün green adj p107

die Gruppe *f* group n p37

günstig inexpensive adj p32

der Gürtel *m* belt n p140

das Transportband conveyor belt p39

gut aussehend handsome adj p105

gut besucht busy (restaurant) adj

gut fine adj p1

Mir geht es gut. I'm fine.

gut good adj p99

gut well adv

Gute Nacht. Good night. p99

Guten Abend. Good evening. p99

Guten Morgen. Good morning. p99

Guten Tag. Good afternoon. p99

der Gutschein *m* voucher n p37

der Essensgutschein meal voucher p37

der Zimmergutschein room voucher p37

H

das Haar *gn* hair n p106

der Haarschnitt *m* haircut n

der Haartrockner *m* hair dryer n p67

haben to have v **p24**

Sex haben to have sex
(intercourse)

der Hafen port (for ship
mooring) n **p54**

das Hähnchen gn chicken
n **p86**

halb half adj **p8**

halb gar medium rare (meat)
adj

halbes Pfund half-pound **p98**

die Hälfte f half n

Hallo hello n **p1**

halten to hold v **p24**

Händchen halten to hold
hands

die Haltestelle f stop n **p52**

die Bushaltestelle bus stop

Haltet den Dieb! Stop, thief!

die Hand f hand n **p168**

das Handbuch gn manual
(instruction booklet) n **p45**

handhaben to handle v **p20**

Vorsicht! Handle with care
p129

der Handschuh m glove n
p161

die Handtasche f purse n **p46**

**Ich habe meine Geldbörse
verloren.** I lost my wallet.
**Meine Geldbörse wurde
gestohlen.** Someone stole
my wallet.

das Handtuch gn towel n

hart hard (firm) adj **p42**

der Hase m hare (bunny)
n **p86**

der Hauch / Zug m puff n
p15

die Hausfrau f homemaker n

die Haut f skin n

das Heilbad gn spa n

heiraten to marry v **p20**

heiß hot adj, warm adj

die heiße Schokolade f hot
chocolate n **p82**

helfen to help / to assist v
p24

hell bright adj

das Hemd gn shirt n

der Herbst m autumn (fall
season) n **p14**

der (Herren-)Frisör m barber
n **p146**

die Herrentoilette men's
restroom

herunterladen to download
v **p24**

das Herz gn heart n **p178**

der Herzinfarkt m heart
attack n

heute today n **p4**

hier here adv **p5**

die Hilfe f assistance n

die Hilfe f help n **p48**

Hilfe! Help! n

das Hin- und Rückreiseticket
round-trip ticket **p32**

hinter behind adj

der Hiphop hip-hop n **p163**

historisch historical adj

das Hobby gn hobby n

hoch high adj **p160**

hoch *high adj* p160
höher *higher*
am höchsten *highest*
hochladen *to upload v* **p24**
die Hochschule *f college n,*
high school n
die Höhe *f altitude n* p155
die höhere Kategorie *f*
upgrade n p44
hören *to hear v*
hören *to listen v* **p20**
hörgeschädigt *hearing-*
impaired adj
die Hose *f pair of pants n*
die Badehose *swim trunks n*
die kurze Hose *shorts*
das Hotel *gn hotel n* p58
der Hund *m dog n* p36
der Blindenhund *service*
dog p62
hundert *hundred adj* p7
die Hupe *f horn n*
der Husten *m cough n*
husten *to cough v* **p20**
der Hut *m hat n* p139
die Hygieneartikel *m, pl*
toiletries n p89

I
Ich hätte gern etwas zu
trinken. *I'd like a drink.*
ich *I pron* p3
ihr *you pron pl (informal)*
Ihr *you pron (formal)*
ihr / ihre *her / their adj* p3
im Voraus *in advance adv*
der Imbiss *m snack n* p172

der Impressionismus *m*
Impressionism n
in der Nähe *near, nearby adj*
nah *near adj*
näher *nearer (comparative)*
am nächsten *nearest*
(superlative)
die Information *f information*
n
der Informationsstand *m*
information booth n p31
der Ingenieur *m,* **die**
Ingenieurin *f engineer n*
p110
innehalten, warten *to hold*
(to pause) v, to wait v
p24, 20
das Insektenschutzmittel *gn*
insect repellent n p176
das Internet *gn Internet n* p31
Wo finde ich ein
Internetcafé? *Where can I*
find an Internet café?
das Internetcafé *gn*
cybercafé n
der Ire *m,* **die Irin** *f Irish n*
p108
irisch *Irish adj*
Irland *Ireland n*
italienisch *Italian adj* p108
der Italiener *m,* **die**
Italienerin *f Italian n* p108

J
ja *yes adv* p1
die Jacke *f coat n* p140
die Jacke *f jacket n* p39

das Jahr *gn year n*

Wie alt sind Sie? (formal) / Wie alt bist du? (informal) *What's your age?*

der Januar *m January n* p13

der Jazz *m jazz n* p116

jemand *someone n* p31

jener / jene / jenes *that (far away) adj* p6

jetzt *now adv* p4

das Joggen *jogging n*

jüdisch *Jewish adj* p115

die Jugendherberge *f hostel n* p58

der Juli *m July n* p13

jung *young adj* p105

der Junge *m boy n, kid n* p103

der Juni *m June n* p13

K

der Käfer *m bug n* p80

der Kaffee (beverage) *m coffee n*

der Eiskaffee *iced coffee*
der Espresso *m espresso n*
das Internetcafé *Internet café*

kahl *bald adj* p15

kalt *cold adj* p113

Kanada *m Canada n*

kanadisch *Canadian adj* p182

kariert *checked (pattern) adj*

die Karte *f card n* p110

die Kreditkarte *credit card* p120

Akzeptieren Sie Kreditkarten? *Do you accept credit cards?*
die Visitenkarte *business card*

die Karte *f map n* p43

der Straßenatlas *road map* p43

der Kartenschalter *ticket counter* p30

der Kartenverkauf *m box office n*

der Kaschmir *m cashmere n*

der Käse *m cheese n* p89

das Kasino *gn casino n* p58

der Katholik *m*, **die Katholikin** *f Catholic n* p115

die Katze *f cat n*

kein *none, no adj adv* p1

keine freien Zimmer *no vacancy*

der Keks *m cookie n* p89

der Kellner / die Kellnerin *m / f waiter n*

kennen *to know (someone) v* p24

das Kennwort *gn password n*

das Kilo *gn kilo n* p10

die Kinder *gn, pl children n pl*

der Kinderarzt / die Kinderärztin *pediatrician n*

das Kinderbett *gn crib n* p61

die Kinderkrippe *f nursery n*

der Kinderwagen *m stroller n*

das Kino *gn cinema n*

die **Kirche** f church n p114
das **Kissen** gn pillow n p40
   das **Daunenkissen** down
   pillow
klar clear adj p159
die **Klarinette** f clarinet n
die **Klasse** f class n p34
   die **Businessklasse** business
   class p34
   die **Economyklasse**
   economy class p34
   die **Erste Klasse** first class p34
klassisch classical (music) adj
das **Klavier** gn piano n p117
das **Kleid** gn dress (garment) n
der **Kleiderbügel** m hanger n
die **Kleidergröße** f size
   (clothing, shoes) n
die **Kleidung** f dress (general
   attire) n p164
klein little adj, small adj p11
   klein small, little
   kleiner smaller, littler
   am kleinsten smallest,
   littlest
der **Kleinbus** m van n p43
das **kleine Mädchen** gn little
   girl n p103
das **Kleinkind** gn infant n p103
Kletter- climbing adj
   die **Kletterausrüstung**
   climbing gear
klettern (mountain) / steigen
(stairs) to climb v p20, 24
   bergsteigen to climb a
   mountain

das **Klettern** gn climbing n
   p155
   das **Felsenklettern** rock
   climbing p155
die **Klimaanlage** f air
   conditioning n p60
der **Knoblauch** m garlic n p95
kochen to cook v **p20**
die **Kochgelegenheit** f
   kitchenette n p61
der **Köder** m bait n p157
der **Koffer** m suitcase / trunk
   (luggage) n p41
der **Kofferraum** m trunk (of
   car) n
der **Kognak** m cognac n p81
die **Koje** f berth n
das **Kondom** gn condom n
   p175
   Hast du ein Kondom? Do
   you have a condom? p175
   nicht ohne Kondom not
   without a condom
können to be able to (can) v,
   may v aux **p26**
   Kann ich _____? May I _____?
konsequent consistent(ly)
   adj/adv **p15**
der **Kontakt für den Notfall**
   m emergency contact n
das **Konto** gn account n p123
der **Kontostand** m balance
   (on bank account) n p123
das **Konzert** gn concert n p118
der **Kopfhörer** m headphones
   n

korrekt *correct adj* p51
korrigieren *to correct v* **p20**
das koschere Essen *kosher meal* p35
kosten *to cost v* **p20**
kosten *to taste v, to try (food) v* **p20**
das Kostüm *gn costume n*
krank *sick adj* p41
der Krankenpfleger / die Krankenpflegerin *m/f nurse n* p110
der Krankenwagen *m ambulance n*
kratzen *to scratch v* **p20**
der Kratzer *m scratch n*
das Kraut *gn herb n*
das Kreditinstitut *gn credit bureau n* p121
der Krieg *m war n* p114
die Krone *f crown (dental) n*
der Kubismus *m Cubism n*
die Küche *f kitchen n* p65
die Kuh *f cow n*
Kunst- *art adj*

das Kunstmuseum *art museum*
der Handwerker *m,* die Handwerkerin *f craftsperson / artisan n*

die Kunst *f art n*

die Kunstausstellung *exhibit of art*

der Künstler / die Künstlerin *m/f artist n*
der Kunststoff *m plastic n* p42
kupferfarben *copper adj*
die Kuppel *f dome n* **p15**

kurz *short adj* p10
der Kurze *m shot (liquor) n*
der Kuss *m kiss n* p169
das Kuvert *gn envelope n* p130

L
laktoseunverträglich *lactose-intolerant adj* p78
das Lämpchen *light (on car dashboard)*
landen *to land v* **p20**
langsamer werden *to slow v* **p24**
das Laufband *gn treadmill n*
laufen *to walk v* **p24**
laut *loud, noisy adj* 68, 69
das Leben *gn life n* p122

Was machen Sie (formal) / machst du (informal) beruflich? *What do you do for a living?* p110

leben *to live v* **p20**

Wo wohnen Sie? (formal) / Wo wohnst du? (informal) *Where do you live?*

die Lebensmittel *gn, pl groceries n*
das Leder *gn leather n* p42
ledig *single (unmarried) adj* p104

Sind Sie ledig? *Are you single?* p104

leid *sorry adj*

Tut mir leid. *I'm sorry.*

letzter / letzte / letztes *last adv* p9
das Licht *gn light (lamp) n* p46
die Liebe *f love n*
lieben *to love v* **p20**

das Lied *gn song n* p168

die Limonade *f soda n* p39

die Diätlimonade *diet soda* p39

die Limousine *f sedan n* p43

links *left adj* p5

das Loch *gn cavity (tooth cavity) n*

die Locke *f curl n*

locker *loose adj* p140

die Loge *f box (seat) n* p153

die Luftpost *air mail*

der Expressversand *express mail*

der Versand erster Klasse *first class mail*

das Einschreiben *registered mail*

Wo befindet sich das Postamt? *Where is the post office?*

M

machen *to do v, to make v* p20

das Mädchen *gn girl n* p166

die Mahlzeit *f meal n* p35

das Essen für Diabetiker *diabetic meal* p35

der Mai *m May (month) n*

das Make-up *gn makeup n*

die Mama *f mom n, mommy n*

der Manager / die Managerin *m / f manager n*

der Mann *m man n*

männlich *male adj*

der Markt *m market n*

der Flohmarkt *flea market* p138

der Freiluftmarkt *open-air market*

der März *m March (month) n*

die Maschine *f machine n* p66

das Röntgengerät *x-ray machine*

der Automat *vending machine*

massieren *to massage v* p20

die Maus *f mouse n*

medium *medium well (meat) adj* p77

die Medizin *f medicine n, medication n*

die Meeresfrüchte *f, pl seafood n* p73

die Menge (things) / der Betrag (money) *f / m amount n* p56

das Menü *gn today's special n* p15

messen *to measure v* p24

der Metalldetektor *m metal detector n*

der Meter *m meter n*

mieten *to rent v*

das Militär *gn military n*

die Milliarde *f billion n* p15

der Milliliter *m milliliter n*

der Millimeter *m millimeter n*

mindestens *at least n*

die Minibar *f minibar n*

die Minute *f minute n* p4

sofort *in a minute*
mischen *to blend v* **p15**
mit *with prep* **p79**
mit Buffet *buffet-style adj*
mit Rollen *wheeled (luggage) adj*
mit wenig Salz *low-salt*
der Mitarbeiter *m,* **die Mitarbeiterin** *f employee n* **p110**
das Mitglied *gn member n*
die Mitgliedschaft *f membership n*
der Mittag *noon n* **p12**
das Mittagessen *gn lunch n* **p74**
mittel *medium adj (size)* **p11**
Mittel- *middle adj* **p28**
Mitternacht *midnight adv* **p12**
der Mittwoch *m Wednesday n*
das Mobiltelefon / Handy *cell phone* **p122**
Geben Sie mir bitte Ihre Telefonnummer? *May I have your phone number?* **p168**
die Telefonvermittlung *f phone operator*
das Prepaid-Telefon *prepaid phones*
der Monat *m month n* **p4**
der Montag *m Monday n* **p12**
der Morgen *m morning n* **p12**
morgens *in the morning* **p65**

morgen *gn tomorrow adv*
die Morgendämmerung *f dawn n* **p12**
bei Tagesanbruch *at dawn*
die Moschee *f mosque n* **p114**
der Motor *m engine n* **p46**
das Motorrad *gn motorcycle n*
müde *tired adj* **p109**
der Mund *m mouth n*
die Münze *f coin n*
das Museum *gn museum n* **p118**
das Musical *gn musical (music genre) n*
die Musik *f music n* **p116**
die Popmusik *pop music*
musikalisch *musical adj*
der Musiker / die Musikerin *m / f musician n* **p110**
der Muslim *m,* **die Muslimin** *f Muslim n* **p115**
die Mutter *f mother n* **p103**
das Muttermal *gn mole (facial feature) n*

N
der Nachbar *m,* **die Nachbarin** *f neighbor n* **p103**
der Nachmittag *m afternoon n* **p12**
nachmittags *in the afternoon*
der Nachname *m last name*
Ich habe meinen Mädchennamen behalten. *I kept my maiden name.*

Nachschenken v refill (of
beverage) v
die Nachspeise f dessert n
p80
die Dessertkarte dessert
menu p80
die Nacht f night n p12
nachts at night n p12, 62
pro Nacht per night
der Nachtclub m nightclub n
nah, in der Nähe close, near
adj p5
nah close p5
näher closer p5
am nächsten closest p5
nähen to sew v p20
der Name m name n p102
der Vorname first name
die Nase f nose n p177
die Nationalität f nationality n
neben next prep p4
der nächste Halt the next
station
der Neffe m nephew n p104
nehmen to take v p24
Wie lange wird das dauern?
How long will this take?
nett nice (kind) adj
das Netzwerk gn network n
neu new adj p150
neun nine adj p7
neunter ninth adj p9
neunzehn nineteen adj p7
neunzig ninety n adj p7
Neuseeland New Zealand n
der Neuseeländer m, die
Neuseeländerin f New
Zealander n

die Nichte f niece n p104
Nichtraucher- nonsmoking
adj
der Nichtraucherbereich
nonsmoking area
das Nichtraucherauto
nonsmoking car
das Nichtraucherzimmer
nonsmoking room
nichts / keine none n p10
der Niederländer m, die
Niederländerin f Dutch
n p108
niedrig low adj p77
niedrig low adj p77
niedriger lower
am niedrigsten lowest
noch einen / eine / ein
another adj p40, 64
der Norweger m, die
Norwegerin f Norwegian
n p109
die Note f grade (school) n
das Notebook gn laptop n
p146
der Notfall m emergency n
der November m November
n
die Nummer f number n
p112
die Nuss f nut n

O
die Öffnungszeiten f, pl
hours (at museum) n
ohne without prep p79

ohnmächtig werden *to faint* v **p24**

OK / in Ordnung *Okay adj adv*

der Oktober *m October n* p14

das Öl *gn oil n* p46, 77

die Olive *f olive n*

der Onkel *m uncle n* p104

die Oper *f opera n* p116

das Opernhaus *gn opera house n* p134

der Optiker / die Optikerin *m/f optometrist n*

orange *orange (color) adj*

der Orangensaft *m orange juice n*

die Orgel *f organ n*

örtlich *local adj* p53

der Österreicher *m*, **die Österreicherin** *f Austrian n* p108

P

das Paket *gn package n* p97

das Papier *paper n* p89

der Papierteller *paper plate* p89

die Papierserviette *paper napkin* p89

die Papiere *gn, pl identification n* p38

der Park *m park n* p119

Park- *parking adj*

parken *to park v* **p20**

Parkverbot *no parking*

die Partei *f political party n* p114

der Partner *m*, **die Partnerin** *f partner n*

der Passagier *m passenger n* p41

passen *to fit (clothes) v* **p20**

passen *to match v* **p20**

passen *to pass (gambling) v* **p20**

die Pause *f intermission n*

das Penthaus *gn penthouse n*

die Person *f person n*

Person mit Sehbehinderung *visually-impaired person*

das Personal *gn staff (employees) n* p70

das Pferd *gn horse n*

die Pizza *f pizza n* p72

der Platz *m court (sport) n*

der Platz *m seat n* p34

der Orchesterplatz *orchestra seat*

platzieren *to place v* **p20**

der Pole *m*, **die Polin** *f Polish n* p109

die Polizei *f police n* p30

die Polizeiwache *f police station n* p30

der Polizist / die Polizistin *m / f officer n* p38

das Poolbillard *gn pool (the game) n*

der Portier *m porter n* p30

die Portion *f portion (of food) n*

das Porträt *gn portrait n*

der Portugiese *m*, **die Portugiesin** *f Portuguese n* p108

der Portwein m port
   (beverage) n
die Post f mail n/post office
   n p128
die Postkarte f postcard n
der Preis eines Gedecks m
   cover charge (in bar) n
   p164
der Preis m price n
   die Eintrittsgebühr
      admission fee n p136
   **in der mittleren
   Preiskategorie** moderately
      priced p58
der Preisnachlass m discount
   n
   der Kinderrabatt children's
      discount
   der Seniorenrabatt senior
      discount
   der Studentenrabatt
      student discount
Privat- home adj
   die Privatadresse home
      address
   die private Telefonnummer
      home telephone number
das Problem gn problem n p2
das Produkt gn product n
professionell professional adj
das Programm gn program n
protestantisch Protestant adj
der Puff m bordello n p15
der Pullover m sweater n p39
die Pumpe f pump n

Q
das Querformat gn
   landscape (painting) n

die Quittung f receipt n p121

R
das Radio gn radio n p43
   das Satellitenradio satellite
      radio p43
die Rampe für Rollstuhlfahrer
   f wheelchair ramp n
das Rauchen gn smoking n
   der Raucherbereich
      smoking area p31
   Rauchen verboten no
      smoking p33
rauchen to smoke v p20
räumen to clear v p20
die Rechte gn, pl rights n pl
   die Bürgerrechte civil rights
rechts right adj p48
   ____ **befindet sich auf der
   rechten Seite.** ____ is on
      the right. p48
   **Biegen Sie an der Ecke nach
   rechts ab.** Turn right at the
      corner.
   Gehen Sie geradeaus. Go
      straight. (giving directions)
der Redakteur m, **die
   Redakteurin** f editor n
   p110
der Regenschirm m umbrella
   n
der Reggae m reggae n p116
regnen to rain v p20
regnerisch rainy adj p113
der Reifen m tire n p45
   der Reservereifen spare tire
      n
die Reise f trip n p99

der Reiseführer *m guide (publication) n*

reisen *to travel v* **p20**

der Reisescheck *m travelers' check n*

die Reklamation *f claim n*

rennen *to run v* **p24**

die Reservierung *f reservation n*

das Restaurant *gn restaurant n*

das Steakhaus *steakhouse*

das Rezept *gn prescription n* p38

die Rezeption *f front desk n*

die Richtung *f direction*

Einbahnstraße *one way (traffic sign)*

riechen *to smell v* **p24**

das Riff *gn reef n* p158

der Rock'n'Roll *m rock and roll n* p116

der Roller *m scooter n* p43

der Rollstuhl *m wheelchair n* p36

der Zugang per Rollstuhl *wheelchair access*

die Rampe für Rollstuhlfahrer *wheelchair ramp*

der elektrisch betriebene Rollstuhl *power wheelchair*

die Rolltreppe *f escalator n*

der Roman *m novel n*

der Mystery-Roman *mystery novel*

der Liebesroman *romance novel*

romantisch *romantic adj*

rosa *pink adj*

die Rose *f rose n*

rot *red adj* p173

rothaarig *redhead adj* p106

der Royal Flush *royal flush*

der Rücken *m back n* p190

die Rückenmassage *f back rub n* p169

rufen *to call (shout) v* **p24**

rufen *to shout v* **p24**

ruhig *quiet adj*

der Rum *m rum n* p81

der Russe *m,* **die Russin** *f Russian n* p109

S

der Saft *m juice n* p89

sagen *to say v* **p20**

der Salat *m salad n* p97

das Salz *gn salt n* p84

sammeln *to collect v* **p20**

der Samstag *m Saturday n* p13

der Satellit *m satellite n* p43

das Satellitenradio *satellite radio* p43

die Satellitenverfolgung *satellite tracking* p43

die Sauerstoffflasche *f oxygen tank n*

scannen *to scan (document) v* **p20**

das Schalentier *gn shellfish n* p79

der Schalter *m window n*

der Abgabeschalter *drop-off window* p130
der Abholschalter *pickup window* p130
Schau her! *Look here!*
der Scheck *m check n* p83
der Scheinwerfer *m headlight n*
schieben *to hold (gambling) v* **p24**
das Schiffswrack *gn shipwreck n*
das Schild „Vorfahrt gewähren" *gn yield sign n*
der Schlafwagen *m sleeping car n*
Schlangenaugen! *Snake eyes! n*
schlecht *adj bad adj*
schlimmer *worse See schlecht*
das Schloss *gn castle n*
das Schloss *gn lock n* p150
schlucken *to swallow v* **p20**
schmal *narrow adj* p11
schmerzen *to hurt (to feel painful) v* **p20**

Autsch! Das tut weh! *Ouch! That hurts!*
die Kopfschmerzen *m, pl headache n* p111
die Zahnschmerzen *m, pl toothache n*
Ich habe Zahnschmerzen. *I have a toothache.*

schminken *to make up (apply cosmetics) v* **p20**

das Schnäppchen *gn deal (bargain) n*
schneiden *to cut v* **p24**
der Schneider / die Schneiderin *m / f tailor n* p66
schnell *fast adj* p49, 128
der Schnitt *m cut (wound) n*
der Schnorchel *m snorkel (breathing tube) n*
der Schnuller *m pacifier n*
schön *beautiful adj* p105
schottisch *Scottish adj*
schreiben *to write v* **p24**

Könnten Sie mir das bitte aufschreiben? *Would you write that down for me?*

der Schuh *m shoe n*
die Schule *f school n*

die Mittelstufe *junior high / middle school*
die juristische Fakultät *law school*
die medizinische Fakultät *medical school*
die Grundschule *primary school*
die weiterführende Schule *high school*

der Schwan *m swan n*
schwanger *pregnant adj*
schwarz *black adj* p106
der Schwede *m*, **die Schwedin** *f Swedish n* p109
das Schwein *gn pig n*

der Schweizer m, **die Schweizerin** f Swiss n p108

die Schwester f sister n

schwierig difficult adj p155

schwimmen to swim v p24

Schwimmen verboten. Swimming prohibited.

die Schwimmweste f life preserver n

sechs six adj p7

sechzehn sixteen adj p7

sechzig sixty adj p7

das Segel gn sail n

das Segeltuch gn canvas (fabric) n p42

sehen to see v p24

Dürfte ich das mal sehen? May I see it?

sehr very p70

seicht shallow adj

die Seide f silk n p139

das Seil gn rope n

sein to be v p23

sein / seine his adj

Selbstbedienungs- self-serve adj

das Selters gn seltzer n p80

senden to send v p20

der September m September n

der Service m service n p36

außer Betrieb out of service

die Servicegebühr f service charge n p64

servieren to serve v p20

die Serviette f napkin n

setzen to put (gambling) v p20

Setzen Sie das auf Rot / Schwarz! Put it on red / black! p173

Beeilen Sie sich bitte! Hurry, please!

sicher safe (secure) adj

die Sicherheit f security n p30

die Sicherheitsschleuse security checkpoint

der Sicherheitsbeamte security guard p30

die Sicherung f fuse n

sie f she / they

sie them pron pl p3

Sie you pron sing/pl (formal)

sieben seven adj p7

siebter seventh adj p9

siebzehn seventeen adj p7

siebzig seventy adj p7

das Sightseeing gn sightseeing n

das Silber gn silver n

Silber- silver adj

silbern silver (color) adj

singen to sing v p24

sitzen to sit v p24

die Skulptur f sculpture n

die Socke f sock n

die Software f software n

der Sohn m son n p105

der Sommer m summer n p14

die Sommersprosse f freckle n

die Sonne f sun n

der Sonnenbrand m sunburn n

die **Sonnenbrille** f sunglasses n p139

die **Sonnencreme** f sunscreen n

sonnig sunny adj p113

der **Sonntag** m Sunday n p12

die **Soße** f sauce n

der **Sozialismus** m socialism n

der **Spanier** m, die **Spanierin** f Spanish n p108

spanisch Spanish adj p108

spät late adj p12

Bitte pünktlich sein. Please don't be late.

später later adv

der **Spaziergang** m walk n

der **Specht** m woodpecker n

die **Speisekarte** f menu n p74

das **Kindermenü** children's menu

das **Diabetikermenü** diabetic menu

die **Spezialität** f special (featured meal) n

das **Spiel** gn match (sport) n

die **Spielekonsole** f game console n p145

spielen to play (a game) v p20

spielen to play (an instrument) v p20

der **Spielplatz** m playground n

der **Spielstand** m score n

das **Spielwarengeschäft** gn toy store n

das **Spielzeug** gn toy n

der **Spind** m locker n p150

der **Umkleideschrank** gym locker

der **Aufbewahrungsschrank** storage locker

der **Split** m split (gambling) n

der **Sport** m sports n

die **Sporthalle** f coliseum n

sprechen to speak v, to talk v p24

Wir sprechen Englisch. English spoken here.

der **Sprung** m crack (in glass object) n

spülen to flush v p20

der **Staat** (gov.) / der **Status** (status) m state n

das **Stadion** gn stadium n p152

die **Stadt** f city n p61

das **Stadtzentrum** gn downtown n p137

der **Stecker** m plug n p145

stehen to stand v p24

die **Steuer** f tax n p143

die **Mehrwertsteuer** (MwSt) value-added tax (VAT)

stillen to nurse v p20

die **Stirn** f forehead n

der **Stoff** m fabric n

STOP STOP (traffic sign)

stornieren to cancel v p20

die **Strafe** f fine (for traffic violation) n p183

die **Strähnchen** gn, pl highlights (hair) n p148

der **Strand** m beach n,p118

stranden to beach v p20

die **Straße** f road n p48

die Straße *f street n* p6

  am Ende der Straße *down the street*

  gegenüber *across the street*

streichen *to paint v* **p24**

das Streichholz *gn match (fire) n*

die Streitkräfte *f pl armed forces n pl*

die Strömung *f current (water) n*

die Stufe *f stair n* p185

die Suche *f search n*

  das Abtasten *hand search*

suchen *to look for (to search) v* **p20**

die Suite *f suite n* p58

der Supermarkt *m supermarket n*

surfen *to surf v* **p20**

  das Surfbrett *surfboard n*

der (Swimming-)Pool *m pool (swimming) n*

die Symphonie *f symphony n*

T

die Tablette *f pill n*

  die Tablette gegen Seekrankheit *f seasickness pill*

der Tacho *m speedometer n*

die Tafel *f board n*

der Tag *m day n* p149

die Tante *f aunt n* p104

tapfer *brave adj* **p15**

die Tariftabelle *f rate plan (cell phone) n*

  Haben Sie eine Tariftabelle? *Do you have a rate plan?*

die Tasche *f / die Tüte f bag n*

tatsächlich *actual adj* p15

taub *deaf adj*

tauchen *to dive v* **p20**

tauchen (mit Atemgerät) *to scuba dive v*

  Ich tauche mit Atemgerät. *I scuba dive.*

  schnorcheln *to snorkel v*

tausend *thousand adj* p7

das Taxi *gn taxi n* p50

  Taxi! *Taxi!*

  der Taxistand *taxi stand*

der Techno *m techno n (music)*

der Tee *m tea n* p82

  Tee mit Milch und Zucker *tea with milk and sugar*

  Tee mit Zitrone *tea with lemon*

  Kräutertee *herbal tea*

das Telefon *gn phone n*

Telefon- *phone adj* p168

der Telefonanruf *m phone call n*

  das R-Gespräch *collect phone call*

  das Auslandsgespräch *international phone call*

  das Ferngespräch *long-distance phone call*

die Telefonauskunft *phone directory*

die Telefonauskunft *f directory assistance*

der Tempel m temple n p114

das Tennis gn tennis n p59

der Termin m appointment n p136

das Terminal gn terminal (airport) n p33

teuer expensive adj p164

das Theater gn theater n p133

das Theaterstück gn play n

die Theke f counter (in bar) n p36

Ticket gn ticket n p30

tief deep adj p157

das Tier gn animal n

der Tisch m table n p21

die Tochter f daughter n p105

die Toilette f toilet n p68

das Toilettenpapier gn toilet paper n

die Tonne f ton n

das Tor gn goal (sport) n

trainieren to train v p20

das Training gn workout n

die Transaktion f transaction n

der Transfer m transfer n

  die Überweisung money transfer p120

transferieren / überweisen to transfer v p20, 24

die Traube f grape n

traurig sad adj p109

der Treff m hangout (hot spot) n

Treppen steigen to climb stairs

der Tresor safe (for storing valuables) n p67

trimmen to trim (hair) v p20

trinken to drink v **p24**

das Trinkgeld gn tip (gratuity) p83

  inklusive Trinkgeld tip included p83

trocken dry adj

trocknen to dry v p20

die Trommel f drum n

die Trompete f trumpet n

tropfen to drip v **p20**

der Truthahn m turkey

der Tscheche m, **die Tschechin** f Czech n p109

die Tür f door n p69

  das Gate gate (at airport) p30

der Türke m, **die Türkin** f Turkish n p109

U

die U-Bahn f subway n

  die U-Bahn-Linie subway line

  die U-Bahn-Haltestelle subway station

  Mit welcher U-Bahn komme ich zu / zur / zum _____? Which subway do I take for _____?

die Übelkeit f nausea n p176

über above adj p69

überall / irgendwo anywhere adv

GERMAN—ENGLISH

überfallen to mug (assault) v p24

überfallen werden to get mugged

überhitzen to overheat v p20

die Übernachtung mit Frühstück f bed-and-breakfast (B & B) n

überprüfen / sich vergewissern to check v p20

die Uhr m clock n, watch n

Uhr o'clock adv p4

zwei Uhr two o'clock

die Uhrzeit f time n p139

die Uhrzeit für das Auschecken check-out time

kein Ausgang not an exit

der Notausgang emergency exit p34

die Umkleide f locker room n

die Umkleidekabine f changing room n

die Umkleidekabine f fitting room n

umsehen to look (observe) v p24

die Umwelt f environment n

der Umzug m parade n

der Unfall m accident n

unfrei collect adj

die Universität f university n

unter below adj p69

unterbrechen to disconnect v p24

das Unternehmen gn business n p37

unterschreiben to sign v p24

Unterschreiben Sie bitte hier. Sign here.

die Untertitel m, pl subtitle n

die Unterwäsche f underwear n

die Unze f ounce n

der Urlaub m vacation n p37

im Urlaub on vacation

in Urlaub gehen to go on vacation

der USB-Anschluss m USB port n

V

der Vater m father n

der Vegetarier m, **die Vegetarierin** f vegetarian n

das vegetarische Essen vegetarian meal p35

der Ventilator m fan n

die Verbindungs-geschwindigkeit f connection speed n p128

verdächtig suspiciously adv p48

Verdammt! Damn! expletive

die Verdauungsstörung f indigestion n

verfügbar available adj p135

verheiratet married adj p104

die Verhütung f birth control n p171, 180

Ich nehme die Pille. I'm on birth control.

verkaufen to sell v p20

der Verkäufer m, **die Verkäuferin** f *salesperson* n p110

der Straßenhändler m, **die Straßenhändlerin** f *street vendor*

der Verkehr m *traffic* n p45

Wie ist der Verkehr? *How's traffic?*

Es ist viel Verkehr. *Traffic is terrible.*

die Verkehrsregeln *traffic rules*

der Verkehrsstau m *congestion (traffic)* n

verkohlt *charred (meat)* adj p77

der Verkostungsraum m *tasting room* n

verlangsamen to *slow* v p20

Fahren Sie bitte langsamer. *Slow down!* v

verlieren to *lose* v p24

der Verlobte m, **die Verlobte** f *fiancé(e)* n

die Vermittlung f *operator (phone)* n p64

verschütten to *spill* v p20

verschwinden to *disappear* v p24

verschwommen *blurry* adj p178

versenden to *ship* v p20

die Versicherung f *insurance* n p183

die Unfallversicherung *collision insurance*

die Haftpflichtversicherung *liability insurance*

die Version f *version* n p128

die Verspätung f *delay* n p36

verstehen to *understand* v p24

Ich verstehe nicht. *I don't understand.*

Verstanden? *Do you understand?*

verstopft *constipated* adj

die Verstopfung f *congestion / constipation* n p176

versuchen to *try (attempt)* v p20

der Verwandte m, **die Verwandte** f *relative* n

verwenden to *use* v p20

verwirrt *confused* adj

verzollen (customs) to *declare* v p20

das Video gn *video* n

der Videorekorder m *VCR* n

viel *a lot* n

viel *much* adj p10

viel Spaß *have fun* pvii

viele *many* adj p10

vier *four* adj p7

vierter *fourth* adj p9

ein Viertel *one quarter, one fourth*

vierzehn *fourteen* adj p7

vierzig *forty* adj

das Vinyl gn *vinyl* n p42

violett *purple* adj

das Visum *gn* visa *n*
der Vogel *m* bird *n*
voll *full adj* p82
vorbereitet *prepared adj*
Vorder- *front adj* p34
vorgestern *the day before yesterday adv* p13
die letzten paar Tage *these last few days*
vorstellen *to introduce v* **p20**
die Vorstellung *f show (performance) n*
vorwärts *forward adj* p6

W
der Wachmann *m* guard *n* p30
der Sicherheitsbeamte *security guard* p30
wachsen *to grow (get larger) v* **p24**
Wo sind Sie (formal) / bist du (informal) aufgewachsen? *Where did you grow up?*
die Wahl *f election n* p114
wählen *to dial (a phone number) v* **p20**
wählen *to vote v* **p20**
wandern *to hike v* **p20**
wenig *little*
wann *when adv* p3
der Wartebereich *m* waiting area *n* p30
die Warze *f wart n*
was *what adv* p3
Was gibt's? *What's up?*

das Waschbecken *gn* sink *n*
das Wasser *gn* water *n* p39
das heiße Wasser *hot water*
das kalte Wasser *cold water*
der Wasserhahn *m* faucet *n*
das Wechselgeld *gn* change (money) *n*
der Wechselkurs *m* exchange rate *n* p121
wechseln *to change (money) v / to change (clothes) v* **p20**
der Wecker *alarm clock* p67
Weckruf *wake-up call n* p67
der Weg *m* trail *n* p156
weiß *white adj*
weich *soft adj*
der Wein *m* wine *n* p47, 76
das Weingut *gn* vineyard *n*
welcher / welche / welches *which adv* p3
weniger *See wenig* p156
wer *who adv* p3
Wem gehört ____? *Whose is ____?*
der Western *western n (movie)*
westlich, abendländisch *western adj*
die Wette *f bet n* p174
Ich gehe mit. *I'll see your bet.* p174
wetten *to bet v* **p20**
der Wetterbericht *m* weather forecast *n*
wie *how adv* p3, 11
wie (viel) *how (much) adv* p3

Wie viel? *How much?* p3
Für wie lange? *For how long?*
wie (viele) *how (many)* adv
wiedergutmachen *to make up (apologize)* v **p20**
wiedergutmachen *to make up (compensate)* v **p20**
wiederholen *to repeat* v **p20**
Könnten Sie das bitte wiederholen? *Would you please repeat that?* p2
Auf Wiedersehen m *goodbye* n p100
wiegen *to weigh* v **p24**
das Wi-Fi gn *wi-fi* n
willkommen *welcome* adj
Gern geschehen. *You're welcome.*
die Wimper f *eyelash* n
die Windel f *diaper* n
die Stoffwindel *cloth diaper*
die Wegwerfwindel *disposable diaper*
windig *windy* adj p113
windsurfen *to windsurf* v
der Winter m *winter* n p14
wir *we* pron pl
wirklich *really* adj
die Wirtschaft f *economy* n
das Wischerblatt gn *wiper blade* n
wissen *to know (something)* v **p33**
die Witwe f *widow* n p104
der Witwer m *widower* p104
Wo ist ____? *Where is ____?*

wo *where* adv p3
die Woche f *week* n p4, 13
diese Woche *this week*
letzte Woche *last week*
nächste Woche *next week*
eine Woche *one week* p13
in einer Woche *a week from now*
der Wodka m *vodka* n
das Wohnmobil (van) / der Wohnwagen (trailer) gn / m *camper* n
wollen *to want* v **p25**
das Wörterbuch gn *dictionary* n
wütend *angry* adj p109

X
XL- *extra-large* adj

Z
der Zahn m *tooth* n p181
der Zahnarzt m *dentist* n p177
zehn *ten* adj p7
zehnter *tenth* adj p9
zeichnen *drawing (activity)* v **p20**
die Zeichnung f *drawing (work of art)* n p117
zeigen *to point* v **p20**
Könnten Sie mir das bitte zeigen? *Would you show me?*
die Zeit f *time* n p156
die Zeitschrift f *magazine* n
die Zeitung f *newspaper* n

der Zeitungsstand *m newsstand n* p31
zelten *to camp v* **p20**
der Zentimeter *m centimeter n*
(zer-)brechen *to break v* **p24**
zerbrechlich *fragile adj* p129
zerkocht *overcooked adj*
zerkratzt *scratched adj* p45
die Ziege *f goat n*
ziehen *to pull v* **p24**
das Ziel *g n destination n*
die Zigarette *f cigarette n*
  die Schachtel Zigaretten *pack of cigarettes*
die Zigarre *f cigar n*
das Zimmer *g n room (hotel) n*
das Zimmermädchen *g n maid (hotel) n*
der Zinssatz *m interest rate n* p121
Zoll *inch*
der Zoll *m customs n* p33
der Zoo *m zoo n* p118
der Zopf *m braid n* p147
zu *too (excessively) adv*
zu *toward prep*
der Zug *m train n* p51
  der Expresszug *express train*
  der Nahverkehrszug *local train*
das Zuhause *g n home n*
zurückgeben *to return (something) v* **p24**

zurückkehren *to return (to a place) v* **p20**
zusätzlich *extra adj* p66
zusehen *to watch v* **p24**
der Zustand *m condition n*
  in gutem / schlechtem Zustand *in good / bad condition*
zuvorkommend *courteous adj* p70
zwanzig *twenty adj* p7
zwei *two adj* p7
zweisprachig *bilingual adj*
zweiter *second adj* p9
zwölf *twelve adj* p7

NOTES

NOTES

NOTES

NOTES

NOTES

NOTES